A Hand Book on
University System

A Hand Book on
University System

R. Ponnusamy
Principal
Madha Engineering College
Chennai, India

J. Pandurangan
Professor and Head
Department of Mathematics
Aarupadai Veedu Institute of Technology
Chennai, India

ALLIED PUBLISHERS PVT. LTD.

New Delhi • Mumbai • Kolkata • Lucknow • Chennai
Nagpur • Bangalore • Hyderabad • Ahmedabad

ALLIED PUBLISHERS PRIVATE LIMITED

1/13-14 Asaf Ali Road, **New Delhi**–110002
Ph.: 011-23239001 • E-mail: delhi.books@alliedpublishers.com

47/9 Prag Narain Road, Near Kalyan Bhawan, **Lucknow**–226001
Ph.: 0522-2209942 • E-mail: lko.books@alliedpublishers.com

17 Chittaranjan Avenue, **Kolkata**–700072
Ph.: 033-22129618 • E-mail: cal.books@alliedpublishers.com

15 J.N. Heredia Marg, Ballard Estate, **Mumbai**–400001
Ph.: 022-42126969 • E-mail: mumbai.books@alliedpublishers.com

60 Shiv Sunder Apartments (Ground Floor), Central Bazar Road,
Bajaj Nagar, **Nagpur**–440010
Ph.: 0712-2234210 • E-mail: ngp.books@alliedpublishers.com

F-1 Sun House (First Floor), C.G. Road, Navrangpura,
Ellisbridge P.O., **Ahmedabad**–380006
Ph.: 079-26465916 • E-mail: ahmbd.books@alliedpublishers.com

751 Anna Salai, **Chennai**–600002
Ph.: 044-28523938 • E-mail: chennai.books@alliedpublishers.com

5th Main Road, Gandhinagar, **Bangalore**–560009
Ph.: 080-22262081 • E-mail: bngl.books@alliedpublishers.com

3-2-844/6 & 7 Kachiguda Station Road, **Hyderabad**–500027
Ph.: 040-24619079 • E-mail: hyd.books@alliedpublishers.com

Website: www.alliedpublishers.com

ISBN: 978-81-8424-904-0

Published by Sunil Sachdev and printed by Ravi Sachdev at Allied Publishers Pvt. Ltd. (Printing Division), A-104 Mayapuri Phase II, New Delhi-110064

Preface

University Systems of different countries have varied backgrounds and have been functioning over a period of few centuries. However they have been having a common thread of binding in that they are trying to impart information, knowledge, ethics, logic, philosophy, astronomy, etc. They are trying to make students/people understand and differentiate between good and bad.

This hand-book is an attempt to give an overall picture of Universities/Institutions of higher-learning describing their mode of functioning, infrastructure necessary and usefulness to society and interests of various stake holders. The breakup cost of higher education in that how the total cost is shared by different groups involved during last decade in a few counties is tabulated.

Though people who are managing the Universities are supposed to know and fully understand their specific role, the authors firmly believe that there is a need for everyone in an organization to have an overall idea about various systems that are in place, rules and regulations that are to be followed, the limitations and freedom that are available so that work can become a pleasure for all. University deals with a large group of students aspiring to enter and those who are already inside the system and consequently their parents/guides. All of them better be aware of a University System and things they can rely upon during students' study period. They should also be familiar with various terminologies that are used in a University, sometimes which may be confusing to any one at the first instant.

The list of top 500 Universities as given by The QS World University Ranking is listed for the sake of students who would like to join Universities abroad. They are listed country wise; if someone is interested in a specific country, of course with ranks and they are provided in a single lot.

How the Indian Universities are governed is outlined.

This handbook is loaded with information about types of Universities and their services, How an University functions, is funded; being managed to deliver to the society, facilities that are to be made available, various support systems and so on, into the reach of everyone who is interested. This book may be useful in saving some money for some of the users and many times save precious time of many who will otherwise be moving from pillar to post for gathering correct information.

The author's wish to state that this hand book is mostly a collection of information from various sources, arranged in a coherent manner presented to help all of course including their views also at possible places with the aim of improving university system in which they are part and parcel.

Who can Look for What

The aspiring students can find useful information about various systems that will be in place, list of world top ranking Institutions/Universities (Annexure–A), the rough cost estimated of higher education in a few countries (Section 12.6) and what kind of financial and other support (Section 7.6) will be available in general.

Students who are already in an University can have information about types of examination, evaluation process, representation regarding any exam related problems getting help to solve even personal problems, their freedom/choices as well as limitations. Also they can have information about how any malpractice will be handled, what types of punishments are in store for such things, whom to approach for any thing. How students will be treated once they have committed doing wrong with staff fellow students or the Institute concerned. The details are available in the chapter titled Checks and balances of University System (Section 9.4 and Chapter 10).

For the teaching fraternity, it is useful to find what kind of work culture is welcomed how to keep abreast of what is going on academically in and around, the need to do student counseling, to improve their qualification, publishing papers in Journals of repute, conducting workshops/seminars/symposiums or taking part in such activities memberships and active participation in academic related associations/chapters interdisciplinary work, joint projects and consultancy work, taking part in the formulation/revision of syllabi, improving competency to handle new/emerging subject contents (Sections 6.3 to 6.8, 7.6 to 7.9, 7.20 to 7.23). How a college teacher gets evaluated during an interview for career advancement is given in detail in Annexure–B.

For industries and companies which think of starting a corporate University, information regarding planning and various steps involved and a suggestion like better to tip-up with an existing traditional university and so on are dealt with (Section 4.7 and 4.8). The cost estimation model is explained in section 12.4 and 12.5. The infrastructure requirement as per GoI guidelines is given in Annexure–III.

For Governments/Officers concerned with Education attention is drawn to the details on how the per candidate cost of education can be arrived at, without any ambiguity (Section 12.4).

For public, this book gives information about how institutes/Universities all over the world find it extremely difficult to get proper funding but meeting the expected level of competency. It gives a birds' eye view of Universities around the world. Also gives in depth details about checks and balances of the systems (Chapter 10). Transparency of the University, preparedness to encompass establishments far and near for the benefit of both on one part the university and on the other part of any organization/industry interested in the interaction, creating a win-win situation for all concerned. How University system has got evolved/history of ancient and modern university can be had at a glance (Chapter 3).

For those who would try to evaluate; compare and contrast universities across the Globe along with various rankings already, available, a new approach in suggested in the 11th chapter. There are many points to ponder.

Contents

Preface ..... *v*
Who can Look for What ..... *vii*

Chapter 1: University System **1**
1.1 Introduction 1
1.2 Objectives of University Education 2
1.3 Characteristics of Good Higher Education System 2
1.3.1 A Well Structured Academic System 3
1.3.2 Enhanced System of Teaching and Learning 4
1.3.3 Good Academic Discipline among Students 4
1.3.4 Well Qualified Faculty Team 5
1.3.5 Structured System of Budgeting and Control 5
1.3.6 Good Infrastructure 5
1.3.7 Student Freedom 6
1.3.8 Academic Freedom 6
1.3.9 Uniform Fees and Service Policy 6
1.3.10 Better Synergy amongst Employer, Staff and Students 6
1.3.12 Evolutionary Development/Promoting New Sources of Innovation ... 7
1.3.13 Well Designed Placement Training Programmes 7
1.3.14 Transparent Administrative System 8
1.3.15 Department Advisory Committee 9
1.3.16 Well Designed Transparent Service Rules and Promotion Policy 9
1.3.17 Good Student Admission Policy 10
1.3.18 Well Structured Student Motivational Mechanism 10
1.3.19 Good System of Counseling and Guidance 11
1.3.20 Emergent Behavior 12
1.3.21 Market Driven Changes 12
1.3.22 Inter-Disciplinary Study 13
1.3.23 Well Planned Annual Campus Events 14
1.3.24 A Good Professional Society Activities 16
1.3.25 A Good Industry-Institute Interaction 17
1.3.26 A Good Research and Development System 18
1.3.27 A Well Structured Academic Feedback System 19
1.4 Conclusion 19

Chapter 2: Components of Well Structured Academic System 20
2.1 Introduction 20
2.2 Governance and Leadership 20
2.3 Institutional Mission and Vision 20
2.4 Well Defined Syllabus 21
2.5 Academic Year/Academic Semester 22
2.6 Academic Calendar 22
2.7 Lesson Plan 23
2.8 Lab manuals 23
2.9 Question Bank 23
2.10 Class Room Teaching 24
2.10.1 Explaining 24
2.10.2 Demonstrating 25
2.10.3 Collaborating 25
2.10.4 Learning by Teaching 26
2.11 Lecture Notes 26
2.12 Course File 26
2.13 Delivery Methods 27
2.13.1 Lectures Sessions 27
2.13.2 Practical Sessions 27
2.13.3 Tutorials 27
2.13.4 Seminars/Workshop 27
2.13.5 Guest Lectures 28
2.13.6 Industrial Visits 28
2.13.7 Mini Projects 28
2.13.8 Academic Tutoring 28
2.13.9 Online Lecture Sessions 28
2.13.10 Video Lecture Sessions 29
2.14 Monitoring 29
2.14.1 Periodic/Internal Assessment Tests 29
2.14.2 Assignments 29
2.14.3 Oral/Model/Final Examinations 30
2.14.4 Student Projects 30
2.14.5 Student Feedback 31
2.14.6 Unit/Experiment Coverage Report 31
2.14.7 Regular Display of Attendance/Exam Percentage 31
2.14.8 Communication to Parents 31
2.15 Grading System 32
2.16 Student Centric Learning and Activities 33
2.17 Student Associations 33
2.18 Laboratories, Workshops and Equipment 33
(Facilities, Maintenance and Utilization)

2.19 Information Access Facilities 34
2.20 Choice Based Credit System (CBCS) 34
2.20.1 Hard Core Course 34
2.20.2 Soft Core Course 35
2.21 Take Home Examination 35
2.22 Student Counseling 35
2.23 Extra-Curricular Activities/Co-Curricular Activities 36
2.24 Student Teacher Relationship 36
2.25 Conclusion 37

Chapter 3: History of University System 38
3.1 Introduction 38
3.2 Early History 38
3.3 Medieval Universities 39
3.4 Modern Universities 41
3.5 National Universities 41
3.6 US University System of Education—History 42
3.6.1 Founding 42
3.6.2 Period 1900–1948 43
3.6.3 Period 1949–1989 44
3.6.4 1990 Onwards 45
3.7 Europe University System of Education—History 46
3.7.1 The First European Universities 46
3.7.2 Representation of a University Class (1350s) 47
3.7.3 The Structure and Spread of Early European Universities 47
3.7.4 Philosophic and External Influences 47
3.7.5 European University Models in the 19th and 20th Centuries 48
3.7.6 The European University Legacies 50
3.8 Indian University System of Education—History 51
3.9 Conclusion 53

Chapter 4: Classification of Universities and their Modes 54
4.1 Introduction 54
4.2 Public/Private Universities 54
4.3 Academic Universities 54
4.4 Vocational Universities 55
4.5 Open/Virtual Universities 55
4.6 International University 55
4.7 Corporate Universities 56
4.7.1 Goals of Corporate Universities 56
4.7.2 Planning for Corporate Universities 57
4.7.3 Curriculum 58

4.8 Different Modes of Education 58
4.8.1 Formal Education 58
4.8.2 Distance Education 59
4.8.3 Web Education 60
4.8.4 Virtual Education 60
4.9 Conclusion 60

Chapter 5: Administrative Structure of University System 62
5.1 Introduction 62
5.2 Academic Ranks 63
5.3 Organizational Structure 65
5.3.1 Academic Administrative Structure 65
5.3.2 Functional Structure 66
5.3.3 Admission Department 67
5.3.4 Academic Department 67
5.3.5 Affiliations Department 68
5.3.6 Research Department 68
5.3.7 Distance Education Department 68
5.3.8 Student Affairs and Service Department 69
5.3.9 Planning and Development Department 69
5.3.10 International Affairs Department 69
5.3.11 Health Department 69
5.3.12 Projects and Consultancy and Institute and Industry Interaction Department 70
5.3.13 Training and Placement Department 70
5.3.14 Human Resource Department 71
5.3.15 Engineering Department(s) 71
5.3.16 Sports and Games Department 71
5.3.17 Finance and Procurement Department 72
5.4 Academic Structure of University 72
5.5 University Councils 73
5.5.1 Senate/Syndicate 73
5.5.2 Board of Studies and Academic Council 73
5.5.3 Research Council 73
5.5.4 Student Council 73
5.5.5 Advisory Board 73
5.5.6 Finance Committee 74
5.5.7 Audit Committee 74
5.5.8 University Ethics Board 74
5.5.9 Ad-hoc Committees 74
5.6 Public Relation Officer 75
5.7 Librarian/Deputy Librarian 75
5.8 Conclusion 76

Chapter 6: Responsibility, Functions and Contribution of Universities 77
6.1 Introduction 77
6.2 Awarding Degrees/Diplomas 77
6.3 Development of New Course/Curriculum/Syllabus 78
6.3.1 Topics Relevant to the Target Group 78
6.3.2 Formulation of Objectives/Learning Outcomes 78
6.3.3 Selecting Appropriate Instructional Methods 79
6.3.4 Implementation of Course or Curriculum 79
6.3.5 Assessments and Evaluation 79
6.4 Imparting Knowledge and Skills 80
6.5 Training Scholarly Approaches 80
6.5.1 Developing Scholarly Approach to One's Profession 81
6.6 Developing Research and Consultancy 81
6.7 Meeting the Expectations of Students and Parents 82
6.7.1 Students Expectations 82
6.7.2 Parental Expectation 83
6.8 Transforming the Society and Livelihood 83
6.9 Establishment and Disestablishment of Academic Programs, Labs, Centers, Departments 83
6.10 Assessing the Quality of Teaching and Student Learning for Improvement ... 84
6.11 Institution of Awards and Fellowships 84
6.12 Conducting of Scholarly Lectures 84
6.13 Conclusion 84

Chapter 7: Special Elements and Components of University System 86
7.1 Introduction 86
7.2 Press 86
7.3 Journals/Magazines 86
7.4 Museum 87
7.5 Newsletters 87
7.6 Fellowship 89
7.7 Scholarship 90
7.8 Industrial Affiliate Programme/Industry-Institute Interaction Programme 91
7.9 Industrial Consultancy Center 92
7.9.1 Industrial Consultancy 92
7.9.2 Sponsored Research 93
7.9.3 Interdisciplinary Project 93
7.10 International-Faculty/Student Exchange Programme/ Industry Exchange Programme 93
7.11 Joint Venture Programme 94

7.12 University Medals 95
7.13 Award/Prize Schemes 97
7.13.1 Employee Award 97
7.13.2 Academic Awards 97
7.13.3 Sports Awards 98
7.14 Professional Societies 98
7.15 Alumni Center 99
7.16 Extra Curricular Activity Center like Dance/Music/Performing Arts, etc. 100
7.17 Faculty Club 100
7.18 Literature Club 100
7.19 Science/Technology Club 100
7.19.1 Membership 101
7.19.2 Meet the Firms 101
7.19.3 Recruitment Conference 101
7.20 Technology Business Incubators 101
7.21 Conferences/Seminars/Symposium/Workshop 102
7.22 Handbooks 103
7.23 Campus Code of Ethics 103
7.24 Campus Map 105
7.25 Mentor Programme 105
7.26 Academic Advisors 107
7.26.1 Function of an Advisor 107
7.27 Endowments 107
7.28 Conclusion 108

Chapter 8: Infrastructure of University System 109
8.1 Introduction 109
8.2 Lecture Halls 109
8.3 Tutorial Halls/Seminar Halls 109
8.4 Board Meeting Room 110
8.5 Interview Room 110
8.6 Laboratories 110
8.7 Drawing Hall 111
8.8 Shopping Malls 112
8.9 Canteen/Food Court 112
8.10 Coffee House 112
8.11 Hostels 113
8.12 General Facilities 113
8.13 Meditation Hall 113
8.14 Locker Facility 113

8.15 Quarters 114
8.16 Guest Houses 114
8.17 Hospitals 114
8.18 Emergency Call Office/Ambulances 114
8.19 Browsing Center 115
8.20 Call Centre 115
8.21 Sports and Games Complex 115
8.22 Theatre/Auditorium/Open-Air Theatre 116
8.23 Transport Facility/Campus Cycles/Trolleys 116
8.24 Language Learning Center 117
8.25 Driving Center/Studio Training Center/Typing, etc. 117
8.26 Bank 118
8.27 Post-Office/Courier Service 118
8.28 Travel Agency 118
8.29 Library/Digital Library 119
8.30 Digital Class Room/Video/Audio Centers 120
8.31 Online/Internet Facility/Web Materials/E-mail/ Web Page Facility/EDUSAT Facility 120
8.32 Exam Cell/Center 121
8.33 Conclusion 121

Chapter 9: System and Processes of University System 122

9.1 Introduction 122
9.2 Admission Process 122
9.2.1 Authority to Admit Students 122
9.2.2 Admission Steps 123
9.3 Recruitment/Appointment of staff Process 123
9.3.1 Recruitment and Selection Process 124
9.3.2 Recruitment Processes: External and Internal 124
9.3.3 Job Description and Grade of Post 124
9.3.4 Authorization to Recruit 125
9.3.5 Advertisement 125
9.3.6 Selection Panel 125
9.3.7 Short-listing 125
9.3.8 Interviews 126
9.3.9 The Offer Letter 127
9.3.10 The Appointment 127
9.3.11 Creation of Faculty Profile/Service Book 127
9.4 Examination System 128
9.4.1 Constitution of Examination Board 131
9.4.2 Process of Examination 132

9.5 Academic Information System 135
9.6 People Identification System/Multi-Purpose Electronic Card 137
9.7 Research and Development Center (RDC) 137
9.7.1 Duties and Responsibilities of RDC 137
9.8 Book Bank 138
9.9 Faculty Development Cell/Continuation-Education Programme 139
9.9.1 Assessment of Skill/Technology Requirement 139
9.9.2 Training Programme 139
9.10 Curriculum Development Cell 139
9.10.1 Book Writing 140
9.10.2 Short Duration Programmes for Teachers 140
9.10.3 Developments Related to Educational Technology 140
9.10.4 Development and Updating of Curriculum 141
9.10.5 Development of Student Evaluation Procedures and Materials on Examination Reforms 141
9.10.6 Technical Education and Vocational Training of Physically Differently Abled Persons 141
9.11 Placement and Training Cell 141
9.12 Planning and Development Office (Budgeting, long-term, short-term) 142
9.13 University Endowment Funds 142
9.13.1 Endowed Professorship 143
9.13.2 Endowed Scholarship/Fellowship 144
9.14 Conclusion 144

Chapter 10: Checks and Balances of University System 145

10.1 Introduction 145
10.2 Academic Discipline Committee 145
10.2.1 The Committee's Authority 145
10.2.2 General Procedures 146
10.2.3 Specific Procedures for Conducting a Hearing 151
10.2.4 Sanctions 152
10.2.5 Disciplinary Notations 153
10.2.6 Appeals 153
10.2.7 Conditions for Early Removal of Disciplinary Note/Sanction 155
10.3 Campus Crime Division 155
10.4 Exam Squad 155
10.5 Visitors' Feedback System/Book 156
10.6 Student Grievance Cell 156
10.7 Faculty/Staff Grievance Cell 156
10.8 Voting Systems 156
10.9 Technical/Maintenance/Service Cell/Centre 157

10.10 General Inspection Committee 157
10.11 Conclusion 157

Chapter 11: World Universities Ranking 158
11.1 Introduction 158
11.2 Survey of Existing World Ranking 159
11.3 Objectives of the Ranking 162
11.4 Type of University Ranking 163
11.5 Surveying Authority 163
11.6 List of Parameters/Attributes for Assessment Suggested 164
11.7 Conclusion 168

Chapter 12: University Financing and Cost Estimation 169
12.1 Introduction 169
12.2 Financing the University/Higher Education 169
12.2.1 The Economic, Social and Political Context 169
12.2.2 The Efficiency and Productivity of the Enterprise 170
12.2.3 Variation in Unit Costs 171
12.2.4 Sources of Revenue for the University 171
12.3 Worldwide Trends in Financing Higher Education 172
12.3.1 Increasing Unit, or Per-Student, Costs of Instruction 173
12.3.2 Increasing Enrollments 173
12.3.3 The Increasingly Knowledge-Based Economy 174
12.3.4 Faltering Governmental (Tax) Revenues 175
12.3.5 Increasing Globalization 176
12.3.6 Increasing Liberalization of Economies 177
12.3.7 Higher Educational Finance and Accessibility 177
12.4 University Cost Estimation 180
12.5 Model for Unit Cost Estimation 181
12.6 Parent Student Total Cost Estimation among Nations 184
12.6.1 Estimated Expenses of Higher Education in India 185
12.6.2 Estimated Expenses of Higher Education in China 186
12.6.3 Estimated Expenses of Higher Education in Australia 186
12.6.4 Estimated Expenses of Higher Education in US 187
12.6.5 Estimated Expenses of Higher Education in Canada 188
12.6.6 Estimated Expenses of Higher Education in France 189
12.6.7 Estimated Expenses of Higher Education in England and Northern Ireland 190
12.6.8 Estimated Expenses of Higher Education in the Russian Federation .. 191
12.6.9 Estimated Expenses of Higher Education in Japan 193
12.7 Conclusion 193

Annexure–A: World University Rankings 2010 193

Annexure–B: In Indian Context: UGC Academic Performance Indicators—2010 212

Annexure–C: In Indian Context: AICTE Norms for Infrastructure–2010: Norms for Land Requirement and Building Space for Technical Institution 238

Annexure–D: Different Data Formats for University/College 252

References 357

CHAPTER 1

University System

1.1 INTRODUCTION

A **University** is an institution of higher education and research, which grants academic degrees at all levels (associate, bachelor, master, and doctorate) in a variety of subjects. A university provides both undergraduate education and postgraduate education. The word *university* is derived from the Latin *universitas magistrorum et scholarium*, roughly meaning "community of teachers and scholars".

Although each institution is differently organized, nearly all universities have a board of trustees; a President, Chancellor, or Rector; at least one Vice President, Vice-Chancellor, or Vice-Rector; and Deans of various divisions. Universities are generally divided into a number of academic departments, schools or faculties. Public university systems are ruled over by government-run higher education boards. They review financial requests and budget proposals and then allocate funds for each university in the system. They also approve new programs of instruction and cancel or make changes to existing programs. In addition, they plan for the coordinated growth and development of various institutions of higher education in the state or country. However, many public universities in the world have a considerable degree of financial, research and pedagogical autonomy. Private universities are privately funded having generally a broader independence from state policies.

Despite the variable policies, or cultural and economic standards available in different geographical locations create a tremendous disparity between universities around the world and even inside a country, the universities are usually among the foremost research and advanced training providers in every society. Most universities not only offer courses in subjects ranging from the natural sciences, engineering, architecture or medicine, to sports sciences, social sciences, law or humanities, they also offer many amenities to their student population including a variety of places like mess, canteen, banks, bookshops, print shops, job centres, and coffee bars. In addition, universities have a range of facilities like libraries, sports centers, students' unions, computer labs, and research laboratories. In a number of countries, major classic universities usually have their own botanical gardens, astronomical observatories, business incubators and university hospitals.

1.2 OBJECTIVES OF UNIVERSITY EDUCATION

The main objectives of an University are:

1. To assist students in developing educational plans those are consistent with their life goals.
2. To provide students with accurate information about academic progression and degree requirements.
3. To help student's access to campus resources that will enhance their ability to be academically successful. To assist students in overcoming educational and personal problems.
4. To review and use available data about students' academic and educational needs, performance, aspirations and problems.
5. To increase student retention by providing a personal contact that students often need and request, thereby connecting them to the institution. Assisting students with decision-making and career direction.
6. Providing clear and accurate information regarding institutional policies, procedures and programmes and to make all concerned to comply with them.
7. Assisting students in the selection of courses and other educational experiences (e.g. internships, study abroad).
8. Evaluating student progress towards established goals.
9. Interpreting various interest/ability inventories that provide students with information related to their career choices.
10. To create socially responsible citizens/leaders in various fields.
11. To do a good research for satisfying the requirements of industry and society.
12. To be an institution of social transformation.

1.3 CHARACTERISTICS OF GOOD HIGHER EDUCATION SYSTEM

Every system in this world has its own inner characteristics that define the inner strength of its system. A University needs a set of good characteristics. These characteristics can be given thus:

1. A well structured academic system
2. Enhanced system of teaching and learning
3. Good academic discipline among students
4. Well qualified teachers
5. Structured system of budgeting and control
6. Good infrastructure
7. Student freedom
8. Good academic freedom
9. Well structured academic library
10. Uniform fees and service policy

11. Operational independence
12. Better synergy among employees and employer
13. Managerial independence
14. Evolutionary development/Promoting new sources of innovation
15. Well designed placement training programmes
16. Transparent decentralized administrative system
17. Department advisory committee
18. De-centralization of responsibilities/work
19. Well designed transparent service rules and promotion policy
20. Good student admission policy
21. Well structured student motivational mechanism
22. Good system of counseling and guidance
23. Emergent behavior
24. Market driven changes
25. Well designed training programmes for better placement opportunities
26. Inter-disciplinary study
27. Well planned annual campus events
28. A good professional society activities
29. A good industry-institute interaction
20. A good research and development system
31. A well structured academic feedback system.

These things are explained in the following section in detail.

1.3.1 A Well Structured Academic System

A well structured academic system having the following system of practices should aim to get a well structured planning, monitoring and coverage of curriculum and syllabus. These attributes are:

1. Governance and leadership
2. Institutional mission and vision
3. A well defined syllabus
4. Class room teaching
5. Academic year gives an idea about the syllabus delivery and contents
6. Academic calendar
7. Course plan
8. Lab manual
9. Full-time/Part-time programmes
10. Well structured planning, monitoring and coverage of curriculum and syllabus
11. Grading System

12. Student centric learning initiatives
13. Student associations
14. System to collect students' feedback and using them to fine tune the system
15. Laboratories, workshops and equipment (facilities, maintenance and utilization)
16. Information access facilities
17. Credit systems
18. Seminar/workshop
19. Industrial visits
20. Take home examination
21. Student counseling
22. Extra-curricular activities/Co-curricular activities
23. Student teacher relationship.

These attributes of a well structured academic system is explained in the chapter 2 in detail.

1.3.2 Enhanced System of Teaching and Learning

Learning is acquiring new knowledge, behaviors, skills, values, preferences or understanding, and may involve synthesizing different types of information. The ability to learn is possessed by humans and gets augmented by using machines at times. Progress over time tends to follow learning curves. Enhancing the competence and status of trainees is not just about creating more degrees; it is also about devising informal ways to update skills from within the relevant sector, and with the help of other trainers. Enhanced system of learning involves usage of various technology and modern devices. For example, facility like a digital library enhances the teaching and learning process. A language lab enhances the learning of that language.

1.3.3 Good Academic Discipline among Students

A University discipline policy can help to control and prevent students' misbehavior by coordinating the University's disciplinary procedures and by informing students what types of behavior are expected of them and what types are forbidden.

Such a policy, however, has inherent limitations. On the one hand, many disruptions occur in the classroom and are inseparable from the student-teacher relationship. On the other hand, even the best policy is only a document, and how it is carried out is important. According to a growing body of literature, the primary determinant of discipline policy's effectiveness is a healthy relationship between University and student—as indicated by such variables as principals' leadership styles and students' perceptions of whether or not they are fairly treated.

The discipline policy should enforce good ethics, moral practice and social responsibilities.

1.3.4 Well Qualified Faculty Team

A well qualified faculty has two components, granting of professionally qualified status and maintaining professionally qualified status. The guiding factor in the granting of professionally qualified status is the development of the faculty member's intellectual capital. This development should be a combination of academic preparation and professional experience. A faculty member generally must possess a master's degree in the area of teaching, but a master's degree in a related field may be acceptable if supplemented with a higher degree of professional experience. With exceptional professional experience, a faculty member may be granted professionally qualified status with only a bachelor's degree. A faculty member must have professional experience that is relevant to the faculty member's teaching assignment, significant in duration and level of responsibility, and current at the time of hiring.

To maintain professionally qualified status, a faculty member must complete at least three "activity units" in the following areas over the five-year period ending with the end of the review period:

- Professional experience
- Involvement in professional activities
- Academic intellectual contributions.

Irrespective of the type of activity the faculty member engages in, to maintain professionally qualified status, the evaluator needs to consider both the quality of the activity and the relevance of the activity to the field of teaching and the specific courses the professionally qualified faculty member will teach. Professionally qualified faculty may maintain the currency of their intellectual capital through intellectual contributions related to the field of teaching, similar to the maintenance requirement for academically qualified faculty.

1.3.5 Structured System of Budgeting and Control

A budget is generally a list of all planned expenses and revenues. It is a plan for saving and spending. The university budget control should give the complete picture of various activities. It should include both recurring and non-recurring expenditures.

1.3.6 Good Infrastructure

A good academic system needs an infrastructure facility. The list of complete infrastructure facilities required for the good academic system is explained in Chapter 7.

1.3.7 Student Freedom

The Student Rights and Responsibilities document should be given to each student highlighting its importance. It should contain guidelines to the rights and duties of students in matters of conduct, academic pursuits, the keeping of records, and publications. This report should describe structures and procedures for the formulation of regulations governing student conduct, for the interpretation and amendment of the guidelines, for the adjudication of student disciplinary cases, and for channeling student complaints, grievances, or concerns to faculty, staff and administrators for appropriate action.

1.3.8 Academic Freedom

Academic freedom is the belief that the freedom of inquiry by students and faculty members is essential to the mission of the academy, and that scholars should have freedom to teach or communicate ideas or facts (including those that are inconvenient to external political groups or to authorities) without being targeted for repression, job loss, or imprisonment.

Still, academic freedom has limits. Teachers should be careful to avoid controversial matter that is unrelated to the subject. When they speak or write in public, they are free to express their opinions without fear from institutional censorship or discipline, but they should show restraint and clearly indicate that they are not speaking for their institution. Academic tenure protects academic freedom by ensuring that teachers can be fired only for causes such as gross professional incompetence or behavior that evokes condemnation from the academic community itself.

1.3.9 Uniform Fees and Service Policy

It is essential to maintain uniform fees for different categories of students. It should be a mandatory for all Universities to introduce fees and funds structure and to give justice to the students and teachers. Further, the University must offer various services uniformly to all students and staff.

1.3.10 Better Synergy amongst Employer, Staff and Students

It is essential to have a good synergy between Employer, Staff and Students. In order to maintain the complete information about concept and ideas of the management it should be spread to all staff and students of the organization uniformly and justified also. This is the first step in creating the synergy among these people. There should not be any misconception about the facts and ideas of the campus. There should be a mechanism through which any one should be able to convey and justify his/her ideas to the top management (Quality Circle/TQM). A discussion or a convincing reply must be forthcoming from the superiors.

1.3.11 Managerial Independence

A system of systems is one where in constituent systems are separately acquired and integrated. The managerial independence is achieved when heads are in either a separate part of an organisation or a completely different organisation from any heads with a vested interest in the outcome of that task, reducing any (intentional or unintentional) pressure. Everywhere it is essential to have, different levels of managerial independence so as to ensure the right functioning of the University/College/School/ Departments.

1.3.12 Evolutionary Development/Promoting New Sources of Innovation

Evolutionary Professional Development is the means by which members of professional associations maintain, improve and broaden their knowledge and skills and develop the personal qualities required in their professional lives. Building on a pilot research, such a project provides an innovative integrated scientific and mathematical context for teachers to implement best practices through inquiry and modeling. It is essential to motivate research to find new products and services. A system of systems comes into existence gradually and continues to change, with functions and purposes added, removed, and modified with experience. This should lead to new innovative development of products and services.

1.3.13 Well Designed Placement Training Programmes

Institution should maintain very strong links with the industry and continue to receive generous support from various organizations. The institution provides opportunities for interaction between students and representatives of the Industry to facilitate placement in suitable jobs. The Training and Placement Officer should maintain liaison with industries for summer placement as well as final placement of students passing out from the college. Institution should also act as a platform to have dialogue between representatives of Govt. organizations, financial institutions, entrepreneurs and students. A partial list is enumerated about where alumni are working, so that they can be contacted for placement purpose at the first instance. Training and Placement cell can also arrange guest lectures, workshops and seminars on career opportunities, entrepreneurship and personality development, etc.

The main functions of the training and placement cell are:

1. Maintaining data base of various recruiting Organizations.
2. Maintaining a comprehensive student data base.
3. Companies are to be requested to mail their requirement to Training and Placement Officer.
4. The resume of students interested in the organization should be collected and forwarded, if so desired.
5. Arranging On-Campus/Off-Campus Interviews
6. The placement schedule should be worked out with mutual consent.
7. The companies are to be advised to give pre placement talk before the selection process at the campus.
8. The final job offers should be routed through Training and Placement cell.

1.3.14 Transparent Administrative System

An academic administration is a branch of university or a set of college employees responsible for the maintenance and supervision of the institution and is separate from the faculty or academics, although some personnel may have joint responsibilities. Some type of separate administrative structure exists at almost all academic institutions, as fewer and fewer schools are governed by employees who are also involved in academic or scholarly work. Many administrators are academics with advanced degrees who fight for time to teach or conduct research actively. Each department needs an advisory committee to fix the further direction of work.

Decentralization is the process of dispersing decision-making administration closer to the staff and/or citizen. All the important decisions and actions at the lower level, are subject to the approval of top management. It includes the dispersal of administration in areas like engineering, management science, sociology and economics. Decentralization is a systematic delegation of authority at all levels of management and in all of the organization. Even in a decentralized situation concern and authority are retained by the top management for taking major decisions and framing policies concerning the whole concern. Rest of the authority may be delegated to the middle level and lower level of management.

Key decentralized administrative responsibilities (and thus administrative units) in an University include the following components:

1. Admissions (Dean—Admissions)
2. Supervision of academic affairs such as hiring, promotion, tenure, and evaluation (with faculty input where appropriate; Dean Academic Affairs and Controller of Examination)
3. Maintenance of official records (Registrar is in charge of all non academic matters)

4. Maintenance and audit of financial flows and records (Finance Officer and Registrar)
5. Oversight of student life and activities, such as religious or cultural groups, career centers and public service centers (Dean Student Affairs)
6. Library and archive management (Chief Librarians)
7. Maintenance and construction of campus buildings (Estate Officer)
8. Maintenance of the campus grounds (Estate Officer, Physical Education Director)
9. Safety and security of people and property on the campus (often organized as an office of public safety or campus police)
10. Supervision and support of campus computers and network (Director Information Technology/Computer Centre)
11. Fundraising from private individuals and foundations ("Director development" or "advancement")
12. Research administration (including grants and contract administration, and institutional compliance with federal and state regulations—Director/Dean Research)
13. Public affairs (including relations with the media, the community, and local, state, and federal governments—Public Relations Officer)
14. Placement and Training (Placement Officer).

1.3.15 Department Advisory Committee

The Academic Advisory Committee is responsible for evaluation of the academic performance of students. One of its goals is to ensure that students continue to make normal academic progress towards graduation. The committee works closely with students, academic advisers and Academic Support Services in assisting students with the needed skills for academic success.

The Academic Advisory Committee consists of representatives from the Teaching Faculty, Students, the Director of the Academic Enrichment Center and the Registrar. At the end of each semester, the committee reviews academic records of students to evaluate academic progress.

1.3.16 Well Designed Transparent Service Rules and Promotion Policy

Every institute must explain clearly about the service rules and promotion policies. The policy must explain the following:

1. Procedure for appointment in different grades
2. Objective, Position and Salary benefits and perks if any
3. Term of appointment
4. Term of Increment and promotion
5. Expected contribution of work

6. Equal Opportunity and Affirmative Action Policies
7. Condition for termination.

1.3.17 Good Student Admission Policy

A good student policy needs to be drafted to give an idea about the institution. It is essential to make the admission policy transparent without any ambiguities. An institution's admissions policy underlies everything it does in the area of the admission of students, from enquiries, recruitment and outreach to making decisions, transmitting data to University, Relationship Building, diversity, transition support, registration and beyond. Closely related to the institution's mission it shows the commitment of the institution to applicants, students and parents. Institutions are urged to have comprehensive admission policies that are easy to understand and are transparent to applicants and their advisors. Details like whether 100% admissions are by students marks alone or else what is the break up and how the other part will be filled. Is any quota system followed? Is there any separate entrance exam to be taken by every one or the marks in the school final level is the only criteria for admission? Such things are to be made clear to all. The Good Practice Statement on Admissions Policies can be drafted to help all the applicants to find their suitability. The admission policy needs to give an idea about the following items.

1. Purpose of the admissions policy and connected legal issues.
2. Responsibility for admissions, mode of admission, quantum, frequency and mode of payment of fees by students.
3. Admissions policy—content, approval, responsibilities and monitoring.
4. Information for applicants about the available infrastructure, courses, faculty and entry requirements.

1.3.18 Well Structured Student Motivational Mechanism

Motivation is the activation or energisation of goal-orientated behavior. The term is generally used for humans but, theoretically, it can also be used to describe the causes for animal behavior as well. According to various theories, motivation may be rooted in the basic need to minimize physical pain and maximize pleasure, or it may include specific needs such as eating and resting, or a desired object, indulging in a hobby, reaching a goal, state of being idle or it may be attributed to less-apparent reasons such as altruism, selfishness, morality, or avoiding mortality. Conceptually, motivation should not be confused with either volition or optimism. Motivation is related to, but distinct from, emotion.

Students are exposed to so many different people (Teachers) in their lives. Everyone and everything at this juncture is trying extremely hard to stimulate the students, make them think, make them work and make them into people the world can be proud of. Because of this overwhelming input of stimulus and influence, students struggle to find their own identity. Motivation at this juncture becomes essential. Once they have recognized this, they tend to deal with the constant environmental pressure by adopting one important policy: "I will only allow others to influence me if they prove to me that they are worth it". This policy is their mechanism of making sure that the right person gets to them at the right time, and it's a good way of doing it. The only time it becomes an issue is when they get impressed by a person who is a bad influence, or when a good person makes no effort to impress them. Motivation can be from a fellow student or a student counselor or any teacher in whom that a student reposes faith.

Motivation mechanisms like giving prizes, rewards and certificates for various activities are also essential in all academic environments.

1.3.19 Good System of Counseling and Guidance

A counselor is an educator who works in colleges/universities to provide academic, career, college access, and personal/social competencies to every student. The interventions used include: Developmental College counseling curriculum lessons and annual planning for every student. Competent group and individual counseling. College/University Counselors use specific skills in advocacy, leadership, systemic change, technology integration, equity assessment, and teaming and collaboration with other stakeholders in a data-driven comprehensive developmental College counseling program.

It is essential to understand the student mentality as well as problems they are to face inside and outside the campus. This will enable university to smoothen the administration, to suit to the student's needs.

In line with the University's mission—'to help the student to succeed'—the Counseling Service aims to enhance student mental wellbeing by providing counseling to students of the University. Through counseling, individuals who are experiencing mental wellbeing difficulties may be facilitated in working towards living a more satisfying and enjoyable life, enabling them to achieve their full potential in their studies at the University as well as in their future lives.

In addition to providing counseling, the service aims to promote a culture of positive mental wellbeing by: reducing stigma through awareness raising campaigns; providing student and staff training sessions and workshops; offering consultation to staff supporting students experiencing difficulties; facilitating access to other University services and external agencies; and instigating and advising on University policies and procedures.

The aim to offer a counseling service of high quality is that the student's experience of the service is positive and helpful one. However, unfortunately this may not always be the case. To make improvements wherever possible, student's feedback about any aspect of the Counseling Service in the form of a compliment, complaint or suggestion is to be obtained. The University should respond to any feedback that is received by considering the issue(s) involved and implementing any changes that will improve the service, where appropriate and possible.

As a general rule, any information relating to student's attendance for counseling will remain confidential to the Counseling Service and will not be disclosed to anyone else unless the student requests so. The Counselors receive ongoing supervision from practitioners external to the University and this supervisory relationship is also usually confidential. However, there are certain circumstances where a Counselor (or Head of Counseling Service) may feel it necessary or be bound by law to break confidentiality, liaising with appropriate persons and/or organizations outside the Counseling Service. Such circumstances usually relate to a concern for the students self or others' wellbeing and usually the counselor (or Head of Counseling Service) would attempt to discuss the situation with the student concerned before taking any action.

The Counseling Service has a core staff team of professionally trained and qualified counselors who are used to working with students experiencing a wide variety of difficulties. At the Department level, the committee consists a Chairman (Deputy Dean of the School) and various members (Academic Advisors). The duties are to assist the mentors to perform their duties as discussed above. The duties are to determine the policies such as objectives, selection, counseling duties, skill training, counseling, honorarium, coordination of the progress of counseling.

1.3.20 Emergent Behavior

A University performs functions and carries out purposes that do not depend on any of its individual department or systems. However it is the socio-technical aspects of the University which are dynamic in nature and involve multiple time scales and uncertainty, and likely so there are to have emergent properties. Voluntary and collaborative interactions among the departments often result in new emergent properties or behavior that are desired and fulfill the primary purpose of the University.

1.3.21 Market Driven Changes

In the modern economy education has become a commercial entity. Institutions generate income through their training, research, consultancy etc. It is essential to offer a training course based on job market. So, the institutions need to adapt the changes according to the market. The marketplace requirements for technical talent are evolving quickly. The best jobs are in client-facing areas—designing advanced systems and sophisticated applications customized to add business value in a specific organization. These new jobs for instance in the IT sector, are much more collaborative, interdisciplinary and broader than the solitary, code-crunching programming jobs of the past. These new jobs require solid technical competence, combined with business and organizational knowledge, as well as good communication skills.

1.3.22 Inter-Disciplinary Study

The adjective interdisciplinary is most often used in educational circles when researchers from two or more disciplines pool their approaches and modify them so that they are better suited to the problem on hand, including the case of the team-taught course where students are required to understand a given subject in terms of multiple traditional disciplines. For example, the subject of land use may appear differently when examined by different disciplines, for instance, biology, chemistry, economics, geography and politics.

In a sense, "interdisciplinary" involves looking a subject from various angles and eventually cutting across disciplines and forming a new method for understanding the subject. A common goal of understanding unites various methods and acknowledges a common or shared subject or problem, even if it spreads to other disciplines.

"Interdisciplinary" in reference to an approach to organizing intellectual inquiry is an evolving field, and stable, consensus definitions are not yet established for some subordinate or closely related fields.

An interdisciplinary community or project is made up of people from multiple disciplines and professions who are engaged in creating and applying new knowledge as they work together as equal stakeholders in addressing a common challenge. The key question is what new knowledge (of an academic discipline nature), which is outside the existing disciplines, is required to address the challenge. Aspects of the challenge cannot be addressed easily with existing distributed knowledge, and new knowledge becomes a primary sub-goal of addressing the common challenge. The nature of the challenge, either its scale or complexity, requires that many people have interactional expertise to improve their efficiency working across multiple disciplines as well as within the new interdisciplinary area. An inter-disciplinarily person is a person with degrees from one or more academic disciplines with additional interactional expertise in one or more additional academic disciplines, and new knowledge that is claimed by more than one discipline. Over time, interdisciplinary work can lead to an increase or a decrease in the number of academic disciplines.

In any academic institution one needs a very good inter-disciplinary study for the birth of new subject of study as well as for the development of new products and services.

Because most participants in interdisciplinary ventures are in general trained in traditional disciplines, they must learn to appreciate differing perspectives and methods. For example, a discipline that places more emphasis on quantitative "rigor" may produce practitioners who think of themselves (and their discipline) as "more scientific" than others; in turn, colleagues in "softer" disciplines may associate quantitative approaches with an inability to grasp the broader dimensions of a problem. An interdisciplinary program may not succeed if its members remain stuck in their disciplines (and in disciplinary attitudes).

Interdisciplinary programs may fail if they are not given sufficient autonomy. For example, interdisciplinary faculties are usually recruited to a joint appointment, with responsibilities in both an interdisciplinary program (such as women's studies) and a traditional discipline (such as history). If the traditional discipline makes the tenure decisions, new interdisciplinary faculty will be hesitant to commit themselves fully to interdisciplinary work. Other barriers include the generally disciplinary orientation of most scholarly journals, leading to the perception, if not the fact, that interdisciplinary research is hard to publish. In addition, since traditional budgetary practices at most universities channel resources through the disciplines, it becomes difficult to account for a given scholar or teacher's salary and time. During periods of budgetary retraction, the natural tendency to serve the primary constituency (i.e., students majoring in the traditional discipline) makes resources scarce for teaching and research comparatively far from the center of the discipline as traditionally understood. For these same reasons, the introduction of new interdisciplinary programs is often perceived as a competition for diminishing funds, and may for this reason meet resistance.

Due to these and other barriers, interdisciplinary research areas are strongly motivated to become disciplines themselves. If they succeed, they can establish their own research funding programs and make their own tenure and promotion decisions. In so doing, they lower the risk of entry.

1.3.23 Well Planned Annual Campus Events

A regular annual campus event planning is essential for any academic institution. The academic calendar is replete with regular annual events. The main objectives of these activities are as follows:

1. To assist, facilitate, promote and undertake research, training and allied activities, in particular, in relation to major problems calling for inter-disciplinary perspectives, through co-operation among various branches of science and technology for example a space mission.
2. To facilitate exchange of information on research and training between institutions.
3. To facilitate co-operative arrangements for research and training between institutions for example mutual arrangements for exchange of research and

training personnel and of research studies and survey and statistical data; to organize strategic training to build capabilities and capacities.

4. To encourage and assist formation of regional and local chapters and study groups from time to time, with a view to (a) facilitating co-operation among interested associations and institutes, (b) reviewing progress in the development of research and training, and (c) suggesting and exploring areas and problems calling for greater attention in future on the part of social scientists and social science institutions.
5. To organize on its own or arrange for conferences/workshops and seminars from time to time on selected problems, especially of an inter-disciplinary nature in co-operation with interested institutions, associations and others interested in promotion of space sciences.
6. To promote greater sharing of infrastructure facilities among members of the Association for research and training in statistical and empirical studies and investigations, for instance, in respect of statistical equipment, computers, library resources, and conference facilities.
7. To create and disseminate information, publish journal, newsletters, reports and studies on ongoing research and training developments and prospective needs and priorities for the information of member institutions and other interested in Promotion of space Sciences.
8. To co-operate and exchange information and Publications with other associations, agencies and organizations, both national and international, pursuing or interested in similar objectives and activities.
9. To foster the training of research workers in fields related to its objects and to undertake training programmes.
10. To promote application of knowledge of space sciences and stimulate development of the profession of space sciences; to facilitate participation of space scientists in major policy making and planning activities at national and state levels and to promote application of space sciences in policy making. For example, different subjects are used for communication, television, weather prediction, cartography, geographical survey and what not, each one being a giant of subjects of their own but have to be understood by a space scientist.
11. To make celebrations on the year achievements and to motivate the students as well as the employees of the institutions.

This plan involves various activities like:

1. Annual Day
2. Cultural Events
3. Sports Days
4. Other Social Day Celebrations
5. Conferences

6. Seminars/Workshops
7. Memorial Lectures
8. Convocation
9. Club Events
10. Association Actives, etc.

The universities/colleges having the convention of celebrating different important days across the year in remembering their service and achievements.

1.3.24 A Good Professional Society Activities

A professional association (also called a professional body, professional organization, or professional society) is a non-profit organization seeking to further a particular profession, the interests of individuals engaged in that profession, and the public interest. Academic institutes need a good set of professional actives. These enable the institutes to associate at the national and international level which may lead to understanding various new concepts and developments.

The roles of these professional associations have been variously defined: "A group of people in a learned occupation who are entrusted with maintaining control or oversight of the legitimate practice of the occupation;" also a body acting "to safeguard the public interest;" organizations which "represent the interest of the professional practitioners," and so "act to maintain their own privileged and powerful position as a controlling body."

Such bodies generally strive to achieve a balance between two often conflicting mandates. Though professional bodies often act to protect the public by maintaining and enforcing standards of training and ethics in their profession, they often also act like a cartel or a labor union (trade union) for the members of the profession, though this description is commonly rejected by the body concerned.

Many professional bodies are involved in the development and monitoring of professional educational programs, and the updating of skills, and thus perform professional certification to indicate that a person possesses qualifications in the subject area. Sometimes membership of a professional body is synonymous with certification, though not always. Membership of a professional body, as a legal requirement, can in some professions form the primary formal basis for gaining entry to and setting up practice within the profession.

Many professional bodies also act as learned societies for the academic disciplines underlying their professions. The students and staff/faculties should enroll as members in the respective professional bodies. The local chapter/section of the professional body should get involved in various activities.

1.3.25 A Good Industry-Institute Interaction

The broad goals of institute-industry interaction can be stated as under:

1. To evolve educational programmes in the institutions which can help the pass-outs to cope with the professional tasks as they enter the service without the need for an elaborate service training programme by the employer.
2. To create adequate activities of continuing education in collaboration with user organizations so that the level of competence of working engineers and the faculty is improved.
3. *Curriculum Development:* Experts from industry are to be actively involved in redrafting the curricula of the educational programmes so that they may emphasize the inclusion of topics which will improve the quality of the engineering graduate and prepare him to face the tasks that will be assigned to him on entering the profession.
4. *Instructional Aids:* Experts from the industry may prepare videotapes or other instructional material/aids on specialized industrial process, quality control measures, instrumentation, manufacturing techniques, etc and present them to the institutions as quite often, it is impossible for the institutions to acquire these facilities within their meager resources. The faculty should be associated in this work so that they can make use of these instructional materials while delivering the concerned courses in which these topics fall.
5. *Student Evaluation:* Experts from the industry may be invited to participate in the evaluation of semester/colloquium of students, their project work, thesis work of postgraduate and research students etc. so that they may be able to offer constructive suggestions for the improvement and applicability of the techniques employed.
6. *Industrial Training of Students:* It is proposed that the industrial training of students may intially be restricted to 4–6 weeks during summer vacation, at the end of third year, and it is fully supervised by the faculty of the institution and the engineers from the industry. The programme should be well defined so that it is taken up seriously by all concerned and is evaluated jointly at the end of the training period.
7. *Industrial Training for Teaching Staff:* As at present a large number of teaching staff members do not have any industrial exposure and experience or both, it is necessary to arrange for them some training in the industry. The nature of training as well as its duration will vary with the level of seniority of the faculty member and the type of participation expected from him when he interacts with the professional engineers. Since it involves a very large number of staff, each institution may have to prepare a plan of action of its own in consultation with the collaborating industries and phase it over a period of 3–4 years. Adequate provision for staff reserves will have to be made, where necessary, to take care of instructional requirements, if the training period extends to the academic session.

8. *Retraining of Supporting Technical Staff:* In many intuitions, the supporting technical staff is not properly qualified and they pick up the skills only through experience. They need to be retrained to improve their skills so that they will be able to handle more sophisticated instruments and equipments, which are replacing the obsolete and in preparing the setups for project work.
9. To permit faculty to gain experience of the industrial practices, quality control and standardisation procedures, safety measures, etc. which in turn will improve their instructional qualities.
10. To permit the experienced engineers to serve as faculty members for specified periods of time, thereby enabling the students to get acquainted with the live problems of the industry and the way in which they were solved.
11. To facilitate the reorientation of project work and to train the students in solving problems keeping the constraints in view.
12. To bring the experts in the two systems together so that they may explore the possibility of collaboration efforts in undertaking research and development projects by pooling the available resources.

1.3.26 A Good Research and Development System

A good research system is essential for better industrial growth and in turn it will pave way for academic development. Research can be defined as the search for knowledge or any systematic investigation to establish facts. The primary purpose for applied research is discovering, interpreting, and the development of methods and systems for the advancement of human knowledge on a wide variety of scientific matters of our world and the universe. Research can use the scientific method, but need not do so always.

Research and development deal with the process of "creative work undertaken on a systematic basis in order to increase the stock of knowledge, including knowledge of man, culture and society, and the use of this stock of knowledge to devise new applications". In a new product design and development plays a crucial role in the success of the company. In an industry that is fast changing, firms must continually revise their design and range of products. This is necessary due to continuous technology change and development as well as to keep pace with the competitors and the changing preference of customers.

Research often refers to basic experimental research; development refers to the exploitation of discoveries. Research involves the identification of possible chemical compounds or theoretical mechanisms. The academic institutions should aid the companies to come out with a new product and services. An R&D alliance is a mutually beneficial formal relationship formed between two or more parties to pursue a set of agreed upon goals while remaining independent organizations, where acquiring new knowledge is a goal by itself.

1.3.27 A Well Structured Academic Feedback System

The Academic Feedback System is a method by which the faculty members are able to provide academic feedback to selected students, if desired, during a semester. The feedback can include rating attendance, participation, tests/quizzes and homework, and entering an anticipated grade.

This is a field where faculty can also offer suggestions for improvement, such as, meeting with the instructor, seeking tutoring, doing make-up assignments, better preparing for class and/or improving time management. This is an important tool for faculty and students, especially students who are struggling in class or are on academic probation, as it gives them a chance to track their progress and seek assistance before they fall behind or it's too late to make a difference in their grade. Of course, the academic feedback system is not intended to replace personal communication with students, but it does provide a record of input and can be viewed by a student's Adviser, allowing him or her objective overview of a student's overall performance.

Apart from this the system must provide a facility to get the feedback from various employees and faculty members of the institution.

1.4 CONCLUSION

This Chapter elucidates different basic practices of university systems which exist around the world. It introduces the objectives and also explains the characteristics of a good education system. Universities are highly independent institutions having separate bodies to decide the aims, models that can be adopted, programmes that are to be started, governing rules to run the show etc and hence do not fall into a fixed frame. Even in existing Universities, anything and everything may be changed and hence the University system as a whole is very dynamic and can be defined and described only in a moving frame of reference which also changes with respect to time.

CHAPTER 2

Components of Well Structured Academic System

2.1 INTRODUCTION

A well structured academic system should have the following system of practices. It should have a well structured planning, monitoring and coverage of curriculum and syllabii. This is to be supported by means of different components and methods. These are covered by having the following items in place with proper perspective.

2.2 GOVERNANCE AND LEADERSHIP

The leadership must provide a clear vision and mission to the University. The functions of the institution and its academic and administrative units are to be governed by the principles of participation and be transparent. Academic and administrative planning in the University should go hand in hand. The institution should practice relevant welfare schemes for all its constituencies. There should be fair and expeditious grievance redressal mechanisms at all levels of the University. The University has to be effective in resource mobilization and planning development strategies. The University has to sustain good practices for governance and leadership.

2.3 INSTITUTIONAL MISSION AND VISION

The vision and mission of the University should be in tune with the objectives of the Higher Education Policies of the nation. The vision statement has to be realized by defining and doing relevant activities. Top management should have commitment, leadership and involvement for effective and efficient transaction of teaching and learning processes. Management and head of the institution should ensure that responsibilities are well defined and communicated to the concerned staff of the institution. Head of the institution has to ensure that valid information is available for the management to review the activities of the institution. Management has to encourage and support involvement of the staff for improvement of the effectiveness and efficiency of the institutional processes.

2.4 WELL DEFINED SYLLABUS

A syllabus is an outline and summary of topics to be covered in an educational or training course. It is descriptive (unlike the prescriptive or specific curriculum). A syllabus is either set out by a board of experts, or prepared by the professor who supervises or controls the course quality.

Both syllabus and curriculum are often combined, and usually given to each student during the first class session so that the objectives and the means of obtaining them are made clear to them. A syllabus usually contains specific information about the course, such as information on how, where and when to contact the lecturer and teaching assistants; an outline of what will be covered in the course; a schedule of test dates and the due dates for assignments; the grading policy for the course; specific classroom rules; etc. With many courses concluding in an exam, syllabi are used to ensure consistency between schools and that all teachers know what must be taught and what is not required (extraneous). Exams can only test knowledge based on information included in the syllabus. With these thoughts in mind, the basic components of a learning-centered syllabus described are to contain the following.

Basic Information: The name and number of the course, meeting times and location, credit hours, and semester, instructor information; office location and hours, appointment scheduling, phone numbers, contact information for teaching or lab assistance and prerequisites of courses, knowledge, or skills students should already have are to be made available.

Required Texts and Materials: List of all required textbooks, technology, and other materials (packets, programs, Internet access, and so on) along with information about editions, volumes, and other details; even hints on locating copies of difficult-to-find materials, are a veritable boon to the students.

Course Description: Summary of what the course covers, with more details than the short catalog descriptions; give the students a more complete picture of what is included.

Course Purpose: Explanation of why students should take this course, how it is relevant to them, will help them now and in the future.

Course Learning Outcomes: List of three to five learning outcomes for each course which may indicate to the students what to really "get" from their experience, and/or ideas/experiences they are likely to remember 5 years from now. These should be linked to students' lives, challenging yet attainable, and inspiring.

Student learning Goals: A space for students to record their own goals and hopes and refer to them often, to achieve their goals.

Classroom Procedures: Summary of the basic routines and learning activities for the course, how the system will assess students' knowledge and skills, what students can expect from teachers and vice versa.

Participation: Explanation of how one expects students to participate in the class, how students should prepare, and how they will be assessed in their participation.

Recommended Study Habits and Other Tips: Helpful tips and hints for students about how to get the most out of each course, how to prepare for the assignments and exams, and other suggestions that will help them excel in the class.

Tips on Using the Syllabus: Explanation of how students can use the syllabus to their best advantage.

Grading Procedures: A breakdown of each assignment and exam, what it is worth, how much weightage is given for various portions, scores and percentages for each grade level. As with learning outcomes, assessments should be linked to students' lives, challenging yet attainable, and inspiring.

Assignment Descriptions: Descriptions and directions for each type of assignment, quiz, exam, and or directions to more detailed directions is the information students need to understand the course assessments.

Course Schedule: Calendar of class days, dates, topic titles, learning outcomes, assignments, exams, and so on, with an explanation of how scheduling changes if necessary will be handled.

Course Policies: Policy statements and standards that are to be met by the students. These may include standard statements from the University, college, or department.

2.5 ACADEMIC YEAR/ACADEMIC SEMESTER

The term academic year explains the pattern of working of the University/Institution. It also gives an idea about the syllabus delivery and examination. Generally two patterns of system are followed around the world. First is the yearly pattern of working system and second one is the semester system pattern. In the yearly pattern a 10 month working duration is followed. In the semester system the academic year is divided into two semesters. The first stretches from the June/July/August till November/December and is called the Fall. The Second one is called as Spring, which starts from December/ January and ends in March/April. Some universities also offer summer courses during summer vacation. Owing to its short duration, not many such countries are on offer.

2.6 ACADEMIC CALENDAR

This is a schedule of important dates and deadlines for an academic year. This should give complete information about various activities like working days, holidays, events and schedule. University Calendar can have various sub-schedules such as 1. Academic Calendar, 2. Athletics Calendar, 3. Alumni Calendar, 4. Theatre Arts and Dance Calendar, 5. Music Performance Calendar, etc.

2.7 LESSON PLAN

A course plan is a teacher's detailed description of the course of instruction for an individual lesson. A daily lesson plan is developed by a teacher to guide class instruction. The details of the plan may vary depending on the preference of the teacher, subject being covered, and the need and/or curiosity of students. There may be requirements mandated by the system regarding the plan.

A well developed lesson plan reflects the interests and needs of students. It incorporates some of the best practices for the educational field. The lesson plan correlates with the teacher's philosophy of education, which is what the teacher feels is the purpose of educating the students.

English program lesson plans, for example, usually center around four topics, namely the literary theme, elements of language and composition, literary history, and literary genre. A broad, thematic lesson plan is preferable, because it allows a teacher to create various research, writing, speaking, and reading assignments. It helps an instructor teach different literature genres and incorporate videotapes, films, and television programs. Also, it facilitates teaching literature and English together. School requirements and a teacher's personal tastes, in that order, determine the exact requirements for a lesson plan.

Unit plans follow much the same format as a lesson plan, but cover an entire unit of work, which may span several days or weeks. Modern constructivist teaching styles may not require individual lesson plans. The unit plan may include specific objectives and timelines, but lesson plans can be more fluid as they can adapt to student needs and learning styles.

2.8 LAB MANUALS

Purpose of Lab Manual is to provide an on-line data source for students of different laboratories. Lab Manual is composed of an assortment of experiments, data, techniques, procedures and experience collected over a long period of time by the authors. Laboratory Safety part of manual should contain a lot of information for training and protection of laboratory workers from potential biological, chemical and physical hazards. Main part should have Standard Operation Procedures (SOP), Guidelines, Reference materials and descriptions of the different laboratory methods. It provides description, working methods and technical support of the laboratory equipment.

2.9 QUESTION BANK

This work involves producing and maintaining a database of questions for all subjects which can be useful for students to get an idea about different perceptions about the subject. The students can use this question bank for preparation of semester exams. This will help the student to have an idea about the depth of the topics, various types of questioning possibilities, and marks that may be assigned for each etc. Needless to say that questions need not be asked from the question bank. It is only a model. It may not contain exhaustive questions.

2.10 CLASS ROOM TEACHING

A good method must be adopted by a teacher for effective teaching. A teacher can choose from various options thereby horning his/her own skill and acquiring his/her personalized style of teaching. The teacher may write lesson plans of their own, borrow plans from other teachers, or search online or within books for lesson plans. When deciding what teaching method to use, a teacher needs to consider students' background knowledge, environment, and learning goals. Teachers are aware that students learn in different ways, based on their background knowledge. Students have different ways of absorbing information and of demonstrating their knowledge. Teachers often use techniques which cater to multiple learning styles to help students retain information and strengthen understanding. A variety of strategies and methods are used to ensure that all students have equal opportunities to learn. A lesson plan may be carried out in several ways: Questioning, explaining, modeling, collaborating, and demonstrating.

A teaching method that includes questioning is similar to testing. A teacher may ask a series of questions to collect information of what students have learned and what needs to be taught. Testing is another application of questioning. A teacher tests the student on what was previously taught in order to identify if a student has learnt the material.

Learning can be done in three ways- Auditory, Visual, and Kinesthetic. It is important to try and include all three as much as possible into the lessons.

2.10.1 Explaining

This form is similar to lecturing. Lecturing is teaching by giving a discourse on a specific subject that is open to the public, usually given in the classroom. This can also be associated with models. Model is used as a visual aid to learning. Students can visualize an object or problem, then use reasoning and hypothesizing to determine an answer.

Students have the opportunity to learn from various types of delivery systems. Usually explaining (lecture) help the auditory learner through the speech of the teacher. If the teacher is to include visuals in the form of overheads or slide shows, his/her lecture can have duality. Although a student might only profit substantially from one form of teaching, all students gain some thing from each of different delivery systems.

2.10.2 Demonstrating

Demonstrations are done to provide an opportunity to learn new exploration and visual learning tasks from a different perspective. A teacher may use experimentation to demonstrate ideas in a science class. A demonstration may be used in the circumstance of proving conclusively a fact, as by reasoning or showing evidence.

The uses of storytelling and examples have long since become standard practice in the realm of textual explanation. But while a more narrative style of presentation is clearly a preferred practice in writing, judging by its prolificacy, this practice sometimes becomes one of the more ignored aspects of lecture. Lectures, especially in a collegiate environment, often become a setting more geared towards presentation of facts than a setting for narrative and/or connective learning. The use of examples and storytelling likely allows for better understanding but also leads to greater individual ability to relate to the information presented. Learning a list of facts provides a detached and impersonal experience while the same list, containing examples and stories, becomes, potentially, personally relatable. Furthermore, storytelling in information presentation may also reinforce memory retention because it provides connections between presentation and real-world examples experience, thus, putting things into a clearer perspective and allowing for increased neural representation in the brain. Therefore, it is important to provide personal, supplementary, examples in all forms of information presentation because this practice likely allows for greater interest in the subject matter and better information-retention rates.

Often in lectures, numbers or statistics are used to explain a subject. However when many numbers are being used it is difficult to comprehend the ideas put forth. Visuals those are bright in color, etc. offer a way for the students to put into perspective the numbers or stats that are being used. If the student can, not only hear but see what is being taught, it is more likely they will grasp fully what is being taught. It allows the student to relate to the subject matter in an effective manner.

2.10.3 Collaborating

Having students work in groups is another way a teacher can direct a lesson. Collaboration allows students to talk with each other and listen to all points of view in the discussion. It helps students' thinking to be less personally biased one. When this lesson plan is carried out, the teacher may be trying to assess the students in their ability to work as a team, leadership skills, or presentation abilities. It is one of the direct instructional methods.

Discussion is a different kind of group work. After some preparation, with clearly defined roles for each in an interesting topic, discussions may well take up most of the lesson, with the teacher only giving short feedback at the end or even in the following lesson. Discussions can take a variety of forms, e.g. fishbowl discussions.

Collaborating (kinesthetic) is useful in that it allows to actively participating in the learning process. These students are who learn by being able to relate the lesson with their physical participation in some way or other. Group projects followed by discussions are a great way to this type of learning.

2.10.4 Learning by Teaching

'To learn a subject teach that subject' is a well known saying. Learning by teaching is a widespread method in Germany, developed by Jean-Pol Martin. The students take the teacher's role and teach their peers.

This method is very effective when done correctly. Having students teach sections of the class as a group or as individuals is a great way to get the students to really study the topic and understand it so as to teach it to their peers. Students participation in the teaching process builds self-confidence, self-efficacy, and strengthens students' speaking and communication skills. Students will not only learn their given topic, but they will gain experience of putting things across the table during discussions.

2.11 LECTURE NOTES

Lecture notes are supplementary learning material given by faculty to the students for clear understanding. One person can easily miss an important point during a lecture through daydreaming or trying to understand the earlier point discussed. Students may also have difficulty deciding what information is important and what is elaboration or example. Creating a lecture notes for various subjects after a lecture gives students a chance to combine all their notes. Those who have missed some information can get it from their peers. The students can also decide what information is critical and give it proper emphasis. Student lecture notes could be done with the entire class, if it is small enough, or with a small set of working students. Student can also compare notes for further discussion and refinement. More over in semester pattern, a considerable coverage of specified topics in all details may be difficult inside the classroom. Lecture notes after discussing the topic will be more appropriate since it can take care of points which could not be covered for lack of time during lecture hours. Problems that require more time to solve can also be given as handout.

2.12 COURSE FILE

A course file is a file that records various materials and resources given to the students. This file is used as an instrument for evaluating the course by doing an analysis in every given interval. The faculty can identify newer methods for teaching a particular topic; problems of students in understanding can be recorded by the teacher. This file records various details like mark analysis, attendance, assignment, teaching resources, lecture notes and etc.

2.13 DELIVERY METHODS

There are different content delivery mechanisms available. It is essential and the prime responsibility of the institution is to arrange such facilities to be available in the campus. These mechanisms are lecture sessions, practical sessions, guest lectures, seminar/workshop, industrial visits, mini projects, tutoring, online and video lectures. These mechanisms are explained in the following sections.

2.13.1 Lectures Sessions

A lecture is oral presentations intended to present information or teach people about a particular topic, for example by a university or college teacher. Lectures are used to convey critical information, history, background, theories and equations. Usually the lecturer will stand in front of the students and deliver information relevant to the lecture's content.

2.13.2 Practical Sessions

A laboratory session implies active learning. It is a chance for students to work with and talk to each other, to experiment, explore, discuss, reflect and draw appropriate conclusions from their work. Some lab sessions aim to acquaint students with practical skills and techniques relevant to the discipline whereas others may focus on the development of skills in scientific inquiry.

2.13.3 Tutorials

More often than not, covering all aspects of a topic on hand during the lecture hour may not be feasible. Hence one extra hour per week may be set aside for tutorial, in which in addition to the concerned lecture, one or more colleagues of mathematics Departments will be helping individual students in solving varieties of problem to take care of all aspects. Usually tutorials are meant for mathematics in addition to other form of training.

2.13.4 Seminars/Workshop

A Seminar is, generally, a form of academic instruction, either at an academic institution or in a professional organization. It has the function of bringing together small groups for recurring meetings, focusing each time on some particular subject, in which everyone present is requested to actively participate. A workshop is another form of academic instruction which consists of experiment, exploration, discussion and drawing appropriate conclusions from their work, in recent trends of the subject. Academic institutions should conduct seminars and workshops to increase the student and faculty learning in advanced topics.

2.13.5 Guest Lectures

A guest lecture is a special lecture given by a field expert from outside agencies arranged for the students by the Department. This is one method to deliver advanced contents to the students.

2.13.6 Industrial Visits

This involves physically taking students for industrial visits during each course. Industry interface enables students to analyze and understand the ever changing dynamics of the industry. These visits provide students with adequate exposure in tackling live problems encountered in the working of an industrial entity. Faculty may take the students at least for one industrial visit per term.

2.13.7 Mini Projects

The individual mini project is by far the most important single piece of work in the degree programme. It provides an opportunity for the students to demonstrate independence and originality, to plan and organize a project over a reasonable period, and to put into practice some of the techniques that have been taught during the course.

2.13.8 Academic Tutoring

Passing down the knowledge to peers in an academic field of study by students currently enrolled in a type of higher education is known as academic tutoring. This seems to be important for students who are struggling to get help from others in an academic setting. A classroom setting is typically not enough for all students to learn the material that they need to know in order to pass the test or to go to next level classes. Academic tutoring from students at a higher grade level or experience in an academic setting can help to encourage and strengthen a student so that they do not fall behind.

2.13.9 Online Lecture Sessions

Today's digital era enables lecture sessions to be accessed remotely from different institutions. If institutions are connected any student from one institute can access the lectures from various advanced institutions. It is essential to give students access to such lectures.

2.13.10 Video Lecture Sessions

Leading universities/organizations have started delivering their lectures in the video format. All the standard topic lectures are available in the form of video. It is the essential responsibility of the faculty to arrange for such lectures in difficult topics. This will help the students to understand the subject in different aspects.

2.14 MONITORING

It is essential to assess the performance of various students in the learning environment. There are different monitoring methods available to asses the student's level of learning. These methods are periodic internal assessment test, assignments, exam and project reviews. The following sections explain these methods in detail.

2.14.1 Periodic/Internal Assessment Tests

Assessment is the process of documentation of the level of attainment of knowledge, skills, attitudes and beliefs usually in measurable terms. Assessment can focus on the individual learner, the learning community, the institution, or the educational system as a whole. This assessment can happen at specific intervals. It can be conducted as a test or take home examination for the students. The faculty of the subject has to decide about the method of assessment. A complex problem/engineering design that require a lot of time to solve may be given as take home examination. This assessment test is a prelude to the final university examination.

For example, in a closed book test, a test taker is often required to rely upon memory to respond to specific items whereas in an open book test, a test taker may use one or more supplementary tools such as a reference book or calculator when responding to an item.

2.14.2 Assignments

Assignment, refers to tasks assigned to students by their teachers to be completed mostly outside of class, and derives its name from the fact that most students do the majority of such work at home. Common homework assignments may include a quantity or period of reading to be performed, writing or typing to be completed, problems to be solved, a small project to be built (such as a diorama or display), or other skills to be practiced. The basic objectives of assigning homework to students are the same as schooling in general: To increase the knowledge and improve the abilities and skills of the students.

2.14.3 Oral/Model/Final Examinations

A standardized exam is one that is administered and scored in a consistent manner to ensure legal defensibility. Questions of the standard exam are fixed by external organizations and subject experts. Standardized exams are widely used, fixed in terms of scope, difficulty and format, and are usually significant in consequences. Standardized exams are usually held on fixed dates as determined by the exam developer, educational institution, or governing body, which may or may not be administered by the instructor, held within the classroom, or constrained by the classroom period. Although there is little variability between different copies of the same type of standardized exam, there is variability between different types of standardized exams. Formal examination often results in a grade or an exam score. This exam score decides the student's result, percentage of marks, etc.

2.14.4 Student Projects

It is essential to asses the quality of the students projects. It is important when choosing a project to understand the way it will be assessed. A good first-class project involves a combination of sound background research, a solid implementation, or a piece of theoretical work, and a thorough evaluation of the project's output in both absolute and relative terms. A good tip is to try to think of the project as an "investigation", rather than an effort to deliver a fully-functioning "product". Proper evaluation of the project becomes crucial to achieve high marks. The very best projects invariably cover some new ground, e.g. by developing a complex application which does not already exist, or by enhancing some existing application or method to improve its functionality, performance etc. A straightforward implementation project is acceptable, but one must appreciate that it is unlikely to gain high marks, regardless of how well it is done. Likewise, projects which are predominantly survey reports, unless they are backed up with experimentation, implementation, or theoretical analysis are not acceptable.

The initial assessment of the project will be undertaken by the supervisor and second marker. The assessment will then be completed by the assessment team which is made up by supervisors and second markers of other projects, and by other teaching staff and researchers who are interested in the subject area. The team members will attend the presentation and agree a team mark. The team marks are later moderated to ensure that the marks are globally consistent. The projects are marked under the following headings:

Background Preparation: This component assesses the way one has arrived at the initial project specification, work programme and list of objectives. It particularly addresses the background research undertaken and the manner in which the approach and programme of work fits in with the current state-of-the-art. It is worth about 15% of the final mark.

General Competence: This assesses one's overall approach to the project and one's ability to overcome the inevitable complications which may arise. The specific areas in which one will be assessed are management and organization, reliability and punctuality, overall technical competence, and individual contribution to the project. This part of the assessment is worth about 25% of the final mark.

Technical Achievement: This assesses the main technical output from the project. It addresses specific issues such as the design, correctness, elegance, usability etc. of the final product and the significance of the work in relation to the state-of-the-art.

2.14.5 Student Feedback

Student feedback is used by students to give in writing about faculty performance in the class rooms. This feedback may be in response to a questioner or a written feedback. This feedback will be used to have a self check by faculty members. This may improve the delivery mechanism and the depth of the contents to suit the particular set of students in a classroom. It may be desirable to obtain once after 10 to 15 hours of teaching and another at the end of the course. Based on feedback faculty should not be punished.

2.14.6 Unit/Experiment Coverage Report

This report is used to know the status of the syllabus completion in the class. It is collected in a regular manner periodically (Once in a month). It also creates awareness to the faculty to complete the syllabus in time.

2.14.7 Regular Display of Attendance/Exam Percentage

In all best University practices, it is mandatory to the students to maintain a certain percentage of attendance to the classes. In order to achieve this Department should display the attendance of students every month. Also, the Department should display the mark score of the students on a regular basis after every internal assessment.

2.14.8 Communication to Parents

Parents are the student's first and best teachers and they always want the best for their wards. As professionals, teachers are a part of their team, helping to educate their children. When parents extend their wholehearted support to teachers, it goes a long way to strengthen their common goal. That is giving good education to their ward. Information and communication are at the heart of this mutual support. It is essential to communicate the results, assessment performance, attendance, interest, activities, special events and student's participations in a regular manner. This will improve a student learning and also improve the image of the institution.

2.15 GRADING SYSTEM

Each college/university has a different system for grading its students. It is imperative that one understands the system in that particular Department. Academic advisor or the registrar's office will provide information that is essential. In order to create competition among students and to understand the different nature of the people, it is essential to have a grading system.

One period/week of lecture class is counted as one credit where as 2 periods of a lab per week is counted as one credit in general.

A course credit is a unit that gives weighting to the value, level or time requirements of an academic course taken at a University or other educational institution.

Grades are standardized measurements of varying levels of comprehension within a subject area. Grades can be assigned in letters (for example, A, B, C, D, E or F), or a range (for example 1.0–4.0), as descriptors (excellent, great, satisfactory, needs improvement), in percentages, or, as is common in some post-secondary institutions in some countries, as a **Grade Point Average** (GPA). The GPA can be used by potential employers or further post-secondary institutions to assess and compare applicants. A *Cumulative Grade Point Average* (CGPA) is a calculation of the average of all of a student's grades for all semesters and courses completed up to a given academic term, whereas the GPA may only refer to one term.

The GPA (Grade Point Average) ranges on a scale from 0 to 10. Each course carries a certain number of credits (usually 1 to 4). The student has to secure a minimum number of credits over the duration of the degree that depends on the program, the department, and specialization. The following letter grades are awarded for each course:

The U grade is failure in the course, and W is the failure to satisfy attendance requirements; in either case, the course is considered failed. The GPA is computed as the cumulative credit-weighted average of the grade points:

where:

- N is the number of courses,
- C_i is credits for the ith course,
- GP_i is grade points for the ith course, and,
- GPA is the grade point average in a semester
- *CGPA* is the cumulative grade point average of all semesters up to that point of time.

Presently, whenever a fail grade is followed by a subsequent pass grade, the fail grade is not used in the computation of *CGPA*; these fail grades are also removed from the transcript and replaced by a footnote indicating the number of attempts made to obtain the pass grade. Some courses are considered *pass-fail* courses which, if a requirement to a student, have to be passed by the student; however, the marks/grade obtained in that course is not considered in the calculation of the CGPA.

2.16 STUDENT CENTRIC LEARNING AND ACTIVITIES

Student-centered learning is an approach to education focusing on the needs of the students, rather than those of others involved in the educational process, such as teachers and administrators. This approach has many implications for the design of curriculum, course content, and interactivity of courses.

For instance, a student-centered course may address the needs of a particular student audience to learn how to solve some job-related problems using some aspects of mathematics. In contrast, a course focused on learning mathematics might choose some areas of mathematics and methods of teaching, which may be considered irrelevant by the student. Apart from academic learning, one should involve them in other activities related to:

1. Higher Education/Competitive Examination Cell
2. National Service Scheme (NSS)
3. National Cadet Corps (NCC)
4. Human Resource Development Cell (HRD)
5. Women Development Cell (WDC), etc.

2.17 STUDENT ASSOCIATIONS

A student society or student Association is an organization, operated by students at a university, whose membership normally consists only of students. They are often affiliated with a university's students' union. Student societies often aim to facilitate a particular activity or promote a belief system; although some (explicitly) require nothing more than that a member is a (former) student. Some are not affiliated with a specific university and/or accept non-university students.

2.18 LABORATORIES, WORKSHOPS AND EQUIPMENT (FACILITIES, MAINTENANCE AND UTILIZATION)

The University needs various academic infrastructures like building, laboratory and other equipments specific to various courses according to curriculum. The infrastructure and laboratory details will differ course to course. The complete details of laboratories and other equipments are given in Annexure–C as per the Indian AICTE Standards.

2.19 INFORMATION ACCESS FACILITIES

In a academic system the information is provided by various means such as: 1. Internet, 2. Telephone 3. Published books, CDs, etc. 4. Information Desk, etc. The Information Desk is a facility provided at the front entrance.

2.20 Choice Based Credit System (CBCS)

The Choice Based Credit System (CBCS) enables a student to obtain a degree by accumulating required number of credits prescribed for that degree. The number of credits earned by the student reflects the knowledge or skill acquired by him/her. Each course is assigned with a fixed number of credits based on the contents to be learnt. The student has the freedom of selecting courses out of those offered by various departments. The grade points earned for each course reflects the student's proficiency in that course. The CBCS enables the students to earn credits across departments and provides flexibility in duration to complete a Program of study. The CBCS facilitates transfer of credits earned in different Departments/Centers of other recognized/accredited universities or institutions of higher education in any country across the world.

In CBCS student representatives take part in designing the curriculum for a program of Study and facilitate in running the academic programs. The courses offered under a Program of Study are designated as Hard Core and Soft Core. A course designated as Hard Core for a particular Program of Study must invariably be completed by the student to receive the degree in that program. The Hard Core Course cannot be substituted by any other course. A student needs to earn certain number of minimum credits by successfully completing Soft core courses to receive the degree. In the event of failure in a Soft-core course the student can substitute the soft core by an equivalent course offered by the parent or other Department. However time tabling (scheduling) is a cumbersome process for the Professors and the students to accommodate more soft courses. Also the ratio of number of staff required to that of the students will get increased. It is a challenging and balancing act, but a desirable system.

2.20.1 Hard Core Course

1. A Hard core subject may be a Theory, Practical, Field based or Project Work based subject which is a compulsory component in the Course Structure. Based on the quantum of time required for teaching—learning, the number of credits for each subject is to be decided within the prescribed limit.
2. Registration for Hard Core courses are also open to students of other departments provided they meet the prerequisites.
3. A Course may be treated as a Hard core or Soft Core Course for students of other Department as per the requirement of Program of Study.

2.20.2 Soft Core Course

1. A Soft core course may be a Theory, Practical, Field based or Project Work, which is optional for the students to register.
2. Students can exercise their choice among a set of Soft core courses from the list of Soft core courses specified for each Programme of study.
3. Students have a choice to register for Soft Core Courses offered by any Department under the advice of the Faculty Advisor.

2.21 TAKE HOME EXAMINATION

Take-home final examinations are sometimes substituted (for example creating architectural design) for regular final examinations. If a course has been assigned a final examination group number, a take-home examination for that course is due on the day on which the final examination has been scheduled. If a course has not been assigned a final examination group number, a take-home examination for the course is due on the day specified in the final examination schedule by the meeting time of the course. If a course does not meet at a time covered by the final examination schedule, a take-home examination may not be due during the first three days of final examination period. No take-home examination may be due during the reading period. Whenever it is due, a take-home examination that requires from students a disproportionate amount of time during reading period for its completion violates the intent of reading period.

The assets of take-home examinations are evident, but they have liabilities as well. One is that they run the risk of inviting improper collaboration. If collaboration on a take-home examination is not to be permitted, or if the take-home examination is to be a closed-book exercise, directions to that effect should be clear, precise, and emphatic. The chief liability, however, is that frequently students spend an excessive amount of time in completing such examinations. This works to the detriment of their other academic obligations at a time when they are attempting to conclude all of their courses in a satisfactory and timely fashion. Instructors are requested, therefore, not to give take-home final examination if a regularly scheduled examination would be equally appropriate to the nature and purpose of that course.

2.22 STUDENT COUNSELING

A crucial element in student counseling is giving training to make decisions beforehand. Counseling Services include psychological, mental or emotional, Education and Career counseling. At the University level, the idea is guiding and assisting students even at entry level to choose an academic major and proper courses as well as a college and then throughout their study at the institute, providing appropriate assistance at each stage of the student's development, growth or progress. They should be advised through conversation and exercises, else students often may fall a prey to unidentified interests. Now a days Career counseling is frequently offered on a one-on-one basis, but at times this service is provided through group workshops, classes, or computerized guidance systems.

A resource library is an essential component of the career services office. These libraries should have a collection of good journals and books on a wide range of counseling and career options including job search manuals and information of employers. Some information formerly provided in book form, such as directories of employers, is increasingly being delivered through the Internet, now days.

Many of the internet web sites do have useful links. This should be carefully scrutinized and updated periodically, so that latest information about the desired options can be made available to the needy students. All aim to increasingly use the internet as a vehicle for counseling, outreach, training, and collaboration. At the time of counseling, it is important that every one knows about others' efforts. This ever-expanding directory contains information on different internet resources set up by counseling centers and how to access them directly from the institute computer.

2.23 EXTRA-CURRICULAR ACTIVITIES/CO-CURRICULAR ACTIVITIES

Extracurricular activities are activities performed by students that fall outside the realm of the normal curriculum of university education. Extracurricular activities exist at all levels of education, college and university education.

Such activities are generally voluntary as opposed to mandatory, non-paying, social, philanthropic as opposed to scholastic, and involve others of the same age. Students often organize and direct these activities under faculty guidance although student-led initiatives, such as independent newspapers, are common.

2.24 STUDENT TEACHER RELATIONSHIP

It is the academic relation between teachers and their students. Relationships give special abilities to players during combat or fame and special items. Relationships can be created and raised by using a certain number of roles. The role of teacher is often formal and ongoing, carried out by way of occupation or profession at a University/College/ School or other place of formal education giving recommendations to students about a decision or course of action.

Classroom management is one of the top issues on teachers minds. Poor classroom management can yield a number of undesirable results, including an overly rigid classroom, a chaotic learning environment, and a focus on discipline rather than learning. Good classroom management produces an environment conducive to learning, exploration, and participation. Teachers who manage their classrooms well typically have students who achieve at higher levels and have more positive attitudes and perceptions. With available resources, teachers can learn the best ways to ensure discipline, and manage their classrooms.

Learning styles are basically the way in which the student best processes information available in the campus or for the course. They are visual, auditory, and kinesthetic. A good teacher realizes this and tries to teach a subject using all three learning styles to help the students find the style, or combination of styles, that works best for them.

2.25 CONCLUSION

The authors opine that it is important to have a well structured academic system in each University in any part of the world. If by definition or by region or by country or by faith or in scope something is found not necessary such component may be omitted/need not find place in such a University. It is possible to be independent and simultaneously be having most of the items discussed, in place, so that expectation of the public and students are met.

Planning saves lot of time during execution; a well planed activity is half done already. Contact hours with students, per course and per week is hardly enough to teach the content related to the prescribed syllabi. The best ways of planning and execution have been narrated in the sections 2.5 to 2.13. Counseling to needy students is an important aspect in the educational institutions. However, many times the system is unable to help all needy persons due to inhibition on the part of students to approach the counselor. Excepting marks/grades, nothing is known about the students' background and problems they do have. Hence general counseling could not penetrate to the desired level. Impartial evaluation should be the order of the day. This helps the students to get used to best practices in their life.

CHAPTER 3

History of University System

3.1 INTRODUCTION

The concept of an university has evolved over quite a long period of time. The histories of Universities are classified in to three categories. These are viz. 1. Early Universities, 2. Medieval Universities 3. Modern Universities. In this Chapter, Section 3.2, Section 3.3 and Section 3.4 deal with the history of Early, Medieval, Modern Universities respectively. Section 3.5 concentrates on the emergence of National Universities. Section 3.6 describes the history of U.S. Universities; Section 3.7 throws light on the history of European Universities, Section 3.8 deliver into the history of Indian Universities and Section 3.9 concludes this Chapter.

3.2 EARLY HISTORY

The original Latin word "Universitas", first used in time of renewed interest in Classical Greek and Roman tradition, tried to reflect this feature of the Academy of Plato (established 385 BC). The term "academia" is sometimes extended to a number of educational institutions of non-Western antiquity, including China, India and Persia:

- Academies such as Shang Hsiang, and later Taixue and Guozijian, succeeded by the medieval Academies of Classical Learning.
- Taxila in Gandhara and the Buddhist Nalanda University in Bihar, India (5th century BC).
- The Sassanid Academy of Gundishapur was founded in the 5th century.

The University of Constantinople, founded as an institution of higher learning in 425 and reorganized as a corporation of students in 849 by the regent Bardas of emperor Michael III, is considered by some to be the earliest institution of higher learning with some of the characteristics we associate today with a university (research and teaching, auto-administration, academic independence, etc.). If a university is defined as "an institution of higher learning" then it is preceded by several others, including the Academy that it was founded to compete with and eventually replaced. If the original meaning of the word is considered "a corporation of students" then this could be the first example of such an institution.

If the definition of a university is assumed to mean an institution of higher education and research which issues academic degrees at all levels (bachelor, master and doctorate) like in the modern sense of the word, then the medieval Madrasahs known as Jami'ah ("University" in Arabic) founded in the 9th century would be the first example of such an institution.

The University of Al Karaouine in Fez, Morocco is thus recognized by the Guinness Book of World Records as the oldest degree-granting university in the world with its founding in 859 by the princess Fatima al-Fihri. Also in the 9th century, Bimaristan medical schools were founded in the medieval Islamic world, where medical degrees and diplomas were issued to students of Islamic medicine who were qualified to be a practicing Doctor of Medicine. Al-Azhar University, founded in Cairo, Egypt in 975, was a Jami'ah university which offered a variety of post-graduate degrees (Ijazah), and had individual faculties for a theological seminary, Islamic law and jurisprudence, Arabic grammar, Islamic astronomy, early Islamic philosophy, and logic in Islamic philosophy.

3.3 MEDIEVAL UNIVERSITIES

The first higher education institution in medieval Europe was the University of Constantinople, followed by the University of Salerno (9th century), the Preslav Literary School and Ohrid Literary School in the Bulgarian Empire (9th century). The first degree-granting universities in Europe were the University of Bologna (1088), the University of Paris (c. 1150, later associated with the Sorbonne), the University of Oxford (1167), the University of Cambridge (1209), the University of Salamanca (1218), the University of Montpellier (1220), the University of Padua (1222), the University of Naples Federico II (1224), and the University of Toulouse (1229). Some scholars such as George Makdisi, John Makdisi and Hugh Goddard argue that these medieval universities were influenced in many ways by the medieval Madrasah institutions in Islamic Spain, the Emirate of Sicily, and the Middle East (during the Crusades).

Many of the medieval universities in Western Europe were developed under the aegis of the Roman Catholic Church, usually as cathedral schools or by papal bull as Studia Generali (NB: The development of cathedral schools into Universities actually appears to be quite rare, with the University of Paris being an exception—see Leff, Paris and Oxford Universities), later they were also founded by Kings (Charles University in Prague, Jagiellonian University in Krakow) or municipal administrations (University of Cologne, University of Erfurt). In the early medieval period, most new universities were founded from pre-existing schools, usually when these schools were deemed to have become primarily sites of higher education. Many historians state that universities and cathedral schools were a continuation of the interest in learning promoted by monasteries.

In Europe, young men proceeded to a university when they had completed their study of the trivium—the preparatory arts of grammar, rhetoric, and dialectic or logic–and the quadrivium: arithmetic, geometry, music, and astronomy.

Outside of Europe, there were many notable institutions of learning throughout history. In China, there was the famous Hanlin Academy, established during the Tang Dynasty (618–907 AD), and was once headed by the Chancellor Shen Kuo (1031–1095), a famous Chinese scientist, inventor, mathematician, and statesman.

The University of Salamanca in Spain was founded in 1218 Prior to their formal establishment, many medieval universities were run for hundreds of years as Christian cathedral schools or monastic schools (Scholae monasticae), in which monks and nuns taught classes; evidence of these immediate forerunners of the later university at many places dates back to the 6th century AD. The first universities were the University of Bologna (1088), the University of Paris (c. 1150, later associated with the Sorbonne), the University of Oxford (1167), the University of Palencia (1208), the University of Cambridge (1209), the University of Salamanca (1218), the University of Montpellier (1220), the University of Padua (1222), the University of Naples Federico II (1224), and the University of Toulouse (1229).

The earliest universities were developed under the aegis of the Catholic Church, usually as cathedral schools or by papal bull as studia generali (n.b. The development of cathedral schools into universities actually appears to be quite rare, with the University of Paris being an exception see Leff, Paris and Oxford Universities), later they were also founded by Kings (University of Naples Federico II, Charles University in Prague, Jagiellonian University in Krakow) or municipal administrations (University of Cologne, University of Erfurt). In the early medieval period, most new universities were founded from pre-existing schools, usually when these schools were deemed to have become primarily sites of higher education. Many historians state that universities and cathedral schools were a continuation of the interest in learning promoted by monasteries.

The University of Bologna began as a law school teaching the *ius gentium* or Roman law of people which was in demand across Europe for those defending the right of incipient nations against empire and church. Bologna's special claim to Alma Mater Studiorum is based on its autonomy, its awarding of degrees, and other structural arrangements, making it the oldest continuously operating institution independent of kings, emperors or any kind of direct religious authority.

The conventional date of 1088, or 1087 according to some, records when a certain Irnerius commences teaching Emperor Justinian's 6th century codification of Roman law, the Corpus Iuris Civilis, recently discovered at Pisa. Many students arrive in the city from lands contracting to gain this knowledge, organizing themselves into 'Learning Nations' of Hungarians, Greeks, North Africans, Arabs, Franks, Germans, Iberians etc. The students "had all the power… and dominated the masters".

Although the university is widely regarded as "the European institution par excellence" in terms of its origins and characteristics, some scholars have argued that early medieval universities were influenced by the religious Madrasah schools in Al-Andalus, the Emirate of Sicily, and the Middle East (during the Crusades). Other scholars oppose this view and argue that there is no actual evidence of the transmission of Arab scholarly methods discernible in medieval universities.

3.4 MODERN UNIVERSITIES

The end of the medieval period marked the beginning of the transformation of universities that would eventually result in the modern research university. Many external influences, such as eras of Humanism, Enlightenment, Reformation, and Revolution, shaped research universities during their development, and the discovery of the New World in 1492 added human rights and international law to the university curriculum.

By the 18th century, universities began to publish their own research journals, and by the 19th century, the German and the French university models had arisen. The German, or Humboldtian model, was conceived by Wilhelm von Humboldt and based on Friedrich Schleiermacher's liberal ideas pertaining to the importance of freedom, seminars, and laboratories in universities. The French university model involved strict discipline and control over every aspect of the university.

Universities concentrated on science in the 19th and 20th centuries, and they started to become accessible to the masses after 1914. Until the 19th century, religion played a significant role in university curriculum; however, the role of religion in research universities decreased in the 19th century, and by the end of the 19th century, the German university model had spread around the world. The British also established universities worldwide, and higher education became available to the masses. In a general sense, the basic structure and aims of universities have remained constant over the years.

The University of Coimbra was the oldest Portuguese University. The end of the medieval period marked the beginning of the transformation of universities that would eventually result in the modern research university.

3.5 NATIONAL UNIVERSITIES

A national university is generally a University created or run by a national state but at the same time represents a state autonomic institution which functions as a completely independent body within the same state. Some national universities are closely associated with national, cultural or political aspirations, for instance the National University of Ireland in the early days of Irish independence collected a large amount of information on the Irish language and Irish culture. Revolutions in Argentina were the result of the university revolution of 1918 and its posterior reforms were by incorporating values that sought for a more equal and good higher education system.

3.6 US UNIVERSITY SYSTEM OF EDUCATION—HISTORY

American University (AU) is a private United Methodist-affiliated research university in Washington, D.C. The main campus is located at the intersection of Nebraska and Massachusetts Avenues at Ward Circle, straddling the Spring Valley, Wesley Heights, and American University Park neighborhoods of Northwest. Roughly 6,000 undergraduate students and around 4,000 graduate students are currently enrolled. Though there is sometimes confusion, American University is separate from most "American Universities" around the world.

It is served by the Tenleytown-AU station on the Washington Metro subway line, which is located roughly one mile from the main campus in the neighborhood of Tenleytown. AU is a member of the Consortium of Universities of the Washington Metropolitan Area, allowing students to enroll in courses offered by other member institutions and students at other member institutions to enroll in courses at AU. A member of the Division I Patriot League, its sports teams compete as the American University Eagles.

3.6.1 Founding

An inspiration for the founding of American University was a letter written by George Washington in which he expressed a desire for a "national university" to be located in the national capital. The university was established in the District of Columbia by an Act of Congress on February 24, 1893, primarily due to the efforts of Methodist Bishop John Fletcher Hurst. It, like most of the universities in the District of Columbia (Georgetown University, like the George Washington University, Howard University, Gallaudet University, and The Catholic University of America, among others), was chartered by an act of Congress, and thus has the seal of Congress appear on all its diplomas. Bishop Hurst and his colleagues were concerned with building an institution that would incorporate the strengths of the best German universities with the strengths of the existing university system in America. As their plans developed during the early years, they began to conceive of American University as an institution that would be:

1. A privately supported university financed principally by the membership of the churches, particularly the Methodist Episcopal Church, which had been the founders of many of the colleges and universities in the early years of American history.
2. An internationally minded institution where scholars from across the nation and from throughout the world would gather to dedicate their combined efforts to the advancement and dissemination of knowledge.
3. A center of higher education and research activities, while independent of the government, would draw freely on the intellectual and scientific resources of the Nation's Capital to supplement and to extend its own capabilities.
4. An institution that would contribute to the general cultural life and development of the capital in much the same manner that state-supported universities in other world capitals contributed to their communities.

3.6.2 Period 1900–1948

After more than three decades devoted principally to securing financial support, the American University was officially dedicated on May 15, 1914. The first instruction began on October 6 of that year, when 28 students were enrolled (19 of them graduate students, nine of them special students who were not candidates for a degree). The First Commencement, at which no degrees were awarded, was held on June 2, 1915. The Second Annual Commencement was held on June 2, 1916 where the first degrees (one master's degree and two doctorates) were awarded.

Shortly after these early commencement ceremonies, classes were interrupted by war. During World War I, the university allowed the U.S. military to use some of its grounds for testing. In 1917, the U.S. military divided American University into two segments, Camp American University and Camp Leach. Camp American University became the birthplace of the United States' chemical weapons program, and chemical weapons were tested on the grounds; this required a major cleanup effort in the 1990s. Camp Leach was home to advanced research, development and testing of modern camouflage techniques. As of 2007, the Army Corps of Engineers is still removing ordnance including mustard gas and mortar shells.

During the next ten years, instruction was offered at the graduate level only, in accordance with the original plan of the founders. In the fall of 1925, the College of Liberal Arts (subsequently named the College of Arts and Sciences) was established. Since that date, the University has offered both undergraduate and graduate degrees and programs. In 1934, the School of Public Affairs was founded.

During World War II, the campus again offered its services to the U.S. government and became home to the U.S. Navy Bomb Disposal School and a WAVE barracks. For AU's role in these wartime efforts, the Victory ship SS *American Victory* was named in honor of the university.

3.6.3 Period 1949–1989

President John F. Kennedy delivered the commencement address at the American University, on June 10, 1963.

The present structure of the university began to emerge in 1949. The Washington College of Law became part of the University in that year, having begun in 1896 as the first coeducational institution for the professional study of law in the District of Columbia. Shortly thereafter, three departments were reorganized as schools: the School of Business Administration in 1955 (subsequently named as the Robert P. and Arlene R. Kogod College of Business Administration and in 1999 renamed the Kogod School of Business); the School of Government and Public Administration in 1957; and the School of International Service in 1958.

In the early 1960s, the Department of Defense and the Central Intelligence Agency operated a think tank under the guise of Operation Camelot at American University. The government abandoned the think tank after the operation came to public attention. AU's political intertwinement was furthered by President John F. Kennedy's Spring 1963 commencement address. In the speech, Kennedy called on the Soviet Union to work with the United States to achieve a nuclear test ban treaty and help reduce the considerable international tensions and the specter of nuclear war during that juncture of the Cold War.

From 1965 to 1977, the College of Continuing Education existed as a degree-granting college with responsibility for on- and off-campus adult education programs. The Lucy Webb Hayes School of Nursing provided undergraduate study in Nursing from 1965 until 1988. In 1972, the School of Government and Public Administration, the School of International Service, the Center for Technology and Administration, and the Center for the Administration of Justice (subsequently named the School of Justice) were incorporated into the College of Public and International Affairs.

In October 1984, President Richard Berendzen announced that the University would purchase the Immaculata Campus in 1986 to help alleviate space problems. This investment would later become the Tenley Campus.

In 1986, construction on the Adnan Khashoggi Sports and Convocation Center began. Financed with $5 million from and named after Saudi Arabian Trustee Adnan Khashoggi, the building was intended to update athletics facilities and provide a new arena, as well as a parking garage and office space for administrative services. Costing an estimated $19 million, the building represented the largest construction project to date, but met with protest by both faculty and students to the University's use of Khashoggi's name on the building due to his involvement in international arms trade.

In 1988, the College of Public and International Affairs was reorganized to create two free-standing schools: the School of International Service and the School of Public

Affairs, incorporating the School of Government and Public Administration and the School of Justice. That same year, construction on the Adnan Khashoggi Sports Center got completed while the Iran-Contra Affair controversy was at its height although his name was not removed from the building until after Khashoggi defaulted on his donation obligation in the mid to late 90's.

3.6.4 1990 Onwards

In 1991, Richard E. Berendzen stepped down as President after admitting to making obscene phone calls. He sought immediate medical treatment and remained a full-time member of the American University faculty until his retirement in 2006.

Berendzen was succeeded by Joseph Duffy, who left after one year to become the head of the United States Information Agency under President Clinton.

The School of Communication became independent from the College of Arts and Sciences in 1993.

In 1997 American University of Sharjah, the only coeducational, liberal arts university in the United Arab Emirates, signed a two year contract with AU to provide academic management, a contract which has since been extended multiple times through August 2009. A team of senior AU administrators relocated to Sharjah to assist in the establishment of the university and guide it through the Middle States Association of Colleges and Schools accreditation process.

In 2003, American launched the largest fund raising campaign in its history. The program, *ANewAU*, has a goal of raising $200 million dollars. As of October, 2009, the University has raised $189.6 million dollars. When the campaign is completed, the University's website states that it "will help to attract and retain the finest faculty, increase scholarship support, create and endow research and policy centers, ensure state-of-the-art resources in all of our schools and colleges, expand global programs, and secure the long-term financial health of the university by boosting the endowment."

In the fall of 2005, the much anticipated Katzen Arts Center opened.

Benjamin Ladner was suspended from his position as president of the university on August 24, 2005, pending an investigation into possible misuse of university funds for his personal expenses. University faculty moved a motion by vote of no confidence against the President Ladner on September 26. On October 10, 2005, the Board of Trustees of American University decided that Ladner would not return to American University as its president. Dr. Cornelius M. Kerwin, a long-time AU administrator, served as interim president and was appointed to the position permanently on September 1, 2007, after two outsiders declined an offer from the Board of Trustees. According to *The Chronicle of Higher Education*, Ladner received a total compensation of

$4,270,665 in his final year of service, the second highest of any university president in the United States.

3.7 EUROPE UNIVERSITY SYSTEM OF EDUCATION—HISTORY

European research universities date from the founding of the University of Bologna in 1088, although the University of Paris (ca. 1160–70) and the University of Magnaura (AD 425) contend for that distinction. In the 19th and 20th centuries, European universities concentrated upon science and research, their structures and philosophies having shaped the contemporary university. The original medieval universities arose from the Roman Catholic Church schools that became "the university". Their purpose included training professionals, scientific investigation, improving society, and teaching critical thinking and research. External influences, such as Renaissance humanism (ca. mid-14th c.), the Age of Enlightenment (18th c.), the Protestant Reformation (1517), political revolution, and the discovery of the New World (1492) added human rights and international law to the university curricula.

By the 18th century, universities published academic journals; by the 19th century, the German and the French university models were established. The German university—the Humboldtian model—established by Wilhelm von Humboldt was based upon Friedrich Schleiermacher's liberal ideas about the importance of freedom, seminars, and laboratories, which, like the French university model, involved strict discipline and control of every aspect of the university. In the 19th and 20th centuries, the universities concentrated upon science, but were not open to the general populace until after 1914. Moreover, until the 19th century's end, religion exerted a significant, limiting influence upon academic curricula and research, by which time the German university model had become the world standard. Elsewhere, the British also had established universities world-wide, thus making higher education available to the world's populace.

3.7.1 The First European Universities

Historically, the University of Bologna, founded in 1088, is considered the "mother of European universities"—symbolic of Italian national unity, which detracts legitimacy from its claim as the first university proper. Said contention is challenged by the definition of "university" as a single, corporate body composed of students and faculties of the disciplines taught, rather than as a corporate body such as the University of Paris, founded in 1208, that might be considered the first university; however, the University at Magnaura Palace, founded in the 9th century as the University of Magnaura, can be defined as such a corpus, because it assembled scholars as a "focal point of medieval Greek science and culture". The first European universities were influenced by the Madrasah institutions in Islamic Spain, the Emirate of Sicily, and the Crusader states.

3.7.2 Representation of a University Class (1350s)

The rediscovery of ancient Græco–Roman knowledge (e.g. Aristotle's works and Roman law), led to the development of Universitates (student guilds), and thus the establishment of the university in the contemporary sense. In turn, the traditional medieval universities—evolved from Catholic and Protestant church schools—then established specialized academic structures for properly educating greater number of students as professionals. Prof. Walter Rüegg, editor of *A History of the University in Europe*, reports that universities then, only trained students to become clerics, lawyers, civil servants, and physicians. Yet rediscovery of Classical-era knowledge transformed the university from the practical arts to developing "knowledge for the sake of knowledge", which, by the 16th century, was considered integral to the civil community's practical requirements. Hence, academic research was effected in furtherance of scientific investigation, because science had become essential to university curricula via "openness to novelty" in the search for the means to control nature to benefit civil society.

3.7.3 The Structure and Spread of Early European Universities

The European Universities multiplied in part because groups decided to succeed from the original universities to promote their own ideals; the University of Paris fostered many universities in Northern Europe, while the University of Bologna fostered many in the South. Some leaders also created universities in order to use them to increase their political power and popularity. For example, Frederick II, Holy Roman Emperor founded the University of Naples in 1224 to train lawyers and administrators who could rival the University of Bologna's influence, which served the hostile Lombard League.

The structure of these early classes involved a teacher reading from texts and commenting on the readings, as well as students learning by teaching other students. Teachers also offered disputed questions to students for discussion. Moving into the 18th century, professors became less focused on simply training university teachers and more focused on "forming the minds of the elite" of a larger society.

3.7.4 Philosophic and External Influences

By the 16th century, the humanist ideas of the Renaissance (14th–16th c.) were slowly accepted; France had propagated them first to Germany, then to England, during the Protestant Reformation (1617). In that intellectual humanist mode, university education began including preparing the student for a civilized life—of culture and civility—and concern for society's public affairs. To achieve that, the curriculum comprised the liberal arts Trivium (grammar, rhetoric, logic), and the Quadrivium (arithmetic, geometry, astronomy, music) meant to prepare students for further specialized education in either theology, the law, or medicine. In 1492, the socio-political consequences of the discovery of the New World expanded European university curricula, as human rights and international law became contemporarily relevant matters. The Spanish enslavement of the native (aboriginal) populaces whom they conquered in the "New World" of the Americas eventually raised ethico-moral questions in Europe about the human rights of the American aboriginals—questions of cultural tolerance evinced by Renaissance humanism, the Bible, and mediæval theories of natural law. In analogy to the ancient world's works, Rüegg relates the "New World" idea to the idea of "new knowledge". In the mid-16th century, scholarly and scientific journals made it feasible to "spread innovations among the learned"; by the 18th century, universities published their own research journals. In the 18th century, the Age of Enlightenment also encouraged education's transition, from the "preservation and transmission of accepted knowledge" to the "discovery and advancement of new knowledge"; the newer universities effected that change more quickly, and adapted Enlightenment ideas about the harmfulness of monarchic Absolutism more readily than did the older universities.

3.7.5 European University Models in the 19th and 20th Centuries

Moving into the 19th century, the objective of universities evolved from repeating facts without understanding to "encourag[ing] productive thinking." Two main university models, the German and the French, arose and gave rise to other models such as the British and Russian. The German model, conceived by Wilhelm von Humboldt, was also known as the Humboldtian model. In 1810, Humboldt convinced the King of Prussia to build a university in Berlin based on Friedrich Schleiermacher's liberal ideas; the goal was to demonstrate the process of the discovery of knowledge and to teach students to "take account of fundamental laws of science in all their thinking," thus, seminars and laboratories started to evolve. Humboldt envisioned the university education as a student-centered activity of research:

> *Just as primary instruction makes the teacher possible, so he renders himself dispensable through schooling at the secondary level. The university teacher is thus no longer a teacher and the student is no longer a pupil. Instead the student conducts research on his own behalf and the professor supervises his research and supports him in it.*

Freedom was an important concept in the German university model, and the system of professors was based on competition and freedom: although professors served as state functionaries, they had the freedom to choose between several states, and their identity and prestige arose from the specialization of scientific disciplines.

The French University model lacked the freedom of the German model, consisting of severe discipline and control over the curriculum, awarding of degrees, conformity of views, and personal habits (for example, there was a ban on beards in 1852). French university professors trained at the École Normale Supérieure, and much of their prestige depended on their schools' reputations. By 1866, though, the German model had begun to influence the strict French model.

The German university model was also used in Russian universities, which hired lecturers trained in Germany and which dedicated themselves to science. At the same time, Russian universities were meant to train the bureaucracy in the same way as the French. Throughout the 19th and 20th centuries, Russian universities underwent much variation in their degrees of strictness and control.

Universities of Oxford and Cambridge

British universities also modeled themselves after the German university. They enjoyed a great deal of freedom because the state granted them an autonomy that allowed them initiative and flexibility. The Universities of Oxford and Cambridge emphasized the importance of research, arguably more authentically implementing Humboldt's idea of a university than even German universities, which were subject to state authority. Overall, science became the focus of universities in the 19th and 20th centuries. Students could conduct research in laboratories and began to produce doctoral theses with more scientific content. According to Humboldt, the mission of the University of Berlin was to pursue scientific knowledge. The German university system fostered professional, bureaucratically regulated scientific research performed in well-equipped laboratories, instead of the kind of research done by private and individual scholars in Great Britain and France. In fact, Ruegg asserts that the German system is responsible for the development of the modern research university because it focused on the idea of "freedom of scientific research, teaching and study."

Professors and Students

Schleiermacher points out that professors, had to "reproduce [their] own realization[s]" so that students could observe the "act of creation" of knowledge. That they serve as models of how to "intelligently produce knowledge". Professorship was awarded to distinguished scholars, and was rescindable only if guilty of a serious crime. From the perspective of James McCain, president emeritus of Kansas State University, professors in 20th century Europe were more prestigious and well-respected than university professors in the US, for having much academic freedom, whilst keeping to formal relationships with the students. Moreover, the professors' professional role expanded from lecturing to investigating, thus research became "an integral part of the professor's task".

The London University, by Thomas Hosmer Shepherd (1827–28), now is an integral part of University College London, a constituent of the University of London.

Popular access to higher education slowly began after 1914, yet the principal remaining obstacle was its expense. For most of the 19th century, the UK continued affording a university education only to aristocrats, and not until the early 20th century, featuring new universities, such as the University of London, was higher education available to the mass populace.

In the 19th and 20th centuries, European university students were mostly responsible for their education; they selected courses of study, professors did not register attendance, and only gave examinations at the end of courses. Ruegg suggests that student propensity to developing student movements, based upon contemporary politics, parallels their attitudes of intellectual freedom and social responsibility.

Progressive educational and political philosophies changed religion's role in the education imparted. During the 18th century, most universities were strongly connected to either a Catholic or a Protestant church, thus the professors' and the students' religion determined employment and matriculation. In the 19th century, religion was deleted from the "compulsory curriculum"; in France, Napoleon's secular Université de France troubled Roman Catholics, because it threatened their educational monopoly. In UK, the new universities (i.e. the University of London), were non-denominational, and the Oxford Act of 1854 rid Oxford and Cambridge universities of required religion with a concomitant decline in chapel attendance, and of religion as integral to a university education.

3.7.6 The European University Legacies

Ultimately, European research universities established the intellectual and academic traditions of university education world-wide; by the 19th century's end, the Humboldtian university model was established in Europe, the US, and Japan. In the Americas, first the Spanish, then the British, and then the French founded universities in the lands they had conquered early in the 16th century, meant to professionally educate their colonists and propagate monotheistic religion to establish formal, administrative rule of their American colonies; like-wise, the British in Canada, Australia, and the Cape Colony; and like-wise Japan, the Near East, and Africa. Those universities disseminated Western European science and technology and trained the natives to develop their countries resources; and, although most promoted the social, political, economic, and cultural aims of the imperial rulers, some promoted revolutionary development of the colonial societies. In the 20th century, urbanization and industrialization made a university education available to the mass populace. Throughout, the basic structure and research purposes of the universities have remained constant; per Clark Kerr, they "are among the least changed of institutions".

3.8 Indian University System of Education—History

Education in India has a history stretching back to the ancient urban centres of learning at Taxila and Nalanda. The Nalanda University was the oldest university-system of education in the world. Western education became ingrained into Indian society with the establishment of the British Raj. Education in India falls under the control of both the Union Government and the states, with some responsibilities lying with the Union and the states having autonomy for others. The various articles of the Indian Constitution provide for education as a fundamental right. Most universities in India are Union or State Government controlled.

India's higher education system is the third largest in the world, after China and the United States. The main governing body at the tertiary level is the University Grants Commission (UGC) India, which enforces its standards, advises the government, and helps coordinate between the centre and the states. Accreditation for higher learning is overseen by 12 autonomous institutions established by the University Grants Commission.

As of 2009, India has 20 central universities, 215 state universities, 169 deemed universities, 5 institutions established and functioning under the State Act, and 13 institutes which are of national importance. Other institutions include 16000 colleges, including 1800 exclusive women's colleges, functioning under these universities and institutions. The emphasis in the tertiary level of education lies on science and technology. Indian educational institutions by 2004 consisted of a large number of technology institutes. Distance learning is also a feature of the Indian higher education system.

Some institutions of India, such as the Indian Institutes of Technology (IITs), have been globally acclaimed for their standard of education. The IITs enroll about 8000 students annually and the alumni have contributed to both the growth of the private sector and the public sectors of India.

The Indian Institutes of Technology (IITs) are a group of fifteen autonomous engineering and technology-oriented institutes of higher education established and declared as Institutes of National Importance by the Parliament of India. The IITs were created to train scientists and engineers, with the aim of developing a skilled workforce to support the economic and social development of India after independence in 1947.

In order of establishment, they are located in Kharagpur (1950; as IIT 1951[1]), Mumbai (1958), Chennai (formerly Madras) (1959), Kanpur (1959), Delhi (1961; as IIT 1963), Guwahati (1994), Roorkee (1847; as IIT 2001), Ropar (2008), Bhubaneswar (2008), Gandhinagar (2008), Hyderabad (2008), Patna (2008), Jodhpur (2008), Indore (2009) and Mandi (2009). Some IITs were established with financial assistance and technical expertise from UNESCO, Germany, the United States, Japan and the Soviet Union. Each IIT is an autonomous university, linked to the others through a common IIT Council, which oversees their administration. They have a common admission process for undergraduate admissions, using the Joint Entrance Examination (popularly known as IIT-JEE) to select around 8,000 undergraduate candidates a year. Postgraduate admissions are done on the basis of the GATE, JMET, JAM and CEED. About 15,500 undergraduate and 12,000 graduate students study in the IITs, in addition to research scholars.

The history of the IIT system dates back to 1946 when Sir Jogendra Singh of the Viceroy's Executive Council set up a committee whose task was to consider the creation of Higher Technical Institutions for post-war industrial development in India. The 22-member committee, headed by Nalini Ranjan Sarkar, recommended the establishment of these institutions in various parts of India, with affiliated secondary institutions.

The first Indian Institute of Technology was founded in May 1950 at the site of the Hijli Detention Camp in Kharagpur. On September 15, 1956, the Parliament of India passed the Indian Institute of Technology (Kharagpur) Act., declaring it as an Institute of National Importance. Jawaharlal Nehru, first Prime Minister of India, in the first convocation address of IIT Kharagpur in 1956, thus spoke "Here in the place of that Hijli Detention Camp stands the fine monument of India, representing India's urges, India's future in the making. This picture seems to me symbolical of the changes that are coming to India."

On the recommendations of the Sarkar Committee, four campuses were established at Mumbai (1958), Chennai (1959), Kanpur (1959), and Delhi (1961). The location of these campuses was chosen to be scattered throughout India to prevent regional imbalance. The Indian Institutes of Technology Act was amended to reflect the addition of new IITs. Student agitations in the state of Assam made Prime Minister Rajiv Gandhi promise the creation of a new IIT in Assam. This led to a sixth campus at Guwahati under the Assam Accord in 1994. The University of Roorkee, India's oldest engineering college, was conferred IIT status in 2001.

Over the past few years, there have been a number of developments toward establishing new IITs. On October 1, 2003, Prime Minister Atal Bihari Vajpayee announced plans to create more IITs "by upgrading existing academic institutions that have the necessary promise and potential". Subsequent developments led to the formation of the S.K. Joshi Committee in November 2003 to guide the selection of the five institutions which would become the five new IITs. Based on the initial recommendations of the Sarkar Committee, it was decided that further IITs should be spread throughout the country. When the government expressed its willingness to correct this regional imbalance, 16 states demanded IITs. Since the S.K. Joshi Committee prescribed strict guidelines for institutions aspiring to be IITs, only seven colleges were selected for final consideration. Plans are also reported to open IITs outside India, though not enough progress has been made in this regard. Eventually in the 11th Five year plan, eight states were identified for establishment of new IITs, and IT-BHU was recommended to be converted into IIT.

Besides top rated universities which provide highly competitive world class education to their pupil, India is also home to many universities which have been founded with the sole objective of making easy money. Regulatory authorities like UGC and AICTE have been trying very hard to extirpate the menace of private universities which are running courses without any affiliation or recognition. Students from rural and semi urban background often fall prey to these institutes and colleges.

From the first Five Year Plan onwards India's emphasis was to develop a pool of scientifically inclined manpower. India's National Policy on Education (NPE) provisioned for an apex body for regulation and development of higher technical education, which came into being as the All India Council for Technical Education (AICTE) in 1987 through an act of the Indian parliament. At the level of the centre the Indian Institutes of Technology and the Indian Institutes of Information Technology are deemed to be of national importance. The Indian Institutes of Management are also among the nation's premier education facilities. Several Regional Engineering Colleges (REC) have been converted into National Institutes of Technology. The UGC has inter-university centres at a number of locations throughout India to promote common research, e.g. the Nuclear Science Centre at the Jawaharlal Nehru University, New Delhi.

In addition to the above institutes, efforts towards the enhancement of technical education are supplemented by a number of recognized Professional Engineering Societies like: (i) the Institution of Engineers (India); (ii) The Institution of Chemical Engineering (India); (iii) The Institution of Electronics and Tele-Communication Engineers (India); (iv) The Indian Institute of Metals; (v) The Institution of Industrial Engineers (India); (vi) The Institute of Town Planners (India); (vii) The Indian Institute of Architects, etc., who conduct Engineering/Technical Examinations at different levels (Degree and diploma) for working professionals desirous of improving their technical qualifications

3.9 CONCLUSION

The authors do not claim that this Chapter consists of the entire history of Universities all over the world; but has given some glimpses of some important University systems in Europe, US and in Asia that is besides mentioning about a few more. This Chapter is an attempt to throw some light on the evolution of the University system over centuries. A comprehensive study of the history of Universities across the world may require a separate volume.

CHAPTER 4

Classification of Universities and their Modes

4.1 INTRODUCTION

The nature and culture of different Universities differ according to their formation. The Universities are normally classified according to i. Funding ii. Mode of teaching and learning iii. Type of Association etc. This chapter explains the different types of Universities as well as modes of Education and their character in detail.

4.2 PUBLIC/PRIVATE UNIVERSITIES

A **public university** is a university that is predominantly funded by public means through a national or sub-national government. A national university may or may not be considered a public university, depending on which region it belongs to.

A **private university** is a university that is run without the direct control of any government entity, as opposed to public universities. Private universities are common in Bangladesh, Brazil, China, Chile, India, Japan, Lebanon, Malaysia, Mexico, Pakistan, Portugal, and the United States but do not exist in some countries. The Netherlands are relatively new to private universities. Tuition fees at private universities tend to be much higher than at public universities.

It is advisable to have some norms fixed by each nation to help the public and students understand what expectations to have about the range of fees and facilities.

4.3 ACADEMIC UNIVERSITIES

An **academic university** is a conventional institution of higher education and research, which grants academic degrees at all levels (associate, bachelor, master, and doctorate) in a variety of subjects. A university provides both undergraduate education and post-graduate education.

4.4 VOCATIONAL UNIVERSITIES

A **vocational university** (professional university or college of higher vocational studies) is an institution of higher education and sometimes research, which provides both tertiary and sometimes quaternary education and grants academic degrees at all levels (bachelor, master, and sometimes doctorate) in a variety of subjects. (More precisely a vocational university grants Professional degrees like Professional Bachelor's degree, Professional Master's degree and Professional doctorates).

The education which takes place at vocational universities combines teaching of both practical skills and theoretical expertise. Higher vocational education might be contrasted with education in a usually broader scientific field, which might concentrate on theory and abstract conceptual knowledge. This has to do with the fact that, in the Middle Ages, an educational institution was called a university only if a certain classical canon of subjects was taught (including, philosophy, medicine and theology). In modern times, other subjects, namely natural and engineering sciences, became more important—but still, institutions of tertiary education focusing on these and not offering the classical canon were denied the prestigious denomination "university", so they had to use the general word (High School in English) *Hochschule* in German, *Haute Ecole* in French (Belgium and Switzerland), *Hogeschool* in Dutch, *Høyskole* in Norwegian, etc.

There exist vocational universities of applied sciences (also named polytechnics or institutes of technology), vocational universities of liberal arts, etc. In recent years, many vocational universities have received full university status, such as the University of Music and Performing Arts, Vienna, Austria (Universität für Musik und darstellende Kunst Wien, formerly Hochschule für Musik und Darstellende Kunst Wien), or the Örebro University, Sweden (formerly Örebro Högskola). There are also some establishments which now have full university status, but continue to use their former names, such as the Royal Institute of Technology in Stockholm, Sweden.

4.5 OPEN/VIRTUAL UNIVERSITIES

Due to the large number and geographical dispersion of students, unlike most conventional universities, working style of the Open University is on the basis of weekend or holidays and adopting various new methods like web orientation or distance learning for imparting knowledge and skills.

4.6 INTERNATIONAL UNIVERSITY

An **International university** can be defined as one which is funded by the governments of many countries and thereby is controlled by the officials from the governments of different countries. Mostly these universities are formed by regional associations.

Another definition is that the **International University** is *international* due to its *international reach*, mainly driven by the curriculum offered, the international student body or the international faculty teaching and researching at the university.

4.7 CORPORATE UNIVERSITIES

Corporate Universities (CUs) are a growing trend in corporations. Corporate Universities are anything from a pumped up training department to a degree granting branch of major companies. Denise Hearn in her article "Education in the Workplace: An Examination of Corporate University Models" cites these statistics: In 1993, corporate universities existed in only 400 companies. In 2001, this number jumped to 2,000. This number is only expected to grow in the future. Although changes in the economy may alter that growth to some extent, this trend is still receiving attention from such companies as Walt Disney, Boeing, and Motorola.

It is important to note that, in most cases, Corporate Universities are not Universities in the strictest sense of the word. The "traditional" definition of a university is an educational institution which grants both undergraduate and postgraduate degrees in a variety of subjects, as well as conducting original scientific research. In contrast, Corporate Universities often limit their scopes to providing job-specific, indeed company-specific, training for the managerial personnel of the mother corporations. For this reason, Corporate Universities are most commonly found in the United States, a nation which has no official definition of a "university". Perhaps the best known Corporate University of all is the Hamburger University operated by McDonald's Corporation in Chicago.

4.7.1 Goals of Corporate Universities

Corporate Universities are set up for a variety of reasons, but most organizations have the same basic needs. According to Hearn, these are to:

1. Organize training
2. Start and support change in the organization
3. Get the most out of the investment in education
4. Bring a common culture, loyalty, and belonging to a company
5. Remain competitive
6. Retain employees.

CUs offer valuable training and education to employees, but they also help organizations retain and promote key employees. Although a CU may sound attractive, there is a lot of work that goes into the planning and implementation of such a project.

4.7.2 Planning for Corporate Universities

Before one jumps into planning a CU, Hearn suggests to conduct "a full learning audit and assessment, a series of design workshops, the creation of a business case and recommendations to senior management, implementation, and finally, further recommendations and review." These steps can help to analyze what work needs to be done. One of the most important goals is to ensure that this project has support from the CEO down. Without funding and support, this project will go nowhere.

According to Jeanne Meister, the president of the consulting firm Corporate University Xchange (CUX), there are ten primary steps to implement and sustain a successful corporate university. These step are reproduced below:

1. First, the executives or top management of an organization must form a governing body for the corporate university, much like that of a traditional university, which will establish and profess the organization's commitment to the program.
2. Secondly, the vision or strategic plan of the corporate university must be crafted; thereby, determining the organization's goals for the program.
3. The organization must then recommend a funding strategy. Most commonly, corporate universities are either funded through corporate allocations or through charges placed on individual business unit budgets.
4. Next the organization must determine its audience or stakeholders who will use the corporate university service.
5. In addition to determining the audience, the organization must also determine how the needs of the audience will be met while continually pursuing the strategic goal of the corporate university.
6. Following the completion of the above tasks, corporate university organizers must develop a template for how products and services will be designed to achieve university goals.
7. The organization must also select suppliers, consultants, traditional universities and for-profit firms who will act as learning partners, if appropriate.
8. The use of technology and resources to be used by the corporate university must then be determined.
9. Additionally, a measurement system should be developed that will allow the organization to continually monitor its progress against the university's strategic goals.
10. Lastly, the governing body must communicate the vision of the corporate university constantly and consistently. All stakeholders should be made aware of the mission, products and programs that make up their organization's corporate university.

Of course, these steps may need to be tweaked depending on the size or goals of the organization. CUs can be outsourced to a consulting firm or planned and implemented inhouse. It is a growing trend for organizations to partner with traditional universities. A traditional university brings organization, structure, and faculty. Universities are often interested in CU opportunities because of the economic gain. There are a number of consulting firms that will help the interested to set up Corporate University, but that can become very expensive. This process can also take a long time, sometimes up to two years.

Hearn also provides overviews of the CUs at Walt Disney, Boeing, and some other large corporations to give ideas of what other organizations have done.

4.7.3 Curriculum

Curriculum of the Corporate Universities are designed in a different manner. For example, Lisa Tanner of the *Dallas Business Journal* cites J.P. Morgan and Co. as an example of a company with an organized curriculum. They have three different types of courses: Business specific courses, organizational learning and communication classes, and management and executive training. What the company decides to offer will depend on the needs (such as sales training, marketing, or soft skills) and the company's business (like manufacturing, consulting, or technology).

Most CUs offer a blended curriculum of online and in person classes. Some organizations offer courses during the workday while others offer them at varying times. Courses can be short workshops or longer, more traditional courses.

Sharon Shinn of BizEd is of the opinion that, unlike traditional universities, CUs demand a return on their investment. There must be concrete evidence that the classroom is delivering results. Many CUs provide hands-on and team learning as a more effective alternative to lecture-based courses, but all CUs agrees that what is learnt in the classroom should be directly applicable to the work environment.

4.8 DIFFERENT MODES OF EDUCATION

There exist different modes of imparting education. They are Formal Education, Virtual Education, Web Education and Distance Education.

4.8.1 Formal Education

Education is the process by which society deliberately transmits its accumulated knowledge, skills and values from one generation to another. Formal Education is a concept, referring to the process in which students can learn something in a predefined area with the help of teachers: Instruction refers to the facilitating of learning toward identified objectives, delivered either by an instructor or other forms.

Teaching refers to the actions of a real live instructor designed to impart learning to the student. Learning refers to learning with a view toward preparing learners with specific knowledge, skills, or abilities that can be applied immediately upon completion.

Full-Time Programme/Part-Time/Weekend Programme

A "Full-time programme" can be used to refer to a student who takes a full load of course work each academic term, commonly 12 credit hours or more. This translates to 12 hours in class per week. Lab hours often count only as one-half or one-third of a credit hour. In the U.S., international students must maintain full-time status for student visas. Often, full-time students pay tuition only for their first 12 hours of class, no matter how many they take beyond that. Adult students (typically up to age 22 or 23) may also fall under their parents' health insurance (and possibly car insurance and other services) if they are full-time, except for one term per year (usually summer). Students may also be eligible for elected office in student government or other student organizations only if they are full-time.

In Indian context the average full load of coursework in each academic term is roughly 20 credits. The fees are same for all students, irrespective of the number of credits for which they register.

Part-Time Programme

A "Part-time Programme" is a programme with reference to a student who takes only a few courses, rather than a full load of coursework each semester or a total of 15 contact hours during a week in evenings only instead of 25 hours a week comes under this category.

Weekend Programme

A weekend comprises the two traditionally non-working days in a seven-day week. The rest of the week is referred to as the workweek. A program devised specifically to suit persons who can attend classes only during all weekends come under this category.

4.8.2 Distance Education

Distance education, or distance learning, is a field of education that focuses on the pedagogy, technology, and instructional system designs that aims to deliver education to students who are not physically "on site" in a traditional classroom or campus. It has been described as "a process to create and provide access to learning when the source of information and the learners are separated by time or distance, or both." In other words, distance learning is the process of creating an educational experience of equal quality for the learner to best suit their needs outside the classroom. Distance education courses that require a physical on-site presence for any reason (including taking examinations) is considered a hybrid or blended course of study. This emerging technology is becoming widely used in Universities and institutions around the globe. With the recent trend of technological advance, distance learning is becoming more recognized for its potential in providing individualized attention and communication with students internationally. The most widely cited pedagogical theory of distance education is that of "transactional distance".

4.8.3 Web Education

E-learning comprises all forms of electronically supported learning and teaching, which are procedural in character and aim to effect the construction of knowledge with reference to individual experience, practice and knowledge of the learner. Information and communication systems, whether networked or not, serve as specific media to implement the learning process.

E-learning is essentially the computer and network enabled transfer of skills and knowledge. E-learning refers to using electronic applications and processes to learn. E-learning applications and processes include Web-based learning, computer-based learning, virtual classrooms and digital collaboration. Content is delivered via the Internet, intranet/extranet, audio or video tape, satellite TV, and CD-ROM. It can be self paced or instructor led and includes media in the form of text, image, animation, streaming video and audio.

4.8.4 Virtual Education

Virtual education refers to instruction in a learning environment where teacher and student are separated by time or space, or both, and the teacher provides course content through course management applications, multimedia resources, the Internet, video-conferencing, etc. Students receive the content and communicate with the teacher using any such mode.

4.9 CONCLUSION

This Chapter classifies different types of Universities that exist around the world. The characters of different Universities vary according to their Nature. The Universities are normally classified according to i) funding ii) Mode of teaching and learning iii) Types of association etc. The Universities are generally classified into Public Universities, Private Universities, Corporate Universities, Vocational Universities, Open/Virtual Universities and International Universities. This chapter also gives an outline about the various modes of education which exist around the world. The mode of education classifies the programmes in to formal education, informal education, Full-time programmes, Part-time programmes, Weekend programmes, Web education and Virtual Education.

University system gains currency/supremacy at the admission counter, class rooms and examination halls which form a cycle. The best university attracts best students.

Since best students are in, only best faculty can thrive there to cope up with the expectations of such students. Best faculty naturally expects best perks and delivers and imparts good knowledge in the minds of students. Strict examination procedures with structured question paper and other practices ensure good output. Good output attract good placements leading to good name to the University and the cycle starts all over again Where to start? only with good infrastructure and best faculty it can start. Otherwise the cycle shall work in the reverse direction and the down fall is imminent to all stake holders.

CHAPTER 5

Administrative Structure of University System

5.1 INTRODUCTION

The University system consists of various functional components and these components are given in the organization structure. The over all general organization structure is given in Figure 5.1. Section 5.2 Explains various Academic Ranks in the University.

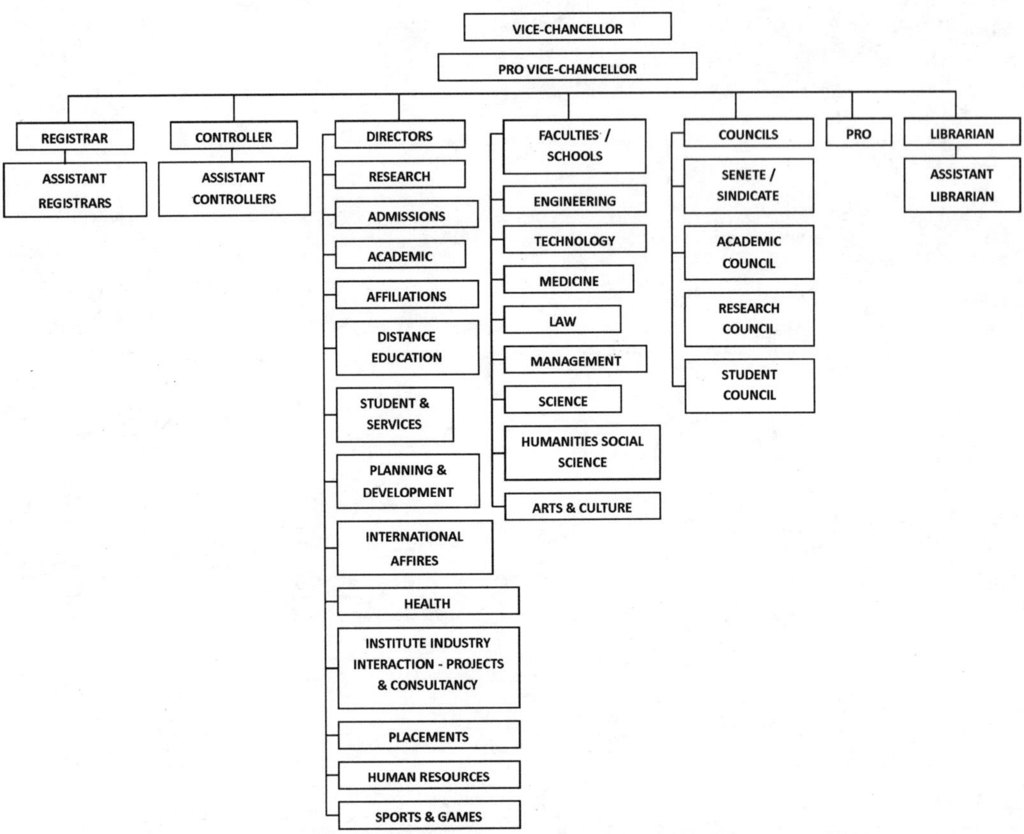

Fig. 5.1: Organisational Structure of an University

Section 5.3 Explains about the organizational structure, Section 5.4 explains the administrative Structure of the University, Section 5.5 explains functional Structure of the University, Section 5.6 explain the Academic structure of the University, Section 5.7 Outlines various boards and councils which exist in the University. Section 5.8 Explains the Public Relation office; Section 5.9 explains the duties of Librarian and Deputy Librarians and Section 5.10 Concludes this chapter. This chapter also gives various position categories available in the education system.

5.2 ACADEMIC RANKS

This list of academic ranks identifies the hierarchical ranking structure found amongst scholars in academia, whether tenured or non-tenured. The lists below refer specifically to colleges and universities throughout the world, although other institutions of higher learning may follow a similar schema.

1. ***Professor:*** Level E appointments, equivalent to Chair Professor in most Asian countries and in the North American universities
2. ***Associate Professor and/or Reader:*** Level D appointments, equivalent to Professor in most Asian countries and North American universities
3. ***Senior Lecturer:*** Level C appointments, equivalent to Associate Professor in North American universities
4. ***Lecturer:*** Level B appointments, equivalent to Assistant Professor in North American universities (Most universities now require applicants for Lecturer positions with PhD degree)
5. ***Associate or Assistant Lecturer, Senior Tutor, Tutor, Research Officer:*** Level A appointments
6. ***Professor Emeritus*** (male) or ***Professor Emerita*** (female) (a title conferred at retirement upon professors who have made significant contributions to their field and/or institution)
7. ***University Professor*** or ***Institute Professor*** or ***Regents Professor*** (a special title not used by all universities)
8. ***Distinguished Professor*** (usually a "Named Chair"; not used by all universities)
9. ***Professor*** ("Named Chair"; that is, the title 'Professor' is preceded by the name of a person who has endowed a chair, such as "Sterling Professor of Playwriting"; not used by all universities; may be a tenured or visiting professorial rank) ***Professor*** ("Full Professor", a tenured rank; this title is used by all institutions)
10. ***Associate Professor*** (generally a tenured rank; some institutions award tenure only to Full Professors)
11. ***Assistant Professor*** (usually tenure-track; always the lowest rank of tenure-track faculty)
12. ***Assistant Professor in Residence*** or ***Faculty in Residence*** (non tenure-track; teaching-track faculty, considered a permanent position in an institution, and

most likely has potential for promotion, to Associate or Professor in Residence. These individuals hold a PhD or terminal degree)

13. ***Adjunct Professor*** (an individual hired by an institution, on a temporary or limited-term basis, in order to teach a specific class or subject, for a specific term. These individuals may hold a Ph.D., though not always, and are typically current practitioners in their field. A second form of adjunct professorship is one in which the individual may be employed in another department or institution and given the title as a form of courtesy or prestige appointment, generally with no obligations or pay, but possibly some benefits, such as access to departmental or university resources...this usage is also called "courtesy" or "affiliate" or "dry" appointment)
14. ***Visiting Professor*** (as the name suggests, a professor visiting from another institution to teach for a limited term.)
15. ***Professor of Practice*** (also ***Associate Professor of Practice***, and ***Assistant Professor of Practice***; non-tenure positions for professionals without traditional academic credentials and/or career paths, but instead recruited for their practical experience and expertise)
16. ***Lecturer*** (Generally have a doctoral (or a terminal master's) degree; non-tenured, focused solely on teaching and sometimes administration, but generally not research. Some institutions may use "Lecturer" and "Instructor" interchangeably)
17. ***Instructor*** (These individuals are on a non-tenured track, may not possess a Ph.D., and are generally not assigned any research. Their primary function is to teach, whether part or full-time. Generally, they are limited to teaching undergraduate students. Sometimes, this rank is used as a place-holder for a "pre" tenure-track person who has not yet completed a doctorate but is slated to become an Assistant Professor upon doing so)
18. ***Postdoctoral Fellow:*** A position to continue Research work after obtaining Ph.D Degree. It is a tenure—track. In some Institutes it may include partial teaching/tutoring per week
19. ***Postdoctoral Associate:*** This is also similar to Post Doctoral Fellow but attached with a sponsored project got by a Professor
20. ***Fellow, Scholar, Teaching Fellow***, or ***Visiting Fellow*** (Generally function as an instructor while working toward a Ph.D., or as postdoctoral research experience; usually funded by an endowment or scholarship)
21. ***Research Associate*** (Graduate students who are sponsored by a professor or institution and tasked with conducting specific research for said professor or institution)
22. ***Research Assistant*** (Usually are undergraduate students doing an internship, or graduate students working under an assistantship at an institution)
23. ***Teaching Assistant*** (This rank usually describes students who are assisting educators with administrative tasks. More commonly, this rank is given to graduate

students who are teaching a course on a professor's behalf, or providing supplemental instruction/tutoring for a specific class. This rank is sometimes used interchangeably with "Teaching Fellow", and some universities distinguish Teaching Assistants from Teaching Fellows, with the latter being a higher rank).

5.3 ORGANIZATIONAL STRUCTURE

The complete structure of the University is given in the Figure 5.1. This involves various sub-structures and positions. This structure consists of administration, functional structure, academic, library, public-relations and list of committees. The following sections explain these structures in detail.

5.3.1 Academic Administrative Structure

An academic administration is a branch of university or college employees responsible for the maintenance and supervision of the institution and is separate from the faculty or academics, although some personnel may have joint responsibilities. Some type of separate administrative structure exists at almost all academic institutions, as fewer and fewer schools are governed by employees who are also involved in academic or scholarly work. Many administrators are academics with advanced degrees but hardly find time to teach or conduct research actively.

Chancellor/President/Rector

All universities have a chancellor as their titular head whose function is largely ceremonial. The Governor of the state, appointed as the Union's representative of state by the President, acts as the Chancellor of the university. The president/Chairman is appointed as the Chancellor of the Private Universities. The de-facto head of the university is the Vice-Chancellor. His equivalent for institutes is the Director.

Vice-Chancellor/Vice-President/Vice-Rector/Director

A Vice-Chancellor is the Chief Executive of a University, who is responsible for smooth functioning of the University, mostly supposed to take care of new initiatives, act as a guide and philosopher of the whole system. Other titles are sometimes used, such as Vice-Rector. These are often active academics who take on significant additional responsibilities. Some of these responsibilities are in charge of Research and Development, International affairs, or Academic and Education affairs.

Registrar/Deputy-Registrar/Assistant-Registrar

A registrar is an official in an academic institution (a college, university) who handles student records. Typically, a registrar processes registration requests, schedules classes and maintains class lists, enforces the rules for entering or leaving classes, and keeps a permanent record of grades and marks. The Registrar is the head of the University's administration. The role is usually combined with that of Secretary of the University's governing bodies and in these cases, the full title will often be "Registrar and Secretary" (or "Secretary and Registrar") to reflect these dual roles. Various grades of professional academic-related staff perform senior administrative and managerial roles in such universities on behalf of the Registrar or Head of Department and head subsections of the administration. Titles afforded to such staff include Academic Registrar, Assistant Registrar, Senior Assistant Registrar and Principal Assistant Registrar, etc.

Controller of Exams/Deputy Controller of Exams

The Controller of Examinations shall be the principal officer-in-charge of the conduct of examinations and tests of the University and declarations of their results. He shall discharge his functions under the superintendence, directions and guidance of the Board of Examinations. He shall be a full-time salaried officer of the university and shall work directly under the direction and control of the Vice-Chancellor within the regulations of the University. His appointment shall be for a term of five years and he shall be eligible for reappointment only one more term of five years. The qualifications and experience for the purpose of selection of the Controller shall be such as may be prescribed. For the functions of COE refer section 8.3.4 and for all minute details section 9.4.

Dean/Principal

A dean is a person with significant authority over a specific academic unit, or over a specific area of concern, or both. They usually run universities or colleges. The Principal is the chief executive and the chief academic officer of a university or college.

5.3.2 Functional Structure

Employees within the functional divisions of an organization tend to perform a specialized set of tasks, for instance the Research Department would be staffed only with Research Staff. This leads to operational efficiencies within that group. As a whole, a functional organization is best suited as a producer of quality graduates. The functional structure involves various activities like Research, Admissions, Academic, Affiliations, Distance Education, Student Affairs and Service, Planning and Development, International Affairs, Health, Institute and Industry Interaction, Projects and Consultancy, Placements, Human Resources, Engineering, Sports and Games and etc. A university system has its own system administration headed by Directors. Its function is to coordinate and integrate system-wide functions and activities. Each constituent unit has its own chief executive officer to whom broad powers are delegated by the governing board for the organization and operation of the constituent unit. The entire activities of these sections are explained as follows.

5.3.3 Admission Department

The main task of the Admission Department is to provide admission to students to all courses offered by the University in various faculties. The Department should prepare the admission policy and procedure, advertise, etc. The department should be responsible for conducting entrance exam for the various courses offered by the University if it is in vogue. Departmental Admission Officers are responsible for ensuring that the department fulfils its responsibilities to university applicants in accordance with the University's admissions policy. Admission Officers are required to fulfill obligations in respect of the admission process, recruitment and the provision of specialist subject advice in the determination of admissions protocols.

Admission Officers are required to work in close collaboration with the Admissions and Partnership Services Office and the International Office in the recruitment and admission of appropriately qualified students. The Admissions and Partnership Services Office publishes on the clear Service Level Statements which articulate the level of support that Admissions Officers can expect from the Office in the performance of their Admissions role. Admissions officer is also responsible for ensuring the right number of graduates.

5.3.4 Academic Department

The academic department is headed by a Dean/Director. Deans/Directors serve both academic and administrative purposes in that they are responsible for hiring department chairs and providing management oversight to bureaucratic processes within the unit. Depending on unit size, deans often have some number of associate and assistant deans to whom they delegate responsibilities associated with administrative functions related to finances, facilities, personnel, and management of academic or curricular programs. The position's uniqueness lies in its routine contact with a broad range of institutional constituents–the president or chancellor, the chief academic affairs officer, the faculty, students, external stakeholders such as donors and corporate supporters, and in some cases the boards that provide institutional or unit oversight. The unique position occupied by academic deans places them at the forefront of institutional change.

Decision-making responsibilities of academic deans typically encompass the following areas: (a) educational program/curriculum; (b) faculty selection, promotion, and development; (c) student affairs; (d) finance; (e) physical facilities development; and (f) public and alumni relations. Given the comprehensiveness of responsibility, it is not uncommon for the role of academic deans in larger, more complex institutions to resemble that of a chief executive officer of a moderately sized business enterprise. Resources under their control are often into the tens, sometimes hundreds of millions of dollars in large research institutions. With diminishing state support of higher education and increased operational costs, the need to identify new sources of revenue has increased considerably, and the work of garnering such support has become a primary function of academic deans in most institutional settings. Responsibilities associated with fundraising, the increasingly complex financial environment presented by issues of student access and equity, and increasing numbers of part-time faculty has made the role of the academic dean far more complex than it has been in the past.

5.3.5 Affiliations Department

A university system is a set of multiple, affiliated universities and colleges that are usually geographically distributed. Typically, all member universities in a university system share a common component among all of their various names. Usually, all member universities of a university system are governed by a system-wide governing body, such as a board of trustees or a board of regents. An Affiliation Department in the University is one that sets courses of study, conducts examinations, and awards educational credentials, but leaves the task of graduate instruction to an array of colleges.

5.3.6 Research Department

The main mission of the University Research Department is to introduce research programs, set up research laboratories, get funding from various agencies and facilitate the students and staff to do research in various fields. The Research Department should support University's mission to be one of the leading research universities in the world by uniting people, resources and opportunities for the creation, preservation and transmission of knowledge. This Department should function with full commitment towards Research and Development of societal importance with the enthusiasm to serve the community.

5.3.7 Distance Education Department

Distance education or distance learning, is a field of education that focuses on teaching methods and technology with the aim of delivering teaching, often on an individual basis, to students who are not physically present in a traditional educational setting such as a classroom. This department is responsible for admitting various off-campus students and should prepare the admission policy, procedure, advertise, etc. The department should be responsible for conducting exam for the various distance education courses offered by the University.

5.3.8 Student Affairs and Service Department

The Department of Student affairs staff provides services and support for students at institutions of higher education to enhance student growth and development. Student affairs professionals are charged with the tasks of developing programming, advising student organizations and student leaders and to meet the needs of the whole student—physical, emotional and mental balance.

5.3.9 Planning and Development Department

The Department of University Planning and Development is responsible for the development of the university capital plan. Staffed with licensed professionals in the fields of architecture, landscape architecture, design and physical planning, Department of University Planning and Development is engaged at the headquarters of the capital project implementation process. The office is involved in the development of the initial scope, site selection and programming of major university capital projects.

Department of University Planning and Development is charged with defining the long-range physical vision of each of the university campuses. Department of University Planning and Development interfaces with state, county and municipal agencies regarding environmental and cultural resource stewardship, and coordination of long-range planning activities working closely with the Office of the Vice-Chancellor for Academic Affairs. Technical services and project support are entrusted to professional consultants and to the university community at large.

5.3.10 International Affairs Department

The Department's goal is to support the students academic success by helping them navigate the challenges they may encounter as an international student or scholar. The Office of International Affairs assists them with the immigration-related aspects of their stay in the Native State. The Department is committed to being a reliable, efficient, and professional resource, and advocates international students in the University both during their tenure and after. The Department also assists individuals in various other statuses and advice departments in regard to immigration-related issues. The Department also provides some tax-related support. Throughout the year, the Department offers various types of orientation and training for international students, scholars, and employees as well as for University administrators and faculty.

5.3.11 Health Department

'A healthy mind in a healthy body' goes an old English axiom. The University Health Center should provide good adequate facilities to students in this regard. The

University Health Center can offer many programs and services to help to meet health and wellness needs. Whether one is interested in primary or urgent care, exploring alternative medicine, or just looking for general health information the staff as Physicians, Nurse Practitioners, Physician Assistants and other health professionals should be in a state of readiness to help. To enrich the lives of students in the principles and skills of health science, contributions to the intellectual foundations of student health, leadership in the public health profession, and collaborations with community partners are to be put in place.

5.3.12 Projects and Consultancy and Institute and Industry Interaction Department

One way of getting funds to the University is through carrying out projects and consultancy. Project and Consultancy Department is responsible for the promotion, facilitation, coordination and administration of all the sponsored and consultancy projects handled by the faculty of University. The departments and research centers, manned by well qualified and motivated engineers, scientists and social scientists, cover wide-ranging areas of specialization. This Department acts as a facilitator between the External Agencies and various Research Departments. The philosophy of encouraging cross flow of knowledge and experience between the Institute and Industries is attained in a continuous time scale.

The institute-industry interaction will have great bearing on the Curriculum, exposure of industrial atmosphere to students and subsequent placement of young graduating students in industries. There is an urgent need to prepare students for jobs in multinational companies, by exposing them to newer technologies and methodologies. These objectives can only be achieved well by bridging the gap between industries and the academic institutes. This can be taken care of by the Institute-industry interaction Department, to some extent.

5.3.13 Training and Placement Department

One of the prime responsibilities of the University is to train and place the students in various organizations and industrial houses. Training and Placement Department is responsible for this task and is an integral part of the University. The University has to provide complete infrastructure for effective functioning of the Department. It should organize training activities throughout the year in an effort towards preparing prospective students for campus selection programmes. The Department should keep inviting various industries and reputed firms for campus recruitment by show casing the strengths of the institute in using updated skills needed for the industries. The Department is to be sensitized to function all through the year towards generating placement and training opportunities for the students.

This Department is responsible for reputed industrial houses across the country to visit the institute regularly for the campus recruitment programmes. The Department should maintain a very cordial relationship with all the recruiting industries and also prepare the candidates to face the competitive world.

5.3.14 Human Resource Department

The Human Resource Department looks after the overall administrative matters relating to the establishment of various Departments. The main task relates to appointment of staff, transfer of staff and the maintenance of the service records and leave accounts of the staff of this Department. The department is responsible for making staffing policy, sound job design, robust task and person specification and versatile selection processes, reward, employment relations and human resource policies, underpinned by a commitment for strong employer branding and employee engagement and on boarding strategies, etc. The Department is also responsible for fixation of salary and perks etc.

Applicant recruitment and employee selection form a major part of an organization's overall resourcing strategies, which identify and secure people needed for the organization to survive and succeed in the short- to medium-term scenario. Recruitment activities need to be responsive to the increasingly competitive market to secure suitably qualified and capable recruits at all levels. To be effective, these initiatives need to include how and when to source the best recruits, internally as well as externally.

It is customary for an organization to undertake all aspects of the recruitment process. This may involve a range of support services, such as: provision of CVs or resumes, identifying recruitment media, advertisement design and media placement for job vacancies, candidate response handling, short-listing, conducting aptitude tests, preliminary interviews or reference and qualification verification, etc.

5.3.15 Engineering Department(s)

The Engineering Department looks after the overall administrative matters relating to the construction and maintenance of the buildings as well as University vehicles. The work mainly relates to fixing up the building plan, architecture, construction, contract, etc. In an University where Engineering education is a part, separate departments exist for each such branch and separate faculty, lab and etc.

5.3.16 Sports and Games Department

Department of Sports and games is responsible for conducting various sports and games and establishing infrastructure in the University/College campus. Physical education, a learning experience, offers a unique opportunity for problem—solving, self-expression and socialization. The objective is to make sports and physical activities an important part of the daily routine making it a way of life and generating fitness awareness among the masses. The programmes of physical education provide opportunities to participate in various competitions inside the campus readying students to take part inter-university competitions and national meets. Sports are in fact a way of life for the student's health and fitness and those looking for professional star status. A well-implemented, comprehensive programme is an essential component for the growth of both mind and body of students. This Department is responsible for providing these things. The Department is responsible for conducting activities like Basketball, Volleyball, Badminton, Table Tennis, Tennis, Cricket, Handball, Softball, Judo, Football, Netball, Chess, Carom, Athletics and Martial Arts. Mental health can be taken care by exposing students to yoga and transcendental meditation. The list of games and sports are only indicative but not exhaustive. It may differ based on preferences and importance in the region of the University.

5.3.17 Finance and Procurement Department

The Finance and Procurement section is responsible for the regulation of all income and expenditure of the University, and for ensuring that the systems of accounting and internal control are adequate and in accordance with laid down standards. The section also deals with insurance and investments, and is responsible for Procurement services. It also fixes the finance policy, preparation of budget, finance statement, distributing salary, etc. This may branch upon a standing committee comprising of experts from various Departments to initiate and support (Technical Details) purchases.

5.4 Academic Structure of University

The academic structure of University exhibits the diversity, comprehensiveness, and depth befitting a University of its age. University is academically organized into one or more large colleges, which contain one or more schools together with research laboratories, which together confer different degrees, majors, and programs. For example, the various faculties are shown in the Figure 5.1. These schools/Department include Engineering, Medicine, Law, Management, Science and Humanities, Arts and Culture, etc. Departments are generally chaired by a member of the department, who may be elected by the faculty of the department, appointed by the dean of the faculty, or assigned by simple rotation among the tenured faculty. The duties, importance, and power of the department chair vary widely among institutions and even among departments within an institution.

5.5 University Councils

The University constitutes various temporary and permanent councils to run the system smoothly. These councils are Senate/Syndicate, Academic Council, Research Council, Student Council, Advisory Board, Finance Committee and Ad-hoc committees. These councils are discussed in detail.

5.5.1 Senate/Syndicate

This body governs all academic matters pertaining to the University, and is made up of the Vice-Chancellor, who is the Chairperson, the Pro Vice-Chancellors, the Registrar cum Secretary, all heads of Faculties, Institutes, Centers, and Departments, all full Professors and two elected members from the Academic Staff, some industrialist and government officials (though many times not mandatory).

5.5.2 Board of Studies and Academic Council

Each Faculty, Institute, centre, and department has its own board of studies whose task is to facilitate the smooth running of the various departments and to make recommendations to the Senate on matters pertaining to their academic or professional activities. Academic Council finalizes and approves the course structures, curriculum and syllabi brought by various boards of studies. Constituent colleges are also representated in this council.

5.5.3 Research Council

The University Research Council (URC) is a standing committee that seeks to "formulate University research policies and procedures" and report these initiatives to the University Vice-Chancellor. By statute, the URC draws its membership from across the University's undergraduate, graduate and professional schools. The URC seeks to create a supportive and enabling environment for research.

5.5.4 Student Council

Student council is a curricular or extra-curricular activity for students and often serves to engage students in learning about democracy and leadership. Cultural events and competitions intramural, intercollegiate and inter University are also come under the purview of student council. However for each such event, a special team of staff will be set up to avoid unnecessary problems.

5.5.5 Advisory Board

The Advisory Board comprises the Vice-Chancellor, the Pro-Vice-Chancellors, all Deans, Directors and Heads of Departments, the Registrar, the Librarian, the Finance

Officer, the Assistant Registrars, the Estates Officer, the University Warden and the Farm Manager. The main duty of the Advisory Board is to advise the officers of the University on the general management of the University.

5.5.6 Finance Committee

The finance committee analyzes the financial position of the University. As and when a project is proposed the finance committee shall look at it from its angle and give a fair picture. The finance committee is by and large responsible for managing the financial position of the University. In general the Vice-Chancellor is the chairman of the Finance committee. A repatriate finance officer equivalent to that of joint secretary of finance in the Government setup (or an outside financial expert) by appointment/deputation. So that he is already in the knowledge of State finance policies, rules and regulations which will help him to handle the University's finance in a smooth fashion.

5.5.7 Audit Committee

The Audit Committee is an independent body answerable directly to the syndicate/ senate and responsible for verifying that the operations of the University have been conducted and its books kept in a proper manner. Usually pre auditing is done in important cases/cases which do not involve only routine committed expenditure. 'Prevention is better than cure' is what drives Universities to have pre-audit system. Though time consuming, many times it avoids complications that may arise otherwise due to the fact all academicians who do administrative work need not be in the know of the intricacies of rules related to finance and its proper handling.

5.5.8 University Ethics Board

The University Ethics Committee reviews protocols submitted by students, staff and all other groups. These Committees which are sub-committees of the University Ethics Committee act in accordance with its published procedures and practices. This committee fixes the code of ethics for the campus students. The committee is also responsible for en-lighting students about ethics code.

5.5.9 Ad-hoc Committees

Apart form the above committees all other temporary committees are constituted by the Vice-chancellor or any other agencies to cater to ad-hoc needs/problems of the University.

5.6 PUBLIC RELATION OFFICER

Public Relations (PR) is about managing reputation. This career field aims to gain understanding and support for clients as well as to influence opinion and behaviour.

PR officers use all forms of media and communication to build, maintain and manage the reputation of the University and Colleges services to businesses and voluntary organizations. They communicate key messages, often using third party endorsements, to defined target audiences in order to establish and maintain goodwill and understanding between the University and the public. They are also in- charge of taking care of the visitors to the University, with the help of the Departments concerned.

Tasks of PRO typically involve:

1. Planning, developing and implementing PR strategies.
2. Liaising with colleagues and key spokespeople.
3. Liaising with and answering enquiries from media, individuals and other organisations, often via telephone and email.
4. Researching, writing and distributing press releases to targeted media.
5. Collating and analysing media coverage.
6. Writing and editing in-house magazines, case studies, speeches, articles and annual reports.
7. Preparing and supervising the production of publicity brochures, handouts, direct mail leaflets, promotional videos, photographs, films and multimedia programmes.
8. Devising and coordinating photo opportunities.
9. Organizing events including press conferences, exhibitions, open days and press tours.
10. Maintaining and updating information on the organization's website.
11. Sourcing and managing speaking and sponsorship opportunities.
12. Commissioning market research.
13. Fostering community relations through events such as open days and through involvement in community initiatives.
14. Managing the PR aspect of a potential crisis situation.

5.7 LIBRARIAN/DEPUTY LIBRARIAN

A librarian is a professional trained in library and information science, which is the organization and management of information services or materials for those with information needs. Typically, librarians work in a public or college library, a library within a business or company, or another information-provision agency like a hospital or law firm. Some librarians are independent entrepreneurs working as information specialists, catalogers, indexers and in other professional, specialized capacities. A deputy Librarian assists the Chief Librarian. A librarian is incharge of making necessary purchase of books, magazines and materials relevant to the specializations in the university along with general category based on periodical requests from various faculties.

5.8 CONCLUSION

This Chapter gives the general structure of Universities which exist around the world. The structure involves various academic and administrative positions and how they function. This chapter also outlines the various councils that manage the system of practice and administration. The basic structure of a University is like the foundation for a multistoried building. The foundation needs to be robust enough to absorb and/or withstand the onslaught of periodic changes. A solid foundation alone can ensure the smooth running of a university.

CHAPTER 6

Responsibility, Functions and Contribution of Universities

6.1 INTRODUCTION

The prime responsibility of any University is to enrich the knowledge of students, mould their character and produce good citizens. This chapter explains the different responsibilities, functions and other contributions of the system.

6.2 AWARDING DEGREES/DIPLOMAS

The first and foremost task of an university is to award degrees and diplomas to the students and scholars. An academic degree is an award conferred by a college or university signifying that the recipient has satisfactorily completed a course of study. Academic degrees were first introduced during middle ages and there was little differentiation between them. Doctoral training was a form of apprenticeship to a guild. The common term of study before new teachers were admitted to the guild of "Master of Arts", was the same as the term of apprenticeship for other occupations. Originally the terms "master" and "doctor" were synonymous, but eventually the doctorate came to be regarded as a higher qualification than the master's degree.

A bachelor's degree is usually an academic degree awarded for an undergraduate course or major that generally lasts for four years, but can range from two to six years depending on the region of the world. An honorary degree or a degree honoris causa is an academic degree for which a university has waived the usual requirements, such as matriculation, residence, study and the passing of examinations. The degree is typically a doctorate or, less commonly, a master's degree, and may be awarded to someone who has no prior connection with the academic institution. Usually the degree is conferred as a way of honoring a distinguished visitor's contributions to a specific field, or to society in general. The university often derives benefits by association with the person in question.

6.3 DEVELOPMENT OF NEW COURSE/CURRICULUM/SYLLABUS

Curriculum development is highly significant as it describes the content structuring and delivery of a training program. The terms aims, objectives, outcomes and competencies are used in describing the intentions of a learning programme in relation to different perspectives. These will be useful in different circumstances and in order, to develop effective and less ambiguous statements in any one of the above categories. The curriculum design process entails gathering industry opinion to understand needs of recruiters and combining this with inputs of academicians to design a course capable of developing competent professionals. Curriculum will serve as the guiding source for lesson planning, teaching methodology, classroom training and testing of students.

The systematic approach for curriculum development involves the following:

6.3.1 Topics Relevant to the Target Group

The range of backgrounds, interests, knowledge, attitudes and skills of students coming on to the course will have a strong influence on course design. Pre-knowledge and any common misconceptions will have to be accounted for, in the design of the course (these may, for example, affect sequence, structure and support mechanisms). The broad thrust of the course content will also have to be considered. Consideration will be given to the sort of people whom the course is trying to develop. The subject area may have traditional aims and directions, but one has to consider the justification of these and/or preparation for future change.

There may be a minimum standard for entry into any course, but this need not always be so. For example, the increasing numbers of non-standard and mature student entrants to higher education will not necessarily have conventional paper qualifications, but may possess skills and qualities which will have an influence on course design. This may have implications in teaching methods; may call for bridge courses, support systems, etc.

6.3.2 Formulation of Objectives/Learning Outcomes

The role of objectives and learning outcomes in a systematic approach to instruction are dealt with in detail in the booklet on 'Specifying the Outcomes of Student Learning'. The objectives and learning outcomes of the course or curriculum element will attempt to encapsulate new skills, knowledge or attitudes which it is intended that the students will acquire. They may be formulated by the learners themselves, by employers, by teaching staff, by a validating, examining or professional body, or by some combination of these and other sources.

6.3.3 Selecting Appropriate Instructional Methods

Having specified the objectives and learning outcomes, we should be in a position to select appropriate teaching/learning methods through which these have a reasonable chance of being achieved. There are far more teaching methods available to choose from than most people realise—one recent book describes no less than 303 different teaching/learning methods! The process of attempting to match appropriate methods to the given objectives and learning outcomes is normally done on the basis of a combination of research and experience. The strengths and weaknesses of different methods are discussed in the booklet on 'Selecting Appropriate Teaching/Learning Methods'.

6.3.4 Implementation of Course or Curriculum

The next element in the system is the actual implementation of the course. This involves all the logistical arrangements associated with running the course, including overall structuring, pacing, implementing the chosen teaching strategies, using appropriate supportive media and materials, and ensuring that all aspects of the course run as smoothly as possible. Booklets providing detailed guidance on how this can be done are to be prepared and supplied.

6.3.5 Assessments and Evaluation

The combined result of the preceding stages is that students are involved in a learning experience that is planned to develop their knowledge, skills and attitudes, taking into account the individual needs and experience of the learners. Just how effective the pre-planning and subsequent operation has been can be measured by studying student performance in continuing and/or post-course assessments. These assessments should be closely related to the specified course objectives and learning outcomes. Poorly-achieved objectives or learning outcomes should typically lead the course designers to examine the entire system in order to identify places where improvements might be made. This could involve a change in the objectives/learning outcomes, a revised assessment of students' pre-knowledge, a critical review of the instructional methods used, an examination of the course structure and organization, a consideration of the assessment methods used, or a combination of some or all of these. These deliberations, together with feedback on the course from staff, students, employers, etc, can be used in an evaluation of the entire concept of the course, which should, in turn, form the basis of an on-going cyclical course development process. The topic of assessment is reviewed in the booklet on 'Assessing Student Performance', with evaluation being covered in the booklet on 'Evaluating the Effectiveness of the Teaching/Learning Process'.

6.4 IMPARTING KNOWLEDGE AND SKILLS

This is an important and primary task of a University Education System. It includes the imparting or acquisition of knowledge; mental and moral training; cultivation of the mind, feelings, and manners. Education in a broad sense, with reference to man, comprehends all that disciplines and enlightens the understanding, corrects the temper, cultivates the taste, and forms the manners and habits; in a narrower sense, it is the special course of training pursued, as by learned professors, to secure any one or all of these ends. Under physical education is included all that relates to the development and care of the organs of sensation and of the muscular and nervous system. Intellectual education comprehends the means by which the powers of the understanding are developed and improved, and knowledge is imparted, logical conclusions are arrived at.

Skills only give teeth to knowledge. Skills are of lower value than knowledge. Skills are often non-contextual. That means, one would learn it exactly the same way irrespective of where it would eventually be applied. If any particular skill is only partially known then it becomes a blunt tooth. Hence, each skill should be acquired to sufficient depth or the skill should be left to someone else entirely.

The Knowledge and Skill development is a review process in the chain of lifelong learning. The main process of imparting knowledge and skill involves:

1. Identifying the knowledge and skills that an individual needs to apply in his/her profession.
2. Helping to identify any gap between the knowledge and skills needed in the job and the current knowledge and skills of the individual and helping to bridge the gap.
3. Helping individuals develop throughout their careers by even providing pay increases based on a agreed system.

6.5 TRAINING SCHOLARLY APPROACHES

A scholarly approach to teaching and learning fosters and preserves the values of good communication, experimentation, critical appraisal and self evaluation. The role of the teacher is to stimulate and challenge, to make connections, encourage students to critically engage in learning activities, to reflect on learning and to adjust current practice to elicit a deeper learning. Engaging in scholarly activities involves continuous reflection on practice, and making decisions about improving the quality of teaching. This includes involvement in research, and in leadership in a range of academic projects.

The teaching and learning environment in which both staff and students participate, provides the best mechanism for staff to put into place learning and assessment opportunities for students to demonstrate that they have understood, practiced and valued academic integrity. Teaching staff at the University are expected to develop student-centred learning approaches to their teaching and to assist their students to access a range of flexible learning options.

6.5.1 Developing Scholarly Approach to One's Profession

This consists of the following approaches:

1. Engaging in collegial activities like peer assessment and mentoring.
2. Grabbing opportunities to involve in research, to present and publish the research work at conferences, workshops and in publications.
3. Communicating with other academics and sharing good practices and ideas.
4. Knowing and using the literature that is appropriate to the concerned discipline.
5. Taking action to improve teaching and learning.
6. Incorporating research and international perspectives in the coursework.
7. Engaging in activities related to the concerned professional associations.
8. Promoting work through grant and award activities.
9. Designing models or case studies that suit one's transnational context, or complete action research that will improve teaching conditions offshore—for one or others.
10. Preparing teaching or online materials in one's discipline, and having them peer reviewed.
11. Reviewing or redeveloping existing materials.

6.6 DEVELOPING RESEARCH AND CONSULTANCY

Research can be defined as the search for knowledge, or as any systematic investigation, with an open mind, to establish novel facts, usually using a scientific method. The primary purpose for applied research (as opposed to basic research) is discovering, interpreting, and the development of methods and systems for the advancement of human knowledge on a wide variety of scientific matters of our world and the universe.

Scientific research relies on the application of the scientific method, a harnessing of curiosity. This research provides scientific information and theories for the explanation of the nature and the properties of the world around us. It makes practical applications possible. Scientific research is funded by public authorities, by charitable organizations and by private groups, including many companies. Scientific research can be subdivided into different groups according to their academic application disciplines.

It is essential for Universities to establish Research facilities and development centers to showcase its ability. Most funding for scientific research comes from two major sources: Corporate research and development departments; and government research councils. Many senior researchers (such as group leaders) spend a significant amount of their time applying for grants for research funds. These grants are necessary not only for researchers to carry out their research, but also as a source of merit.

A consultant is usually an expert or a professional in a specific field and has a wide knowledge of the subject matter. A consultant usually works for a consultancy firm or is self-employed, and engages simultaneously with multiple and changing clients. Thus, clients have access to deeper levels of expertise than would be feasible for them to retain in-house, and may purchase only as much service from the outside consultant as desired. It is essential to have a good consultancy to expose the scholarly knowledge of the students.

Some consultants are employed by a consult staffing University, a University that provides consultants to clients. This is particularly common in the technology sector. Consultants are often called contractors in the technology sector in reference to their employment contract. Strategy consultants are common in upper management in many industries. There are also independent consultants who act as interim executives with decision-making power under corporate policies or statutes. They may sit on specially constituted boards or committees.

6.7 MEETING THE EXPECTATIONS OF STUDENTS AND PARENTS

6.7.1 Students Expectations

1. Students expect teachers to explain everything to them fully, particularly the details of what they are expected to do in the course and how grades are assigned.
2. Students value teachers who are friendly and open, communicating something about themselves as people.
3. Students may want teachers to interact with them in class, encourage student participation and deal gently with incorrect responses.
4. Students prefer teachers who make their classes interesting by using a lively presentation style, "relevant" and intriguing examples, and humour.
5. Students respect teachers who are knowledgeable, but who are also willing to admit that they do not know something when that is the case.
6. Students expect that they must be trained to set their own personal development goals and take responsibility for their own learning.
7. Students expect that they must be trained to learn and to be intellectually challenged; strive for excellence in their studies and seek to achieve high academic expectations in all of their courses.
8. Students expect that they must be trained to acquire an inquisitive mind; respect for human diversity and individuality; a sense of civic and global responsibility; sound ethical principles; effective writing, speaking, and quantitative skills; and a healthy lifestyle.
9. Students expect that they must be trained to involve in the campus community; and take full advantage of opportunities to develop and implement career plans.

6.7.2 Parental Expectation

Parents are trying to give their children every opportunity to enrich themselves, to excel, to become super kids, in a highly structured and supervised environment. This is a positive situation in one sense: today's children have far more exposure to Saturday morning classes in dance, art, science, politics, and computers and greater specialized focus and training in athletics and music. But as the bar continues to be raised higher and higher and the academics become more and more challenging, this culture of high expectations sets up a classic situation for stress and early burnout.

The situation can be particularly stressful in immigrant families. In these cases, some hopeful and ambitious parents push their kids hard to move up from just-off-the-boat working-class status to - middle-class professionalism. This syndrome leaves no time or tolerance for exploring life or self.

It is with the best of intentions that parents raise the bar on minimum expectations. But a large number of sound studies have found that the results of this increased pressure from home have a part to play in the epidemic of mental health issues on campus.

The system has to be balance between the expectations of both parents and students.

6.8 TRANSFORMING THE SOCIETY AND LIVELIHOOD

Many Universities have been institutions of social transformations. It is possible since the students are young and bubbling. Social transformation is the process by which an individual alters the socially ascribed social status of their parents into a socially achieved status for themselves. However another definition refers to large scale social change as in cultural reforms or transformations. Social transformation in this context requires a shift in collective consciousness of a society—local, state, national or global—so that reality is refined by consensus. This often happens by external stimulus and sometimes intentionally.

6.9 ESTABLISHMENT AND DISESTABLISHMENT OF ACADEMIC PROGRAMS, LABS, CENTERS, DEPARTMENTS

The University should provide some space for eminent personalities to establish and de-establish the programs, labs and centers. The University must provide the funding and infrastructure for establishing all these systems. The university should provide the facility to conduct regular conferences, workshop, seminars, etc. Apart from this, the University should provide the facility for starting new courses.

In the same way the academic personality should actively monitor social value of all these programs, labs, centers. If the system feels that the programs, labs and centers have no value then it can be disestablished. These processes are socially or market driven one.

6.10 ASSESSING THE QUALITY OF TEACHING AND STUDENT LEARNING FOR IMPROVEMENT

Assessing quality in higher education makes for some important ethical assumptions, some of which may be questionable. A more satisfactory ethical view is required if assessing quality in higher education is to be sound. However, political intrusion in system-wide assessment brings an influence which, preoccupied with market forces and technological development, goes beyond appropriate technical excellence to technical excess. This generates a climate inimical to ethical quality and conflicts with academic work.

Academic development units have a special role in regard to academic quality, but tend to be conceived of in a technical way. It is essential to asses the teaching quality, continuously monitor the student learning and must device various strategies to improve the over all quality.

6.11 INSTITUTION OF AWARDS AND FELLOWSHIPS

The institute/university should institute a fellowship or award to recognize the leaders of the field in recognition of outstanding achievement in the field, which is the highest honour the Academy can bestow. The Fellowship recipients have been mainly academic achievers, notable writers, scholars, etc.

6.12 CONDUCTING OF SCHOLARLY LECTURES

The Scholarly Lecture offers a selection of outstanding lectures by notable personalities like world leaders, Nobel laureates, field specialists, etc., from across the disciplines on a variety of subjects. Academic and scientific awards routinely include a lecture as part of the honor, and academic conferences often center on "keynote addresses", i.e., lectures. This is sometimes organized in the form of public lecture. These personalities present the renewed scholarly knowledge to the public/audience. A public lecture is a means employed for educating the public in the sciences and medicine.

The Royal Institution has a long history of public lectures and demonstrations given by prominent experts in the field. Likewise, the University should invite eminent world leaders to present their achievements and ideas.

6.13 CONCLUSION

Universities in general are places of knowledge generation, accumulation and dissemination in the interest of public at large. This cannot be done by a few persons who excel in their fields alone. Each need a band of colleagues and students interested in the topics concerned, besides necessary materials like books, journals, laboratory equipment, ambience and freedom. All these are to be put in under set of rules and regulations. Total freedom and strict rules and regulations cannot co-exist. One has to have a thin line of demarcation between them. Self imposed discipline is the best way of life in a university system. Freedom of every stake holder is to be preserved and enjoyed without infringing into others freedom without affecting other groups. Competitive spirit is to be encouraged to excel in the subject, but simultaneously avoiding un-ceremonial activities.

Students form an inevitable part of any university conducting and developing of any new research and joint ventures. All need the support of student's involvements leading to a win win situation to the staff, students, the university and other partners if any.

CHAPTER 7

Special Elements and Components of University System

7.1 INTRODUCTION

In every University system there are several special components and elements that add value to the system. These components will facilitate the faculty, scholars and students to perform special tasks and motivate them to excel in research. A few components will help them to achieve better research results. This chapter gives various additional components and elements that give special value to the system.

7.2 PRESS

Every University needs to have a support for publishing work generated through various academic, research and other activities. This needs to be done via establishment of press. For example the famous American Institute MIT (Mechachetus Institute of Technology) (http://mitpress.mit.edu/main/home) has its own press to support their own academic activities. It publishes various books and journals in their field of specialization. It publishes only world class books and journals in subjects like Architecture, Arts, Bioethics, Biology and Medicine, Cognition Brain and Behavior, Computer Science and Intelligent Systems, Economics, Finance and Business, Environmental Studies and Nature, Humanities, Law, Linguistics, Neuroscience, New Media, Philosophy, Photography, Physical and Earth Sciences, Political Science, Science Technology and Society and etc.

7.3 JOURNALS/MAGAZINES

The identity of an university is, most often, tied to its area of focused research. It is the most important activity for Universities to acquire state of art technology or knowledge and disseminate the same. This will show their scholarliness in specific areas of technology/knowledge. This can be done through publishing journals/magazines in the field of research/specialization. These journals/magazines are having review committee members, field experts and editorial board members derived from various eminent institutions across the world. These publications are also sold across the world to different famous libraries and other subscribers.

7.4 MUSEUM

'The only constant in this world is change' goes an old adage. Technology too evolves with time. Every organization has its own style of upgrading their components and equipments. It always gives a pleasure to see and know the old technology and components. This can be achieved by maintaining a museum to keep the old technology components rather than simply auctioning them to the public. It will enable the new generations to learn about the new things in that how they differ from the older things and create a history of scientific equipments. This kind of museum is available at Harvard University. It has been purchasing scientific instruments on a continuous basis for teaching and research since 1764. The Collection of Historical Scientific Instruments in a museum was established in 1949 to preserve this apparatus as a resource for teaching and research in the history of science and technology, has become one of the three largest university collections of its kind in the world. Originally associated with the Harvard library system, the Collection became affiliated with the Department of History of Science in 1987.

With the addition of instruments from various departments and donations from private benefactors, the collection now contains over 20,000 objects dating from about 1400 to the present. A broad range of scientific disciplines are represented, including astronomy, navigation, horology, surveying, geology, calculating, physics, biology, medicine, psychology, electricity and communication. Significant instruments, made obsolete by new technologies, continue to be incorporated. Many of the documents detailing the purchase and use of the instruments have been preserved, and are available for research in the Collection's adjunct library.

7.5 NEWSLETTERS

Every Department/Society/Center/Group/Association is doing various activities in the campus and it is essential to disseminate information about these activities to all since many times people staying in the same group may not be aware about (hidden) the activities going on in the same association or community. In order to avoid such a situation it is always better to circulate newsletters throwing light on all activities. It will also avoid the misunderstanding of the activities going on in the particular organization. A sample Mathematics Department news letter of MIT is given as follows:

Autumn 2006
Volume 1
Massachusetts Institute of Technology

Integral

NEWS FROM THE MATHEMATICS DEPARTMENT AT MIT

Inside

- **Faculty News and Awards**

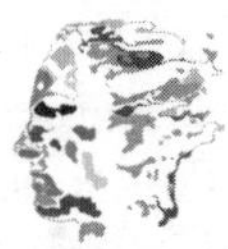

- **Abel Laureate Isadore Singer Wins Killian Award**
- **Richard Melrose Appointed to Simons Chair**
- **Gerald Sacks Retires**
- **Putnam Competition**
- **Lusztig Conference**
- **$15 Million Campaign**
- **Alumni & Friends**

Dear Friends,

I am pleased to introduce *Integral*, the newsletter from MIT's Mathematics Department. *Integral* will bring you news of our faculty, alumni, staff, and students, as well as updates on recent developments of note. Our plan is for *Integral* to announce what is new, celebrate our achievements, define our challenges, and bring together our mathematical community. *Integral* will be available in hardcopy and on the web at http://math.mit.edu. Looking over the alumni of our department, I see a remarkable group of people. Many have gone on to distinguished careers in mathematics and other fields in academia and business. We're proud of you! Now you can stay in touch with us through *Integral*. Tell us what you've been up to and give us stories about your time at MIT. Your suggestions on ways to improve the department are also welcome. Let us know what you'd like to see in future issues of our newsletter. Do you like the title? If not, please suggest something better! To steal a phrase from Paul Erdös, "Our minds are open."

Among Our Faculty

MIT is an extraordinary place, and mathematics is central to nearly everything the Institute does. Here's an interesting statistic: Among the MIT faculty outside the Mathematics Department, 13 hold degrees from our department, including the current head of Electrical Engineering and Computer Science (EECS), a former MIT provost, and a Nobel Prize winner in biology.

Highest Honors

The Abel Prize for research in mathematics was established by Norway about three years ago, although it had been conceived a century earlier. Similar in many respects to a Nobel Prize, the Abel Prize is still relatively unknown. We need to work on raising public awareness of this major award in our field. At MIT, we're most fortunate to have a faculty member who is one of these rare creatures, an Abel Laureate: Isadore Singer. "Is" holds the position of Institute Professor, one of the very highest honors that MIT bestows upon its faculty, and in March he gave the 2006 Killian Lecture.

Simons Lectures

Our Simons Lecture Series has been running annually for five years, bringing in distinguished speakers, such as Laurent Lafforgue, Peter Shor, Robert MacPherson, Wendelin Werner, Grigory Perelman, Nigel Hitchin, and Noga Alon. This year, we were privileged to hear speakers Akshay Venkatesh and Yves Couder. In 2007, we will hear from David Donoho and Terry Tao.

Off the Infinite Corridor

A few other happenings are worth mentioning. We've completed a renovation of the second-floor common room. It now has three enormous blackboards, a new kitchen, comfortable furniture, and boardgames. We've also renovated the third-floor applied math laboratory, where John Bush and Martin Bazant conduct experiments on how to walk on water and other miracles.

Reaching Out

David Jerison is taking over RSI (Research Science Institute) and SPUR (Summer Program for Undergraduate Research) from Hartley Rogers, who has been running them for many years. These wonderful programs match our graduate students with high-school students and MIT undergraduates for an intensive summer research experience. This year, two students, Kimberly Scott and Yi Sun, ranked among the top-10 winners in the Intel Science Talent Search for their work in the RSI program, summer 2005. To transmit excitement about mathematics, we've recently developed a pilot program called "ProveIt," which joins MIT undergraduates with Cambridge-area middle-school and high-school students.

Moving Forward

Our department is entering a critical period. Over the next few years, we will be recruiting new faculty most actively. The choices we make now about faculty hiring and research direction will determine the character of our department for a generation. If you have thoughts on the future of mathematics at MIT, we're eager for your advice and help. Please email me directly at sipser@math.mit.edu. I hope to hear from many of you.

MSirn

Michael Sipser
Department Head

7.6 FELLOWSHIP

A fellowship is a financial and intellectual reward for personal and academic achievements as well as the recognition of future potential or a financial reward that is given to graduate students based on academic and personal achievements. It may or may not include a tuition waiver. Usually it is awarded by an institution, government, or a private organization and can fund anywhere between 1 and 5 years of study.

Most of the fellowships provide financial support for graduate study either abroad or in the native states; however, a few provide support for the last two years of undergraduate study as well. Since fellowships open doors to opportunities that would otherwise seem beyond reach many students apply for them. Most fellowships are prestigious and highly competitive.

The Fellowships Office has to create this site to establish a functional, user-friendly, multifaceted, digital interface between the Fellowships Office and the student constituency. Through this website, students can access a treasure trove of fellowship information including, detailed descriptions in the extensive fellowship database, applications, deadlines, guidelines, helpful hints, and additional resources. Also, students can gain access to exclusive internships and membership to the Fellowships bi-weekly letters. The fellowship is also called as Research fellow, Graduate fellow, etc.

Full/Half Fellowship—If financial reward given to a fellow/student supports the complete process of research/course study by single agency then it is called as full fellowship. One agency may give a partial support and other may give a partial support for research or course study. This kind of facility called as Half Fellowship or Partial fellowship.

Teaching Fellowship—It is financial assistance provided to students (usually graduate students) through part-time academic employment, assisting a faculty member with teaching. Typical duties include teaching sections of classes, grading, and tutoring.

Research Assistanceship—Financial assistance provided to students (usually graduate students) through part-time academic employment, assisting a faculty member with his or her research.

Book Writing/Thesis Writing Fellowship—It is a short time financial assistance provided to the faculty member/student through academic institution to assist him for book writing or thesis writing. It also provides a faculty member/student to acquire and share his knowledge with other members of the institutions.

Short-Term/Long-Term Research Fellowship—Financial assistance provided to the faculty member/student for less than a year is called as short term fellowship; if it is given for more than one year and more period of time then it is called as long term fellowship.

Visitors Fellowship—Financial assistance provided to the faculty member/student for collecting information and academic other interaction from the higher learning institutions for a specific period of time is called as visiting fellowship. Normally this kind of fellowship may be given by the host institution or any other agency.

Travel Fellowship—Financial assistance provided to the faculty member/student for attending a seminar/conference/workshop or presentation of papers either with in the country or abroad is called as travel fellowship. Some of these are described in section 5.2 also to make that compartment of information complete.

7.7 SCHOLARSHIP

A scholarship is an award of access to an institution, or a financial aid award for an individual student scholar, for the purpose of furthering their education. Scholarships are awarded based on a range of criteria which usually reflect the values and purposes of the donor or founder of the award.

Types of scholarships may be classified into the following primary groups.

Merit-based—financial aid for which financial need is not used to determine the recipient. The recipient may be determined by students' athletic, academic, artistic or other abilities. The actual monetary value of the scholarship may be negligible, the scholarship being meant to motivate the student and promote the study of the subject. However, this is not always the case and the largest scholarships are almost always merit-based.

Need-based—financial aid for which the student and family's financial situation is a primary factor in determining the recipient. Usually such scholarship will cover all or part of the tuition and may even cover living-costs. Very often even need-based private scholarships require the awardees to be distinguished students, as the deed founding the award may include a phrase like: "for the studies of *founder's favourite subject* in *founder's favourite institution of higher education* for a talented youth of limited means from *founder's home town/county/state etc.*"

Ethnicity-based—financial aid where applicants must initially qualify by race, religion, or national origin. After filtering the applicants based on their ethnicity, additional factors are taken into consideration to determine the final recipients.

Institutional-based—scholarships awarded by a specific college or university (institution) to a student planning to attend that institution.

General—Other scholarships which are awarded for a variety of reasons which do not fall into one of the above categories. These may be for reasons of the student's association with the objectives of the sponsoring organization. For example, some corporations give scholarships to their employees' children or based upon academic success.

7.8 INDUSTRIAL AFFILIATE PROGRAMME/INDUSTRY-INSTITUTE INTERACTION PROGRAMME

The main objective of the Industrial Affiliates Program is to support the mutual needs of business, industry, and academia in any subject of their choice. This is accomplished by providing appropriate mechanisms for technical exchange and collaboration and employment of students. There is the opportunity to participate in long-range technical assessments of problems and directions in the field. Contacts with prospective employees can be established easily; affiliates have early access to student resumes and student and faculty publications. Special seminars and short courses can be arranged. Faculty members are available for informal technical discussions and more formal presentations.

The advantages to the University are also substantial. Staff and students can learn about current problems in industries. Students become acquainted with industrial needs. The co-op program and summer internships in local and national industries provide students with a complementary element to their education. The result of the interaction is greater excellence in both research and teaching missions of the department.

At a more general level, the Affiliates Program is an example of a constructive relationship between industry and the University—a relationship that stimulates developments in both segments of our society and it is a win-win situation for both.

The benefits of the program to member companies include:

1. Attendance at an annual Industrial Affiliates Program meeting that features research overviews by faculty, in-depth research presentations and demonstrations by students on current work, working sessions on common technical areas with both faculty and students, and opportunities to interview prospective employees.
2. Seminars by faculty members at the affiliate company's site (upon request).
3. Online resumes submitted by graduating students at all degree levels.
4. Announcement of interesting seminars and presentations.
5. Contact with technical and administrative representatives of other affiliate companies.

The annual meeting is an opportunity for the department and affiliates to come together and discuss topics and issues of mutual interest. The entire faculty attends, as well as most of the students, and over all it includes at least one to three representatives from each member company to attend. The meeting may span up to two days and may feature the following:

1. Research overviews by faculty, and updates on recent developments and research results within the department.
2. Small focused sessions organized by research areas where students, faculty, and affiliates can interact in a workshop setting and discuss research areas in depth.

3. Demonstrations of software and hardware systems developed by the research projects.
4. One-on-one meetings with individual faculty and students to create/continue collaborations.
5. Discussion of the educational mission of the department and the continuous changes and improvements made to the curriculum.
6. Interaction with other affiliate members; and opportunities to interview and discuss employment opportunities with undergraduate and graduate students for both permanent and co-op/internship positions.

7.9 INDUSTRIAL CONSULTANCY CENTER

The Center for Industrial Consultancy and Sponsored Research (IC&SR) is set up to promote interaction between the Industry and the Institute. This centre plays a vital role in bringing together the people from the Industry and the faculty of the Institute resulting in important contributions to design and development in the country.

The Centre for Industrial Consultancy and Sponsored research fosters institute-industry interaction and serves as a link between the Institute and the Industries and aims at encouraging and promoting consultancy research work by the faculty serving as a catalyst in the discharge of these tasks. Over the years, the consultancy and sponsored research activities shall have an impressive growth both on scope and in extent. The Centre administers the consultancy and sponsored projects; compiles and disseminates scientific and technical information and coordinates patenting of products and processes developed in-house. The Centre also co-ordinates activities relating to joint collaborative programmes with institutes in other countries, Entrepreneurship Development programme and Industrial Associateship Scheme.

7.9.1 Industrial Consultancy

Apart from teaching and research, faculty and technical staff of the Institute take up many assignments of direct relevance to the Industry. This activity is known as Industrial Consultancy and many include one or more of the following.

1. Testing and certification of Industrial products.
2. Development of prototypes and their testing.
3. Exploring new approaches to Design and Manufacturing.
4. Help design new products.
5. Investigate/correct problems, manufacturing of equipment.
6. Offer specialized programs to the Industry to keep them abreast of latest developments.

7.9.2 Sponsored Research

Sponsored Research relates to specific academic assignments proposed by the faculty. These include research in areas of current relevance, new investigations, product or system development, etc. Sponsored projects are funded by national organizations and quite often by Government agencies.

Sponsored projects provide for bringing in new resources to the Institute and also permit technical staff to be employed for specific durations to carry out the research. Though sponsored projects are basically academic in nature, useful results for the Industry are often achieved.

7.9.3 Interdisciplinary Project

A project which needs expertise from different fields of specialization falls under this category. For example in Anna University Chennai, a project of building a Micro satellite was undertaken, which was funded by ISRO (Indian Space Research Organization) to the tune of Rs 5.5 cores. This needed a team of 10 Professors from various Departments like Aeronautical, Electronics and Communication Engineering, Electrical and Electronics Engineering, Mechanical Engineering, Civil Engineering, Computer Science, Mathematics and a team of Research Scholars, a handfull of Project Associates and Graduate Students. Being the first of its kind it took a period of more than 5 years and had to make international purchases using Govt. rules. Apart from this, team members had to do hard work burning midnight oil and coordinating with ISRO officials every now and then for ensuring the progress from time to time. Finally it was completed successfully and launched by ISRO in 2009.

Such projects not only boost the image of the university but also act as a morale booster for the team members in particular. The importance of expertise in each field is appreciated by every other department person. The secrecy of working in isolation gets broken and the persons involved attain better understanding of their and other subjects.

7.10 INTERNATIONAL-FACULTY/STUDENT EXCHANGE PROGRAMME/INDUSTRY EXCHANGE PROGRAMME

International Faculty/Student exchange programme enable scholars (Faculty/Students) to exchange their views and knowledge about various types of education, technology, arts, culture etc between the different countries across the world. This will also increase the mutual relation between the organizations, countries. This must be designed with the help of the academic or national or Government organizations.

For example over 50 years, the Council for International Exchange of Scholars (CIES) has helped administer the Fulbright Scholar Program. The CIES is U.S. government's flagship academic exchange effort, on behalf of the United States Department of State, Bureau of Educational and Cultural Affairs. Founded in 1947, CIES is a private organization. It is a division of the Institute of International Education (IIE). CIES maintains deep ties with the U.S. higher education community, including individual universities and colleges and major scholarly organizations. It also works with a network of bi-national Fulbright Commissions in 50 countries and 90 U.S. diplomatic posts around the world, as well as international universities and higher education associations.

The day-to-day work of CIES is carried out by over 60 program officers and staff organized by world region. A six-person external relations unit assists program officers with recruitment and works with U.S. colleges and universities, professional and scholarly associations and the media to publicize the Fulbright Scholar Program and other CIES undertakings.

Nearly 300 academics and professionals serve without compensation on CIES discipline and peer review committees, reviewing applications of American scholars and some foreign scholars. The committees meet throughout the year at CIES offices to evaluate and recommend candidates for the available Fulbright awards. CIES also has a network of 2200 Fulbright representatives on college and university campuses who help promote the Fulbright Scholar Program and assist faculty and administrators in applying.

In Boston, New York, Los Angeles, San Francisco, Chicago and Washington, DC, CIES-appointed metropolitan coordinators arrange cultural and social activities for foreign Fulbright Scholars.

Like wise the industrial exchange programme enables the academicians to learn about the industrial technology. So, the academician can design the curriculum/syllabi according to the needs of the industry. Every industry must design such a special programme to help out the academicians to join hands with the industry. Consortium of academic organizations, industrial organizations also must involve themselves in designing such a program.

7.11 JOINT VENTURE PROGRAMME

Joint projects are positive, usually local, activities performed by members of two or more groups that are or have been in conflict with one another. Such projects allow individuals from opposing sides of a conflict to encounter one another in a conflict-free zone of cooperation. One example of a joint project is Croats and Muslims in Bosnia, former enemies, jointly rebuilding houses destroyed during their conflict. Other examples of joint projects are:

1. Interstate water distribution system, by the states concerned.
2. International border monitoring jointly by the neighbours.

3. A Philippine bakery that employs Muslims and Christians
4. The Galilee Bilingual School for Arab and Jewish Children, in which all classes are co-taught by an Arab and a Jew.
5. Some even consider the European Union to be a kind of joint project, since it came about following World War II and has served as a galvanizing force for former enemies.

The goals of joint projects are three-fold. First, they lead to the construction of specific structures, organizations, relationships, and institutions that will be useful to those on both sides of a conflict. Secondly, joint projects are also intended to lead to grass root level reconciliation and conflict transformation that can then spread to society as a whole. And thirdly, once a joint project is completed, it is hoped that the manifestation of the joint project, for instance a home, a school, or even a coalition government, will serve as a symbol of peace and cooperation.

Joint projects may seem entirely positive; however, there are potential negatives to working closely with one's enemies. While the separation of opposing parties usually leads to negative stereotypes, working in proximity with opposing parties can lead to first-hand verification of such stereotypes. In addition, joint projects can potentially further separate opposing parties if one side feels that the resulting structure or institution will benefit the other group more. Also, joint projects are often conceived of and organized by third parties, such as Non-Governmental Organizations (NGOs) sometimes leading to a lack of the important feeling of ownership that a successful joint project must have.

Ideally, individuals who are members of conflicting groups cooperate to organize joint projects. For example, academics, religious leaders, or parents who have lost children to the conflict have begun joint projects. These joint projects begun by individuals close to the conflict tend to have the most promise of success, due to the sense of project ownership and the direct transformation that tends to occur as the projects are undertaken.

Once initiated by outside third parties, ideally such projects should be transferred to the participants themselves, at least to some extent, so that they feel as if the project is their own, not something they are doing for someone else. Funding and other constraints, however, often make this difficult to do.

7.12 UNIVERSITY MEDALS

The Fields Medal is a prize awarded to two, three, or four mathematicians not over 40 years of age at each International Congress of the International Mathematical Union, a meeting that takes place every four years. The Fields Medal is widely viewed as the top honor a mathematician can receive. It comes with a monetary award, which in 2006 was C$15,000 (US$15,000 or 10,000). Founded at the behest of Canadian mathematician John Charles Fields, the medal was first awarded in 1936, to Finnish mathematician Lars Ahlfors and American mathematician Jesse Douglas and has been regularly awarded since 1950. Its purpose is to give recognition and support to younger mathematical researchers who have made major contributions. It is to be noted that there is no Nobel Prize for mathematics subject.

Same way every organization can take a lead in one subject area in the world and can award special medals like this. This shows the commitment of the organizations for the field development.

A **University Medal** is one of several different types of awards, bestowed by universities upon outstanding students or members of staff. The usage and status of university medals differ between countries.

In Australia, the University Medal is usually awarded upon completion of Honours degrees based on academic merit. The criteria for bestowing the University Medal are stringent, and the number of medals awarded is limited. The usual criterion is very high marks across all the subjects undertaken in the 4-year Honours degree. In some universities (such as the University of Sydney), the University Medal is treated as a distinct division or class of the Honours degree ("First class Honours and University Medal").

The University Medal is often awarded to the most distinguished undergraduate student upon graduation. In addition to stringent academic criteria, students are also judged on extra-curricular activities, publications, and other qualities. In some universities, the University Medal is bestowed upon members of the University for their extraordinary contribution to the University. Such an award is often conferred upon retirement of a staff member.

These medals are awarded in the following way. The university announces the medals and all those eligible for the same need to apply for the same with in the last date of application. Sometimes others can also nominate persons for the award of the medals from their observations.

1. The Medals Committee may award the University Medal to any outstanding graduate of the University.
2. A Faculty shall nominate for the consideration of the Medals Committee all graduands who have shown exceptional academic merit.

A list of the graduands arranged in rank order:

(a) within the Faculty;
(b) within the program; and (where applicable)
(c) within the discipline (major).

3. The Secretary shall prepare a list of all the nominees in rank order and listing the number of courses completed at High Distinction and Distinction levels.
4. The Medals Committee shall examine, consider and review all information provided by the Faculties, and determine the award of Medals.
5. The Medals Committee shall use the following guidelines to assist in its deliberations:
   (a) Only one Medal will be awarded within each program or discipline (major) where more than one discipline (major) can be undertaken in a program.
   (b) Where the two (or more) highest candidates within the one program/ discipline are equal in terms of the GPA, the candidate with the greater number of High Distinctions, or, if this does not separate the candidates, the candidate with the greater number of High Distinctions and Distinctions shall be awarded the medal. If this still does not separate the candidates, the Committee may award the Medal jointly.
   (c) Where two candidates within a program or discipline are of exceptional merit, and are high in rank order within the University and/or the Faculty, they may both be awarded a Medal.

7.13 AWARD/PRIZE SCHEMES

Awards/Prizes serve multiple objectives. The primary objective is to increase the interest of workers and motivate them in the right direction. First important thing is that the organization must decide a dimension for the development and then it can fix a different set of prizes/awards either to give the monitory benefit or to increase the social value of the organization as well as the stake holders. These awards may be given to rank holders, best book writers, best projects/theses, researchers, papers, innovations, etc.

University can make any custom award or certificate like the following, to encourage betterment in every field.

7.13.1 Employee Award

For employee of various cadre awards for the best performance, based on feedback; excellence achieved decided by their supervisors and for perfect attendance may be instituted.

7.13.2 Academic Awards

The academic awards are of the following categories Academic Achievement Award, Best All Round Student, Researcher Award.

7.13.3 Sports Awards

The Sports awards can be given to the various individual and team games

7.14 PROFESSIONAL SOCIETIES

A **profession** is an occupation, vocation or career where specialized knowledge of a subject, field, or science is applied. It is usually applied to occupations that involve prolonged academic training and a formal qualification. It is axiomatic that *"professional activity involves systematic knowledge and proficiency."* Professions are usually regulated by professional bodies that may set examinations of competence, act as a licensing authority for practitioners, and enforce adherence to an ethical code of practice.

Professions include, for example: Doctors/Surgeons, Lawyers, Engineers, Teachers, Diplomats, Professors, Priests, Architects, Accountants, Physical Therapists and some other specialized technical occupations.

A professional body or professional organization, also known as a Professional Association or Professional Society, is an organization, usually non-profit, that exists to further a particular profession, to protect both the public interest and the interests of professional. The balance between those two may be a matter of opinion. The professional bodies may act to protect standards of training and ethics of their profession. Many professional bodies perform professional certification to indicate that a person possesses qualification in the subject area, and sometimes membership in a professional body is synonymous with certification, but not always. Sometimes membership in a professional body is required for one to be loyal to practice the profession. Many professional bodies also act as learned societies for the academic disciplines underlying their professions. Membership of a professional body does not necessarily mean that a person possesses qualifications in the subject area, or that they are legally permitted to practice their profession.

All academic institutions must have a very close relation to help each other to improve the activities related to teaching profession. It is inevitable for the academic institutions to start the chapter or involve in various activities of the profession to improve the academic standards.

List of a Few International Professional Organizations

- AABB (formerly American Association of Blood Banks)
- American College of Forensic Examiners—International (ACFEI)
- Association for Computing Machinery (ACM)
- Association of Clinical Research Professionals (ACRP)
- Association of International Product Marketing and Management (AIPMM)

- Association of Records Managers and Administrators (ARMA International)
- Commonwealth Lawyers Association
- Drug Information Association (DIA)
- Institute of Electrical and Electronics Engineers (IEEE)
- Institute of Food Technologists
- Institute of Internal Auditors (IIA)
- Institute of Management Accountants (IMA)
- Institute of Professional Psychologists (IPP)
- Institute of Transportation Engineers
- Information Systems Audit and Control Association (ISACA)
- International Association for Bridge and Structural Engineering (IABSE)
- International Association for Plant Taxonomy (IAPT)
- International Facility Management Association (IFMA)
- International Federation for Information Processing (IFIP)
- International Federation of Intellectual Property Attorneys (FICPI)
- International Public Health Forum (IPHF)
- Latin American Studies Association (LASA)
- Society of Automotive Engineers (SAE International)
- Society for Clinical Data Management (SCDM)
- Society for Technical Communication (STC)
- Society of Clinical Research Associates (SoCRA)
- World Organization of Web Professionals (WOW)
- Indian Society for Technical Education (ISTE)
- Computer Society of India (CSI).

7.15 ALUMNI CENTER

The Alumni Center is available for use by the Alumni Association, University Advancement, University Development, and University Foundation. It is also available to university faculty, staff, centers, departments and colleges. All groups requesting the use of the center space are subject to the approval of the Alumni Center Director or a representative.

The Alumni Center is reserved for functions and activities in keeping with the University alumni and University Advancement. The university reserves the right to prioritize and control the type of functions and activities that take place in the building.

For example Anna University, Chennai has an alumni centre inside University Campus. The alumni also has a separate club outside the campus used as a meeting place to members and guests with all facilities like outdoor stadium, games and sports venues, conference hall, dining hall and guest house.

7.16 EXTRA CURRICULAR ACTIVITY CENTER LIKE DANCE/MUSIC/PERFORMING ARTS, ETC.

The University can nurture various extracurricular activities like Dance, Music and performing arts etc. For example the University of Alberta Dance Club is the largest dance group on campus with over 1700 active members yearly, and offers an extensive range of classes and activities. Regardless of one's dancing ability, there is something in the club for everyone. If anyone is interested in instruction, the club can offer 10 classes each week for nine weeks per term, ranging from beginner to advanced (Newcomer to Silver). Overall, the club teaches the 10 dances found in International Ballroom Syllabus, including Waltz, Viennese Waltz, Quickstep, Foxtrot, Tango, Cha Cha, Rumba, Samba, Jive, and Paso Doble.

7.17 FACULTY CLUB

The faculty club is formed by the members of the faculty of the University. The Purpose of having such a club in the campus is to have a platform where the faculty and their family members can interact and participate in myriad and meaningful activities. All round the year the club organizes events, both cultural and sports for faculty, their spouses and children.

7.18 LITERATURE CLUB

Literature Club can be formed with a number of member groups that would provide a regular gathering of those who wished to share their reading experiences with others. The members of the organization may gather periodically to review and critique readings. This club may include its own collection of books for members.

The club can maintain two series of records; these can be administrative records, and records of club activities. Administrative records include minutes, correspondence, club histories, lists of presidents and their activities, an incomplete collection of yearbooks, and photographs. Records of club activities include reading lists and book reviews.

7.19 SCIENCE/TECHNOLOGY CLUB

A Science Club at the University exists to help students in their study of specific areas of science and facilitates communication between students and prospective employers. It can be done through a variety of activities and events.

A sample of the many activities and events can be as under.

The primary aim of the Technology Club is to foster liaison between its members with a view to promoting the development of Science, Technology and Acquisition within the community. It will develop contacts with the industry, explore research and development opportunities, and seek to advance academic understanding within the community. It is also about keeping in touch with those who have been served with and creating an important network.

7.19.1 Membership

Members consist of all current members of the particular technology group. Membership is open to serving industrial employees on appointment to a post in the Technical employment field. There can be an annual membership fee of nominal amount which will be collected from each member. Also different grades may be given to each member based on their year of stay in the club.

7.19.2 Meet the Firms

Many companies are expected to visit the campus in order to give students a chance to gather information about them. Meet the Firms is facilitated by the Science Club. It provides students a more casual way to get to meet recruiters than an interview format and come to know about suitable opportunities.

7.19.3 Recruitment Conference

Annual Recruitment Conference can take place once in a year, allowing students to interview with employers for summer internship or full-time positions. Some firms can be expected to come every year, in what is always a highly successful event. The conference is very convenient for students, who would otherwise need to travel all over to track down interviews.

7.20 TECHNOLOGY BUSINESS INCUBATORS

Technology Business Incubator's (TBI) focus is to create commercially successful high-tech ventures by nurturing them with the resources these ventures need. For example, in the early stage, TBI will assist the incubatee in assessing the market potential of the business idea by guiding through the process, which the incubatee has to implement on his own with his resources and some assistance from TBI.

Such early stage advice and consultancy offered by TBI will be a free service. When the promoter and TBI is satisfied with the project idea and its success potential, the incubatee will enter in to an agreement with TBI for availing the services of the TBI on mutually agreed terms and conditions.

TBI may collect a nominal fee for the services and the space and technical support provided. As all the tenant incubates are sharing these resources from a common pool, the incubates will benefit from the lower cost of resources in the early stages. The form of compensation and the payment mode can be tailored to specific needs and based on individual case.

Broadly all the activities referred to in four stages above can be summed up as following:

- Ideation/Innovation stage has Concept development/Opportunity spotting, Market assessment/Competition analysis, First level Business Planning/Business Modeling, Founding Team formation, Intellectual property safe guarding and Seed Funding. (A)
- Incubation Stage has Mentoring, Advisory board, Proof of Concept/Prototyping, Financial Assistance, Test marketing and Full scale business planning. (B)
- Implementation Stage has Full scale Business Planning, Pitching for Venture Funding, Scaling up operations, Large scale commercialization and Mature Team Formation. (C)
- Take off stage has Going National/Global, Initial Public Offering, Exit provisioning for Venture Capitalists and Full scale business Graduation. (D)

The TBI can assist potential and qualifying ventures/incubatees by supporting them from stage A to C, as described above and if needed, can extend the support during stage D also. The role of TBI will also depend on the individual cases, their strengths, weaknesses and extent of support required by the tenet incubatees.

The TBI can, only assist the venture promoters in all these stages, but can never replace entrepreneurship demanded from the promoters for business. Hence, the entrepreneurship of the promoters play a very important role in the success of these ventures. To encourage entrepreneurship, TBI will train the potential entrepreneurs and guide them through the process of business venturing through interactive workshops and constant nurturing. A part of the profit by TBI will go to the University.

7.21 CONFERENCES/SEMINARS/SYMPOSIUM/WORKSHOP

Academic meeting, in science and academia, a formalized event where researchers present their results in speeches, workshops, seminar or by other means. All the Departments/ Schools/Colleges/University are expected to conduct seminar/conference/symposia.

An **academic conference** is a conference for researchers (not always academics) to present and discuss their work. Together with academic or scientific journals, conferences provide an important channel for exchange of information between researchers.

A **Seminar** is, generally, a form of academic instruction, either at a university or offered by a commercial or professional organization. It has the function of bringing together small groups for recurring meetings, focusing each time on some particular subject, in which everyone present is requested to actively participate. This is often accomplished through an ongoing Socratic dialogue with a seminar leader or instructor, or through a more formal presentation of research. Normally, participants must not be beginners in the field under discussion. The idea behind the seminar system is to familiarize students more extensively with the methodology of their chosen subject and also to allow them to interact with examples of the practical problems that always crop up during research work. It is essentially a place where assigned readings are discussed, questions can be raised and debates conducted. It is relatively informal, at least compared to the lecture system of academic instruction.

Symposium originally referred to a drinking party (the Greek verb *sympotein* means "to drink together") but has since come to refer to any academic conference, whether or not drinking takes place. The sympotic elegies of Theognis of Megara and two Socratic dialogues, Plato's *Symposium* and Xenophon's *Symposium* all describe symposia in the original sense.

7.22 HANDBOOKS

A **handbook** is a type of reference work, or other collection of instructions, that is intended to provide ready reference. A **vade mecum** (lat. "go with me") or **pocket reference** is intended to be carried at all times.

Handbooks deal with several topics, and are generally compendiums of information in a particular field or about a particular technique. They are designed to be easily consulted and provide quick answers in a certain area.

For example, the Stanford University Graduate Student Handbook is a compendium of information about Stanford University policies, requirements, and resources relevant to all Stanford graduate students irrespective of their school, department, or program affiliation. This manual also links to other resources, e.g. other departmental or external web sites."Handbook" is sometimes applied to documents that are produced within an organization that are not designed for publication—such as a company handbook for HR, for instance. In this case, the term is used nearly synonymously with "manual."

Every work in the university needs to be documented as a handbook and so nobody will suffer to understand the working nature of the University in any corner. One can refer the Stanford University website to learn more about the handbooks. (www.stanford.edu/handbooks)

7.23 CAMPUS CODE OF ETHICS

Every campus needs a responsibility, ethics at all different levels. This will enable people to trust the system in which they are and add value to the whole system. It is always better for the campus to define the code of ethics. Here is an example code of ethics (Virginia University of Technology).

Approved October 2, 2004 by the Board of Visitors of the University of Virginia

1. "We perform our public responsibilities, services and activities ethically, competently, efficiently and honestly, in keeping with University policy and applicable law.
2. We expect that all necessary and proper controls safeguarding public resources are in place and observed, with periodic auditing of functions and departments by the State Auditor of Public Accounts and/or the University Auditor who shall report directly to the Board of Visitors' Audit and Compliance Committee.
3. While in the service of the University, we conduct ourselves free of personal conflicts or appearances of impropriety, mindful that our exercise of authority on behalf of the University has been delegated fundamentally for the public good. Conflicting interests or influences are promptly disclosed to our superiors and appropriate steps are undertaken to promote the integrity of University business and other transactions.
4. We do not accept anything of value offered in consideration of performing our public duties, other than the compensation, benefits and reimbursement of expenses duly authorized by the University or otherwise permitted by law. We do not accept any favor, loan, service, business or professional opportunity from anyone knowing (or when it should be known) that it is offered in order to improperly influence the performance of our public duties, or when acceptance thereof may reasonably be perceived as an impropriety in violation of University policy or state law. University procurements of goods or services are undertaken only by authorized personnel and, when competitive principles apply, decisions are made impartially and objectively in accordance with established policy and state law.
5. We preserve and respect the confidentiality of University records, including patient and student records. We do not externally disclose confidential records or other nonpublic information without appropriate authorization, and any confidential record or information we access as a result of our position or duty is neither exploited for personal benefit nor misused for any unauthorized purpose.
6. We are committed to the principles of federal and state law guaranteeing equal opportunity and nondiscrimination with respect to University services, programs, activities and employment, and we support an environment that respects the rights and opinions of all people which, in the words of our founder, promote "the illimitable freedom of the human mind." Complaints of discrimination, harassment and retaliation are investigated and when warranted appropriate corrective action is taken and disciplined in accordance with University policy and applicable law.
7. Our communications on behalf of the University with all persons, including co-employees, clients, customers, patients, students, guests and vendors, are conducted professionally and with civility.

8. We do not condone dishonesty in any form by anyone, including misuse of University funds or property, fraud, theft, cheating, plagiarism or lying. We encourage and expect reporting of any form of dishonesty, and our managers and supervisors to appropriately investigate such reports. We also expect that the police and/or State Auditor of Public Accounts will be notified when circumstances reasonably indicate fraud or theft of University funds.
9. We strive for continuous improvement in our performance of public duties for the University, mindful of the public cost to our activities which must be reasonable and appropriately authorized.
10. We bring to the attention of supervisors and managers, the University auditor or other responsible University office, any violation of these principles or circumstances reasonably indicating that a violation has occurred or may occur. Such reporting in good faith in order to promote the ethical integrity of operations is expected and encouraged by the University, and retaliation by any University employee as a result against the person making such good faith report shall be subject to disciplinary action. We appropriately investigate all such reports and, when warranted by the facts, require corrective action and discipline in accordance with University policy and state law".

The above is quoted to inform all concerned to take cognizance of the same and for implementation by every University.

7.24 CAMPUS MAP

Every campus of big universities must give guideline to travel across the campus in printed form and it must be displayed in every street. This will help the visitors to move across the campus without any difficulty. A sample map of the Stanford University is given here for the reference. (Figure 7.1)

7.25 MENTOR PROGRAMME

As an international student in the University one will have many opportunities to meet new people, get to know a new language and a different culture. The person will experience new things, discover different aspects of life and meet people with different ideas, values and views on life. Every University offers lots of activities, both academic and social. In order to help the student to settle down and adjust to that system one can apply for a student mentor. The Mentor Programme engages students at the University to help the student in practical matters and to guide him into University's student life.

A mentor group consists of 3-4 local students assigned to 15–20 international students. The mentors do this voluntarily because they think it will be fun helping them to get to know the campus student life and at the same time make new friends from all over the

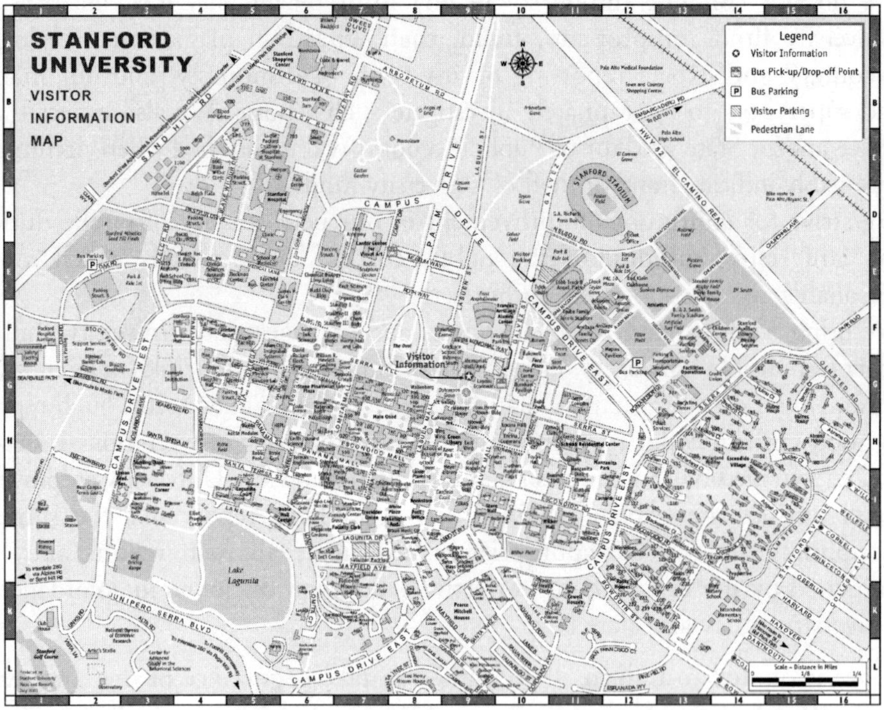

Buildings

GRID	BUILDING NAME	GRID	BUILDING NAME	GRID	BUILDING NAME	GRID	BUILDING NAME
F-5	Allen Ctr. for Integrated Systems (CIS)	H-8	Clock Tower	C-3	HOME	F-4	Pine Hall
G-5	Applied Physics Bldg.	I-8	Clubhouse	H-9	Hoover, Herbert Memorial Bldg.	H-13	Police Services
A-8	Arboretum Children's Center	F-5	Cogeneration Facility	L-8	Hoover House, Lou Henry	G-4	Polya Hall
F-10	Arrilaga Alumni Center, Frances	F-4	Codura Hall	G-9	Hoover, Lou Henry Bldg	F-4	Poplar Hall
G-8/9	Art Gallery and Bookshop	G-14	Credit Union (see also Tresidder)	A-8	Hoover Pavilion	I-8	Post Office
F-10	Bakewell	G-9	Cummings Art Bldg.	G-9	Hoover Tower	H/I-6/7	Press bldg.
H-5	Bambi	G-5	Cypress Hall	C-5	Hospital, Stanford	B-7	Psychiatry
J-6	Bechtel International Center	F-14	Dining Services	E/F-5/6	James H. Clark Center	G-13	Recycling Center
E-5	Beckman Center	H-6	Durand Bldg.	F-4	Juniper	I-1	Red Barn
J-9	Bike Shop	H-8	Education, School of	E-7	Keck Science Bldg.	F-4	Redwood Hall
K-13/14	Bing Nursery School	F/G-6	Electrical Engineering Building	J-6	Kingscote Gardens	I-3	Ricker Dining Center
F-4	Birch	I-4	Elliott Program Center	K-6/7	Knoll, The	J-9	Rogers House
I-6	Black Community Services Center	H-10	Encina Commons, Hall	G-9	Landau Economics	K-7	Row Housing Office
C-4	Blake Wilbur Clinic	F-1	Env. Safety Facility and Annex (ESF)	F-4	Laurel	G-7	Sequoia Hall
G/H-7/8	Bldgs. 1-460 (See Main Quad)	K-14	Escondido Elementary School	I8/9	Law, School of	G-11	Serra Complex (651&655)
I/H-7/8	Bldgs. 500-610	J-14	Escondido Village Office	D-4	Lucas Center	J-9	Serra House
B-4	Blood Center (800 Welch)	G-13	Facilities Operations Bldgs.	G/H-7/8	Main Quad	H-6	Skilling Bldg.
K-9/10	Bolivar House	I/J-7	Faculty Club	J-8/9	Mariposa House	G-4	Spruce Hall
I-8	Bookstore	E-5	Fairchild Center (Fairchild Aud., Fairchild Sci.)	C-8	Mausoleum	F-14	Stanford Auxiliary Library (SAL)
I-7	Bowman Alumni House	C-6	Falk Center	E-4	Mayer Cancer Biology	B-6	Stanford Barn
J-8	Braun Music Center	G/H-13	Fire Station	G/H-6	McCullough Bldg.	C-5	Stanford Hospital
J-9	Bridge, The	I-7	Fire Truck House	E-3/4	Medical School Office Bldg.	J-10	Stanford Hum. Ctr. (SHC Annex)
I-8	Building 590	G-4	Forsythe Hall	E-5	Medicine, School of	E/F-6/7	Stauffer Bldgs. I, II, III
G-9	Business, Graduate School of	F-9	Frost, Laurence, Amphitheater	H-7	Memorial Church	I-6	Storke Student Publications
D/E-7	Cantor Arts Center (Stanford Museum)	H-9	Galvez Module	G-9	Memorial Auditorium	J-9	Student Services Center
H/I-8	Career Planning Center	F-6	Gates Computer Sciences	H-9	Meyer Library	I-9	Sweet Hall
G-3	Carnegie Institution	F-6/7	Gilbert Biological Sciences Bldg.	H-6	Mitchell Earth Sciences Bldg.	H-6	Terman Engineering Center
G-5	Cedar Hall	G-5	Ginzton Laboratory & Module	H-6	Moore Materials Research	I-6	Thornton Center
L-3	Ctr. for Adv. Study in Behav. Science	H-5	Godzilla	E-6	Mudd Chemistry Bldg.	E-10	Track House
E-4	Ctr. for Clinical Sciences Research (CCSR)	K-9	Gould Center	L-3	National Bureau of Econ. Research	I-7	Tresidder Union
I-9	Ctr. for Educ. Res. at Stanford (CERAS)	H-6	Green Earth Sciences Bldg.	F-4	Oak	J-10	Vaden Health Center
F-5	CIS (see Allen Ctr. for Integrated Systems)	H-9	Green Library	F-7	Old Chemistry Bldg.	G-6	Varian Laboratory
H/I-8	Ctr. for Turbulence Research (CTR)	G-5	Gyro Relativity Bldg. (GP-B)	I-7/8	Old Union (Student Services)	F-4	Ventura Hall
E-6/7	Chemical Biology Lorry Lokey	J-9	Haas Center	E-7	Organic Chemistry Bldg.	G-8	Wallenberg Hall
F-14	Children's Center	I-6	Harmony House	J-9	Owen House	I/J-11	Wilbur Modules
D-5	Clinic, Stanford	G-6, H-5	High Energy Physics Lab (HEPL)	C-5	Packard Children's Hospital	G-6	William R. Hewlett Teaching Center

Residences

GRID	NAME	GRID	NAME	GRID	NAME	GRID	NAME
K-7	680 Lomita	J/K-7	Florence Moore Hall: Alondra, Cardenal, Faisan, Gavilan, Loro, Mirlo, Paloma	I-2/3	Lyman Graduate Residences	J-8	Sigma Chi (□□)
K-8	Bob (Moore South)	I-4	Governor's Corner: Murray, Treat, Yost	I-11/12	Manzanita Park: Castano, Kimball Hall, Lantana	J-8	Sigma Nu (□□)
H/I-11	Branner Hall	K-8	Grove Lasuen	J-8	MARS	H-3	Sterling Quad: Adams, Potter, Robinson, Schiff
K-8	Casa Italiana (Moore North)	K-8	Grove Mayfield	J-12	Mirrielees House	I-9	Stern Hall: Burbank, Casa Zapata, Donner, Larkin, Serra, Twain
J-9	Chi Theta Chi (□□□)	K-10	Hammarskjold	J-8	Muwekma-Tah-Ruk	J-8	Storey
J-8	Columbae	L-9	Haus Mitteleuropa	L-5/6	Narnia	I-3	Suites: Anderson, Griffen, Jenkins, Marx
K-11	Cowell Cluster Houses: □□□, □□□, Terra, □□□, ZAP	L-9	Kairos	K/L-9	Phi Kappa Psi (□□□)	L-8	Synergy
H-9/10	Crothers Hall, Crothers Memorial Hall	K-6	Kappa Alpha (□□)	K-8	Phi Sig	K-7/8	Theta Delta Chi (□□□)
L-9	Durand	K/L-7	Kappa Sigma (□□)	J/K-12	Rains Houses	H-10	Toyon Hall
L-6	Enchanted Broccoli Forest	I-5	Lagunita Court: Adelfa, Eucalipto, Granada, Naranja, Ujamaa	I-5/6	Roble Hall	I-10	Wilbur Hall: Arroyo, Cedro, Junipero, Okada, Otero, Rinconada, Soto, Trancos
H-14	Escondido Village	L-9	La Maison Francaise	L-9	Roth	J-8	Xanadu
		K-6	Lambda Nu (□□)	H-11	Schwab Residential Center		
				L-7	Sigma Alpha Epsilon (□□□)		

Fig. 7.1: A Map of Stanford University

world. Mentors are already familiar with the campus/town and the way things work around there. They know the best places to socialize at, as well as the best place to go for a workout.

One of the mentors will contact foreign student shortly after his arrival in country (possibly even before). Maybe the new student will tour the city, have dinner, and go to one of the "nations'" parties or something similar. The mentor groups are not obliged to follow a certain schedule, so what is done together is up to each mentor group to decide. The students can always contact the mentors for any kind of advice. The Mentor Programme has proven to be quite successful and it provides an opportunity to socialize with an international student.

Remember that this is a give and take situation and the mentors need students input and participation as much as the student needs them. If there is something the student want to do or see, he/she can always contact their respective mentors and see if the group can do it together.

7.26 ACADEMIC ADVISORS

Each student will be allocated an academic staff who will serve as the student's academic advisor for the entire duration of the student's study at the School/Department/College. The academic advisor has to advise, on course registration and monitor the students' academic progress. Students are urged to discuss with their respective academic advisors on any problem they may face.

This system is primarily to assist and advise student under supervision. An advisor can be a lecturer, instructor, teacher, graduate and whoever is interested in helping students to overcome studying problems. Advisor activities are organized and monitored by the Dean or Director or Head of the Department.

7.26.1 Function of an Advisor

1. To overcome academic problems faced by students.
2. To assist students overcome personal problems which may hinder the student's academic performances.

In order to carry out the duties effectively, the advisor can make use of the facilities which are readily available at the University such as Management Information System, assistance from the teaching/learning and counseling unit and hostel head, etc.

7.27 ENDOWMENTS

In every University, individuals or an associated group can come forward to constitute a endowment to carry out various activities like Lecture, Creation of Physical Facilities, or fellowship or Scholarship. This will help the University to have more activities and better visibility. The University can also propose to organise endowment activity in honour of the donor would like the University to organise. For this, the donor has to make a contribution. The series of lectures or activity carried out would be some time of International or National repute. Most of the US Universities do have this type of endowment activities.

7.28 CONCLUSION

As all are aware that any University is an independent body having its own ambitions, visions and missions cut for the needs for each University may definitely vary from those of others. It is impossible to start specifying Universities and the systems that are needed for each one of them. However, our aim has been to bring it to the attention of all concerned about what components in place could collectively represent a good University. Hopefully we have succeeded in bringing in many special elements in this chapter, at least a part of which will definitely be needed for each one of the Universities around the world, based on the type of University, its students, availability of resources.

It is important to make the system as a complete one and it is possible only when the system serve the society. These special components and elements will facilitate a few people to achieve better results. The special components and elements will not only enable the research scholars and professors to do better research results; but also drive other students to achieve better professionalism and morals. Every University can have a better unique system for the betterment of the University and world at large.

CHAPTER 8

Infrastructure of University System

8.1 INTRODUCTION

The major strength of university is its infrastructure. The University should provide a conducive atmosphere for students to learn and all required facilities to the community at large. The University should provide a good living atmosphere for students and faculty alike. This chapter explains the different types of infrastructure required for a modern University.

8.2 LECTURE HALLS

A lecture hall is a large room used for instruction, typically at a college or university. Unlike a traditional classroom with a capacity from one to four dozen, the capacity of lecture halls is typically measured in hundreds. Lecture halls almost always have a pitched floor, so that those in the rear are elevated higher than those in front of them, giving them visual access to the instructor.

Modern lecture halls often feature audio-visual equipment to aid instruction of large population. A microphone and speakers are common to help the instructor be heard, and projection screens may be used for large displays.

8.3 TUTORIAL HALLS/SEMINAR HALLS

A tutorial is a small class of one, or only a few students, in which the tutor (a lecturer or any other academic staff member) gives individual attention to the students. The tutorial system is fundamental to methods of teaching at universities, but it is by no means peculiar to them. Internet computer tutorials can take the form of a screen recording, a written document (either online or downloadable), or an audio file, where a person delivers step by step instructions on how to do something.

The Seminar Hall stands at the heart of University with a stipulated capacity. It has to be designed with a perfect echo system. An excellent lighting facility adds to its grace. All the major University, college events like Counseling, Seminars and other cultural events and competitions take place here in this hall. It is an open to all hall with various artists from in and out of college performing their best in annual competitions like Confluence, Literati and other major events organized by the college societies.

In a computer based education, a tutorial is a computer program whose purpose is to assist users in learning how to use (parts of) a software product such as an office suite or any other application, operating system interface, programming tool, or game. There are two kinds of software tutorials: movie tutorials that you watch and interactive tutorials where you follow on-screen instructions (and in some cases watch short instruction movies), whereupon you do the tutorial exercises and get feedback depending on your actions. Some computer based tutorials can also be put up on the web.

8.4 BOARD MEETING ROOM

Its name seems up the purpose of this hall. All important decisions about the day to day affairs are made to happen in this room only. It is here that all the VIPs along with the Principal/Vice-Chancellor and the governing body sit together in a round table conference to make their decisions.

8.5 INTERVIEW ROOM

This hall is the most important room in a University student's life. All the PPTs and interviews take place in this room. This room is to be quite a big one, fully air conditioned, equipped with all new modern sophisticated gadgets required by the company officials during their presentation like a fully multimedia enabled PC, a laser OHP attached to it, Internet facility, wireless microphones, TV, VCR, etc. and a good sound system too.

8.6 LABORATORIES

A laboratory (informally, lab) is a facility that provides controlled conditions in which scientific research, experiments, and measurements may be performed. The title of *laboratory* is also used for certain other facilities where the processes or equipment used are similar to those in scientific laboratories.

Scientific laboratories can be found in schools and universities, in industry, in government or military facilities, and even aboard ships and spacecraft. A laboratory might offer work space for just one to more than thirty researchers depending on its size and purpose.

Labs used for scientific research take many forms because of the differing requirements of specialists in the various fields of science. A physics lab might contain a particle accelerator or vacuum chamber, while a metallurgy lab could have apparatus for casting or refining metals or for testing their strength. An aeronautical lab might use a wind tunnel. A chemist or biologist might use a wet laboratory, while a psychologist's or economist's lab might be a room with one-way mirrors and hidden cameras to observe behavior. In some laboratories, such as those commonly used by computer scientists, computers (sometimes supercomputers) are used for either simulations or analysis of data collected elsewhere. Scientists in other fields will use still other types of laboratories. Despite varied differences among laboratories, some features are common. The use of workbenches or countertops at which the scientist may choose to either sit or stand is a common way to ensure comfortable working conditions for the researcher, who may spend a large portion of his or her working day in the laboratory. The provision of cabinets for the storage of laboratory equipment is quite common. It is traditional for a scientist to record an experiment's progress in a laboratory notebook, but modern labs almost always contain at least one computer workstation for data collection and analysis.

8.7 DRAWING HALL

Technical drawing, also known as **drafting**, is the "art and practice of creating accurate representations of objects for technical, architectural and engineering needs." A practitioner of the craft is known as a *draftsman*, and recently, "drafter".

Technical drawing includes the various fields and technologies underpinning electronics, which has in turn revolutionized the art with new tools in the form of Computer Aided Design (CAD). Most technical fields, even those not generally considered as highly technical such as plumbing have their own conventions and practices—the symbols and shorthand notations convey a lot of information in minimal space. All of these are specialized communications. The foundation of the modern computerized world is directly founded on the accurate scale drawings on synthetic *vellums* that enabled the integrated circuits and printed circuit boards under modern electronics, as discussed in the section below Before CAD. The development and progress of the industrial revolution on the whole depends on the art, usually taught and classed as one of the Industrial arts. Engineering and architectural students are introduced to the art, generally in freshman level courses.

This basic drafting system requires an accurate table and constant attention to the positioning of the tools. A common error is to allow the triangles to push the top of the T-square down slightly, thereby throwing off all angles. Even tasks as simple as drawing two angled lines meeting at a point require a number of moves of the T-square and triangles, and in general drafting can be a time consuming process in the conventional sense.

A solution to these problems was the introduction of the mechanical "drafting machine", an application of the pantograph (sometimes referred to incorrectly as a "pentagraph" in these situations) which allowed the draftsman to have an accurate right angle at any point on the page quite quickly. These machines often included the ability to change the angle, thereby removing the need for the triangles as well.

8.8 SHOPPING MALLS

A shopping mall or shopping centre is a building or set of buildings that contain a variety of retail units, with interconnecting walkways enabling visitors to easily walk from unit to unit. A shopping mall (or outlet centre) is a type of shopping place in which manufacturers sell their products directly to the public through their own stores. Other stores in outlet malls are operated by retailers selling returned goods and discontinued products, often at heavily reduced prices. When the size of residential students and staff is small such a smaller sized facility may suffice.

8.9 CANTEEN/FOOD COURT

A cafeteria is a type of food service location in which there is a little or no table service. A school dining location is also referred to as a canteen or dining hall. Cafeterias are different from coffeehouses, although that is the Spanish meaning of the American word. Instead of table service, there are food-serving counters/stalls, either in a line or allowing arbitrary walking paths. Customers take the food they require as they walk along, placing it on a tray. In addition, there are often stations where customers order food and wait while it is prepared, particularly for items such as hamburgers or tacos or dosas and vadas as the case may be served hot and can be quickly prepared. Alternatively, the patron is given a number and the item is brought to their table. Sometimes, for some food items and drinks, customers collect an empty container, pay at the check-out, and fill the container after the check-out. Free second servings are often allowed under this system. For legal purposes (and the consumption patterns of customers), this system is rarely or never used for alcoholic beverages, if it is permitted in the University/Country.

A food court is a plaza that is contiguous with the counters of multiple food vendors and provides a common area for self-serve dining. At a typical food court, food is ordered at one of the vendors and then consumed at a seating area, which is normally a plaza surrounded by the counters of the multiple food vendors.

8.10 COFFEE HOUSE

A Coffee house is a social event, usually held to raise awareness for a social cause or other event. Coffeehouses get their name from the fact that most Coffee houses are held in an actual coffee house, either that or they serve coffee as one of the primary beverages.

Also common are soda, milk, and tea. Common foods include cookies, crackers, muffins, and various other snack foods.

8.11 HOSTELS

Hostels provide budget-oriented accommodation where guests can rent a bed, sometimes a bunk bed in a dormitory and share a bathroom, lounge and sometimes a kitchen. Rooms can be mixed or single-sex, although private rooms may also be available. Hostels are generally cheaper for both the operator and the occupant; many hostels employ their long-term residents as desk clerks or housekeeping staff in exchange for free accommodation. An effort should be made to distinguish between establishments that provide longer term accommodation and those offering short term accommodation to students.

Essentially the apartment hostel combines the flexibility of apartment living with the service of a hostel. Many of the apartments take advantage of prime locations with panoramic views of cities seen through wall to ceiling windows. Suites usually include high quality finishes, broadband connection and interactive TV, servicing and integrated kitchen and bathroom. High quality leather sofas in the living area and king size beds bring the hotel experience to a whole new level. Some come with the basics: satellite or cable TV, washer, dryer, dishwasher, cooker, oven, fridge, freezer, sink, shower, bath, wardrobes, all the furnishings to be expected in a luxury home. In Indian contacts it is dormitory type (2 to 3 persons) per room having dining halls at very close proximity. Single rooms are also provided for graduates.

8.12 GENERAL FACILITIES

A corner having separate shops for tailor, laundry, hair stylist, phone booth, reprographic facility, printing and binding, etc. is an absolute necessity.

8.13 MEDITATION HALL

A yoga hall is a medium sized, air-conditioned building that is used for yoga sessions, rehearsal space and intimated performances. This space can double up as a dormitory for retreats. Dormitory facilities may include separate men's and women's lockers, showers and restrooms and can accommodate a few students. This space can also be used to screen films for residents. Early morning and evening meditations, yoga, special performances, rehearsals, workshops and exhibitions all can take place in this space.

8.14 LOCKER FACILITY

A locker is a temporary storage place for students clothing and personal possessions. Self storage refers to a business that owns and operates a facility that is subdivided into self storage spaces which are rented to tenants, usually on a monthly basis. These lockers are given to the students to store their ornaments and other important things like certificates, etc.

8.15 QUARTERS

Employee quarters are those parts of a building, traditionally in a private house, which contain the domestic offices and staff accommodation. From the late 17th century until the early 20th century they were a common feature in all large houses. Sometimes they are an integral part of a smaller house—in the basements and attics, especially in a town house, while in larger houses they are often a purpose-built adjacent wing or block. In architectural descriptions and guide books of stately homes the servants' quarters are frequently overlooked, yet they form an important piece of social history, often as interesting as the principal part of the house itself. Good universities/institutes provide apartments of various sizes depending on the cadre for a nominal rent. This may be available for 10 to 25% of the total staff.

8.16 GUEST HOUSES

A guest house in the US is a private home which has been converted for the exclusive use of guest accommodation. The owner usually lives in an entirely separate area within the property and the guest house may serve as a form of lodging business, similar to a bed and breakfast. In other parts of the world guest houses are the only kind of accommodation available for visitors with no local relatives.

Among the features that distinguish a guest house from a hotel or bed and breakfast is the lack of full time staff. Bed and breakfasts are usually family owned, with the family living on the premises. Hotels maintain a staff presence 24x7. A guest house on the other hand will have limited staff presence. Because of the limited staff presence check-in is often by appointment. Food at guest houses may be available only on prior intimation. Morning coffee/tea with bread and omelet may be made available in short notice.

8.17 HOSPITALS

An University should have a hospital with inpatient facilities atleast for a few, and have a clinic kept open 24×7 with atleast skeleton staff with waiting ambulances which can be utilized to transship patients in emergency to the needed places.

8.18 EMERGENCY CALL OFFICE/AMBULANCES

Many universities have a single emergency telephone number, that allows a caller to contact local emergency services for assistance. The emergency telephone number may differ from country to country. It is typically a three-digit number so that it can be easily remembered and dialed quickly. Some universities have a different emergency number for each of the different emergency services; these often differ only by last digit. This emergency office provides the ambulances, police help and other urgent services.

8.19 BROWSING CENTER

An **internet café** or **cyber café** is a place where one can use a computer with Internet access, most for a fee, usually per hour or minute; sometimes one can have unmetered access with a pass for a day or month, etc. It may serve as a regular café as well, with food and drinks being served.

Internet cafés are located world-wide, and many people use them while traveling to access web mail and instant messaging services to keep in touch with family and friends. Apart from travelers, in many developing countries Internet cafés are the primary form of Internet access for citizens as a shared-access model is more affordable than personal ownership of equipment. A variation on the Internet café business model is the LAN gaming center, used for multiplayer gaming. These cafés have several computer stations connected to a LAN. The connected computers are custom-assembled for game play, supporting popular multiplayer games. This is reducing the need for video arcades and arcade games, many of which are being closed down or merged into Internet cafés.

8.20 CALL CENTRE

A call centre is a must for an university, which can provide updated information about anything and everything about the University for outsiders as well as students and staff of the University. It can provide all sorts of information and clear doubts about rules and regulations of the University, locations, dates and times of ongoing events, relevant contact persons for any matter/procedures to be adopted and so on. A well updated website can extend such a help to a very great extent. Call centre gives information in an interactive mode and have been well appreciated by every needy person.

8.21 SPORTS AND GAMES COMPLEX

The University Sports Complex is a sports and entertainment facility located in University owned and operated by the University Sports Authority. The sports complex should include various facilities like Tennis practice wall, Indoor Multipurpose Stadium, Badminton, glass back wall Squash Courts, Table Tennis, Billiards/Snooker, Basket Ball, Hockey, Cricket, Cricket Practice pitches, Football, Jogging Track, Children Park, Skating, Golf Driving Range, Pitch and Putt Course, Olympic Size Swimming Pool, Toddlers Pool, Air Rifle/Pistol Shooting Range, Aerobics, Yoga, Taekwondo,

Fitness Centre, Naturopathy Centre, Health and Nutrition Centre, Reiki, Sports Shop, Snack Bars, Swimming Pool, etc. The university should provide a right access to students to access these facilities. Above list is neither exhaustive, nor it may be necessary/possible to have all, in all University locations/countries. Based on need or specialization in which the University wants to concentrate the facilities can be created.

8.22 THEATRE/AUDITORIUM/OPEN-AIR THEATRE

An auditorium is a room built to enable an audience to hear and watch performances at venues such as theatres. For movie theaters, the number of auditoriums is expressed as the number of screens. The audiences in a modern theatre are usually separated from the performers by the proscenium arch, although other types of stage are common.

The theatre may be situated at a central place of the University. With a capacity of more than 1000–3000 people, it can serve as a multi-purpose hall for various activities. And a perfect echo system with excellent lighting facilities will add to its grace. All the major college/University events like college day, conferences and other cultural events and competitions can take place here. It is an open to all hall with various artists from in and out of college performing their best in annual competitions like Confluence, Literati and other major events organized by various associations. In some places it may be an open air theater.

8.23 TRANSPORT FACILITY/CAMPUS CYCLES/TROLLEYS

Buses may be used for University transportation either by private hire or owned by the University. Longer distance transportation are also carried out by bus, either on a turn up and go basis or through a transport operator. As a minimum, many countries require that a bus carrying students displays a sign, and may also adopt yellow liveries. Student transport often uses older buses cascaded from service use, retro-fitted with more seats and/or seatbelts. Student transport may be operated by local authorities or private contr-actors. Institutions may also own and operate their own buses for other transport needs.

Bicycle sharing systems are schemes in which numbers of bicycles are made available for shared use by individuals who do not own them. Publicly shared bicycles are a mobility service, mainly useful in urban environment for proximity travels. This removes disadvantages to the individual rider, including loss from theft or vandalism, lack of parking space, storage, and maintenance requirements.

Mini buses can be used to transport the students, staff and parents to the various locations inside the campus. This will help the students/hostellers/parents to do internal transportation quickly and conveniently. If it is a big campus it is essential to maintain one such facility.

8.24 LANGUAGE LEARNING CENTER

Self access language learning centers are educational facilities designed for student learning that is partially self-directed. Students have access to resources ranging from photocopied exercises with answer keys to computer software for language learning. These centers are an outgrowth of a style of learning that can go by several names: learner-centered approach, learner autonomy or self-directed learning. The theory behind this style of learning is that students, especially foreign language students, learn better if they have a say in how they learn. The structure of established self access centers varies from completely student-directed work with classroom immersion to those which provide primarily tutor or instructor guidance for student work.

8.25 DRIVING CENTER/STUDIO TRAINING CENTER/TYPING, ETC.

In order to equip the students to be independent in their life, different vocational programmes can be offered by any University. These trainings include car driving, photography, video-grapy, etc.

Driver's education is a formal class or program that prepares a new driver to obtain a learner's permit and or driver's license. It may take place in a classroom, in a vehicle, online, or a combination of the above. Topics of instruction include traffic code or laws and vehicle operation in that country. Typically, instruction will warn of dangerous conditions in driving. Even a person who has a valid driving license in a country, even with international license is not ready to drive in many countries as per their regulations. There are countries which have left handed driven vehicles alone and movement permitted on a road on the right side with free right turns where ever convenient. This is just opposite to what is practiced in UK, India, etc. Even among European countries there are such variations. Hence training and obtaining a license in other countries becomes a must even if one is a seasoned driver knowledge of road conditions, driver impairments, and hazardous weather are to be know. Instructional videos may also be shown, demonstrating proper driving strategies and the consequences for not observing the rules.

A photography course can be an interesting proposition for a creative individual interested in aesthetics, creativity and technical expertise. An inherent passion for photography coupled with professional training can make commercial and digital photography a lucrative profession. The importance of the electronic and print media in today's world has created a huge demand for professional photographers. A professional photographer desirous of having a career should have adequate knowledge about light, color, shades, human expressions, visual effect, nature and wildlife.

A videographer is a person who works in the video medium—recording moving images and sound on tape, disk, other electro-mechanical devices, or broadcasting live. On a set, he or she is usually responsible for the camera, sound, and lighting. As part of a typical field production crew, videographers usually work underneath a producer. However, for smaller productions (e.g. corporate and event videos), a videographer often works alone or as part of a two or three person team of camera operators and lighting and sound technicians.

Typically, videographers are distinguished from cinematographers in that they manage smaller, event scale productions (commercials, documentaries, live events, short films, training videos, weddings), differing from individualized large production team members. Due to reduced budget compared to full-length feature productions, videographers typically use electro-mechanical cameras while cinematographers record images on film. The advent of digital cinematography, however, has reduced this distinction.

8.26 BANK

A branch of any one (at least) bank with ATM facility in the University campus is a must to take care of payments by students to the University, payments to all workers and teachers can be made through this branch. All students and staff are supposed to keep a savings bank account in the branch. Of course all other services provided by any other branch shall also be made available to all concerned. This saves time and effort of the University in having a sufficiently sized separate set up to deal with all money transactions. It also facilitates to make transactions at their convenience.

8.27 POST-OFFICE/COURIER SERVICE

A University post office is a facility authorized by a postal system for the posting, receipt, sorting, handling, transmission or delivery of mail. Post offices offer mail-related services such as post office boxes, postage and packaging supplies and all existing services of Post office in that Country.

A University courier is a person or a company who delivers messages, packages, and mail. Couriers within the University campus are distinguished from ordinary mail services by features such as speed, security, tracking, signature, specialization and individualization of services, and committed delivery times, which are optional for most everyday mail services. As a premium service, couriers are usually more expensive than usual mail services, and their use is typically restricted to packages where one or more of these features are considered important enough to warrant the cost. The University should provide the space and other facilities for the post office as well as courier service.

8.28 TRAVEL AGENCY

A University travel agency is a retail business that sells travel related products and services to customers on behalf of suppliers such as airlines, car rentals, hotels, railways, sightseeing tours and package holidays that combine several products. In addition to dealing with students and staff most travel agencies have a separate department devoted to making travel arrangements for business travelers and some travel agencies specialize in commercial travel. This helps the university student and staff to schedule and plan their trips, through them saving time.

8.29 LIBRARY/DIGITAL LIBRARY

An academic library is a library which serves an institution of higher learning, such as a college or university library. These libraries serve two complementary purposes: to support the school's curriculum, and to support the research of the faculty and students, in the university.

The support of teaching requires material for class readings and for student papers. In the past, the material for class readings, intended to supplement lectures as prescribed by the instructor, has been called reserves. In the period before electronic resources became available, the reserves were supplied as actual books or as photocopies of appropriate journal articles. Traditionally, one copy of a book was made available for each 10 students—this is practical for large classes only if paperback copies are available, and the books reused from term to term.

Academic libraries must decide what focus they take in collecting materials since no single library can supply everything. When there are particular areas of specialization in academic libraries these are often referred to as niche collections. These collections are often the basis of a special collection department and may include original papers, artwork, and artifacts written or created by a single author or about a specific subject. In the traditional sense, a university library is a collection of books and journals. Large university libraries are considered research libraries, and often contain many specialized branch research libraries. A research library is a library which contains an in-depth collection of material on one or several subjects. A research library will generally include primary sources as well as secondary sources.

A digital library is a library in which collections are stored in digital formats (as opposed to print, microform, or other media) and accessible by computers. The digital content may be stored locally, or accessed remotely via computer networks. A digital library is a type of information retrieval system.

Many academic libraries are actively involved in building institutional repositories of the institution's books, papers, theses, and other works which can be digitized or were 'born digital'. Many of these repositories are made available to the general public with few restrictions, in accordance with the goals of open access, in contrast to the publication of research in commercial journals, where the publishers often limit access rights. Institutional, truly free, and corporate repositories are sometimes referred to as digital libraries.

8.30 DIGITAL CLASS ROOM/VIDEO/AUDIO CENTERS

The digital classroom takes advantage of being able to write on the tablet in a variety of programs because it makes that written work available anytime and anywhere. Students can submit their assignments to digital drop-boxes before class even begins, and teachers can carry them anywhere with their tablets. Students and teachers both retain copies of documents shared with each other, and they can collaborate online. The teachers can retain copies of annotations made on student work. In the digital classroom it is understood that students must gain fluency in searching, evaluating, manipulating, creating, and publishing information in a variety of media forms and formats. It is more convenient for the student to get access to the resources than doing in the normal classroom.

Audio-Video classroom is a facility standard for distance learning that aim to deliver education to students who are not physically "on site". Rather than attending courses in person, teachers and students may communicate at times of their own choice by exchanging printed or electronically stored, or through technology that allows them to communicate in real time and through other online ways. The standard video lectures can be made available to the students. Student can take the video lectures and can learn leisurely. Some universities offer high definition video communications to education practitioners, students, researchers and administrators.

8.31 ONLINE/INTERNET FACILITY/WEB MATERIALS/E-MAIL/ WEB PAGE FACILITY/EDUSAT FACILITY

Web-based teaching materials are a subset of Computer-Based Training (CBT) or electronic learning (eLearning) used to leverage the World Wide Web for the delivery of instructional materials.

Several teachers and institutions provide access to Web-based teaching materials through links on Web pages. University professors and departments often provide similar resource pages to augment learning opportunities for their students. These resources are especially helpful when they provide an extension beyond what is covered in the classroom (i.e. materials on specific disciplines created by experts who may have deep knowledge in that discipline).

Several companies and cooperative efforts have emerged to provide online access to Web-based teaching materials. These entities range from companies producing their own education media to sites provided to aggregate links to other existing content. While the missions of these organizations may differ, they all focus on furthering the World Wide Web as the delivery medium for teaching materials.

Web-based teaching materials emerged as elements on personal Web sites with the proliferation and adoption of the Internet. Beyond personal publishing, Web-based teaching materials were often published online as samples and supplemental materials by commercial entities experimenting with the World Wide Web.

8.32 EXAM CELL/CENTER

The controller of examination is responsible for the conduct of semester/end year examinations as needed in the University and affiliated colleges if any. Printing, stationary for exam, appointing experts for setting question papers, appointing a board of experts to do rerating of question papers for correctness, clarity, coverage, etc., before being printed and or sent to colleges. Arranging for collection of answer books every day even from faraway places, arranging for central valuation, verifying/ monitoring the same, making entries, processing the marks and publication of results; processing objections from student and parents about valuation and taking appropriate corrective measures wherever necessary. For example in Tamil Nadu of India there are almost hundreds of colleges under Anna University and it is a mammoth task for the controller of examination to plan and execute flawlessly and all these well within a short time frame. At one point of time it was around fifty thousand scripts from the University and two million scripts from colleges per semester which were manually evaluated, results processed by machine and published in 35 to 45 days of time after the last examination. For a complete and comprehensive description of whole examination system refer section 8.4 and 9.4.

The Examination Cell co-ordinates the conduct of mid term as well as end semester examination. Exam Cell at the university/college is responsible for providing the managed services for conducting online, offline and mock examinations. The operations performed include, the receipt of applications from students including payment of fee, attendance upload, the internal marks upload and printing of hall tickets for the students. The major parts of the operations at the exam centre of a college includes the receipt of question papers from the university just before the examination, printing the question papers and or distributing question papers in print form received from the University and conduct the examinations.

8.33 CONCLUSION

This Chapter first gives the various infrastructure facilities required in an University. Their importance and need in an University set up have been highlighted. Though many of them are needed, some of them may not be necessary, if the University is small in size or is situated inside a city where such facilities are readily available nearby. However sufficient floor space, well equipped and maintained labs, class rooms and library are to be in excess of requirements at any point of time. Then new programmes when devised can have a kick start at short notice. The infrastructure and systems should be able to cater to the needs of conduction of national/international level programmes and have to be overbalanced periodically. Large Universities should more or less be like mini cities with all facilities.

CHAPTER 9

System and Processes of University System

9.1 INTRODUCTION

A good university system provides a secured and structured system to ensure the right functioning. This chapter explains the different types of processes involved in the functioning of any University System.

9.2 ADMISSION PROCESS

A university/college admission refers to the annual/semester process of applying to institutions of higher education for undergraduate/graduate study. This usually takes place during the senior year of high school/undergraduate. While dates and deadlines vary, the entire application process usually begins in the autumn and concludes in the spring of the final year of high school/under graduation programme.

In the recruitment and selection of students the only consideration must be that the individual meets, or is likely to meet, the requirements of the programme or course. These requirements being met, no applicant should be discriminated against on the basis of their gender, race, colour, ethnic origin, nationality (within current legislation), disability, sexual orientation, marital status, caring or parental responsibilities, age, or beliefs on any matters such as religion and politics.

The above policy must be adhered to in all matters concerning student recruitment and admissions. The University is committed to a programme of action to ensure that its policy is implemented and monitored at an organizational and individual level. Each department has a Departmental Equal Opportunities Liaison Officer who disseminates information on good practice and training.

9.2.1 Authority to Admit Students

University Statutes vest with the Vice-Chancellor the power to admit as a student to University anyone having the qualifications required for admission as stipulated in University Regulations. The Statutes further grant the Vice-Chancellor the power to delegate his power to admit students, to any Officer of University or other person or body as he may think fit. The arrangements for the admission of students as outlined in this and other sections of the Academic Manual present the current position as regards the delegation of the Vice-Chancellor's power to admit students. The Vice-Chancellor reserves the rights, at any time, to delegate the power to admit students to other Officers of University, persons or bodies deemed suitable by him should any particular circumstances require it.

9.2.2 Admission Steps

The University admission has to be done by the University Admission Committee. The admission committee has to be constituted by the Vice-Chancellor. The Vice-chancellor shall be the Chairman for the admission committee. The admission committee may function with a Secretary and who shall be responsible for conducting admission. The Process of Admission involves various steps like

1. Preparation of Policy for Admission.
2. Preparation of Plan/Schedule for Admission.
3. Preparation of Application and Information Brochure for Students.
4. Preparation of Guidelines for the various admission staff working in admission process.
5. Printing Application/Creation of Web Application Facility.
6. Issuance of Application.
7. Preparation of Question Paper for Entrance Examination if any and conducting entrance Examination; Publication of marks/grades of students in the Entrance Exam.
8. Conducting a Counseling session to the Students for Selection of Courses.
9. Conducting Medical Examination and Verification of Certificates.
10. Issuance of Admission Cards.
11. Guidance to hostel facilities whenever needed.

9.3 RECRUITMENT/APPOINTMENT OF STAFF PROCESS

The aim of the HRD is to find the mechanisms in place for performance assessment of faculty and staff and use these findings to improve teaching, research and service of the faculty and other staff. Develop Strategies and implementation plans of the institution to recruit and retain diverse faculty and other staff who have the desired qualifications, knowledge and skills.

Recruitment is the process of selecting the most suitable candidate for a specific job requirement. Recruitment and selection are step by step processes involving both, the employer and the employee, in a way that both of them are mutually benefited. This section will help to understand how this works.

9.3.1 Recruitment and Selection Process

Employers are always concerned about how to find and hire the right employees. Employers recruit for the present and future needs of the University. There are usually two types of recruitment processes.

9.3.2 Recruitment Processes: External and Internal

Internal recruitment applies to the people working at present in the university. They are given a chance to apply for a given vacant position first. This may include a change in profile on the part of the employee. Internal recruitment is more economical and less time consuming for the University. In contrast, external recruitment has to do with external candidates applying for an available position. Naturally, the resources spent for such a selection process are more.

Individual department heads based on workload and available staff makes an equipment list of positions to be filled and send the same to HRD (Human Resources Department) which plays a significant role in the recruitment process of every University. Whenever a vacancy arises in an University, it is the responsibility of the HRD to place the information in the public domain through various media, such as newspapers and various job sites. However, it is of utmost importance that the advertisement designed clearly defines the designation, job profile the skill set required and the range of compensation offered.

The requirement is either to recruit for a new post, or to refill an existing post. One has to check the following aspects before putting the vacancy in the public domain.

1. Is the role/function still required?
2. Could the role/function be carried out by redistributing duties to other staff?
3. Could the duties be outsourced—cost implications?
4. Is the post full-time or part-time?
5. Does the job description need updating?

9.3.3 Job Description and Grade of Post

All new posts, and existing posts which have substantially revised job descriptions, must be graded using the job evaluation scheme before they can be advertised.

Existing posts: A review of the current job description and selection criteria is to be made. If there are no significant changes, the grade of the post will remain the same. If changes are required, a revised job description is to be sent to the HRD for grading.

New posts: A job description has to be made and submitted to the HRD for grading. Advice on job design, defining appropriate selection criteria, and grading matters, can be obtained from HRD.

Posts at grade: The grade and salary for appointments at this level must be approved by the Syndicate/Senate Council.

9.3.4 Authorization to Recruit

Prior to advertisement for any vacant or new post, approval must be obtained from the appropriate authority. For all posts it is the Head of each Department to initiate and get approval from the appropriate Finance Officer and the Registrar via the recruitment panel. Once the necessary approval has been obtained the Head of Department will be initiating the next process of notification.

9.3.5 Advertisement

A draft of advertisement to be released has to be prepared first. It is advisable to include the interview date(s) in the advertisement, in which case, the date(s) must be checked with the members of the selection panel before the advertisement is placed. Consider the most appropriate media for advertisements. Note that all advertisements will also appear on the Universities Job Opportunities Web Page and at least in two National News Papers both in national language and common language and in the language of instruction.

9.3.6 Selection Panel

Identify members of the selection panel (note the requirement for those chairing selection panels to have attended one of the University's recruitment and selection briefings in the last few years. For the panel normally members of both sexes are to be considered). HRD Personnel Administrator is to be informed of the identity of the panel chair and of the names of the other panel members using the Advertising Request Form. Confirm closing date, dates of short listing meeting, and interviews with panel members and advise your HRD Personnel Administrator using the Advertising Request Form. Whether the selection process should include a test of some kind to assess in written or numerical skills, ability to use spreadsheets or manipulate data, a short presentation has to be decided. Once these decisions have been made, the Advertising Request Form may be created and sent to HRD Personnel Administrator.

9.3.7 Short-listing

Copies of all applications will be sent to the panel chair and panel members, normally within three working days of the closing date. Then a short-listing meeting has to be arranged and attended by all members of the selection panel. Ideally the date for the short-listing meeting should be agreed upon at the time the advertisement is placed. At this meeting, the panel will.

1. Assess each application against, and only against, the published selection criteria and record the results on the short-listing form. This form will be provided with the applications and will include the unique 'recruitment reference' number.
2. Decide which candidates should be invited for interview (it would be expected normally to invite up to six candidates) and whether a test or presentation will be required.

At the short-listing meeting (or at some point before the interviews):

1. Decisions on the format of the interviews, the questions to be asked, and which of the selection criteria will be addressed by which members of the panel are to be closed. If not done already, consider whether any exercises or presentations are to be included.
2. If exercises or presentations are to be included, specific arrangements (e.g. venue, availability of computer/printer, PowerPoint, nature of tests in relation to the selection criteria, how exercises will be scored etc.) are to be worked out in detail. The same is to be communicated to HR Personnel for making arrangements.

This note should also include provision for information to be added verbatim to the letter of invitation for interview. Short-listed candidates will be invited for interview by HRD Personnel. Note that candidates normally expect to be given a minimum of 7 working days notice prior to interview. All other applicants not invited for interview or held in reserve will be declined.

9.3.8 Interviews

It is imperative that the panel knows how to conduct an interview. Job interviews play an important role in the entire recruitment process. It is very important to put the candidate at ease, so as to eliminate initial nervousness and to break the ice. It is better to start with general questions, so that the candidate feels relaxed. Later, queries should be job related, objective in nature and understandable to the candidate.

All ambiguities should be done away with, when describing the responsibilities of the slot available. It is to be ensured that panel members are familiar with the University's Code of Practice on Staff Recruitment and Selection. A copy of this Code has to be provided to the Chair of the panel along with the applications. Assessment of each candidate against, and only against, the published selection criteria are to be considered along with the results of any exercises. Candidates are to be informed at which stage referees may be approached. List of preferred candidate, and any reserve candidate(s) has to be obtained from the chairperson of the committee.

9.3.9 The Offer Letter

The start date (according to candidate's availability) and starting salary based upon qualifications, experience, current salary, comparability with existing staff salary and, where appropriate, the University's pay policy are to be decided. With regard to starting salary, the panel chair should normally aim to offer a salary at the point on the scale that is immediately above the candidate's current salary.

As soon as conveniently possible the HR personnel should contact the preferred candidate to make a provisional offer conditional upon Acceptable References, the return of a satisfactory Medical Questionnaire, Confirmation of the candidate's right to work in the University, evidence of qualifications where these are essential to the role.

When making the provisional offer, it is essential to emphasize that the offer is provisional, that it is subject to the conditions described above, and that the offer will be confirmed in writing, subject to meeting those conditions. References will be requested by HRD Personnel Administrator and forwarded to the panel chair as soon as received. The panel chair should then confirm to the HRD in writing whether or not the references are acceptable.

Once the four conditions (references, medical questionnaire, right to work in University, qualifications) have been met, a formal 'letter of appointment' (contract) signed by the HRD Personnel Manager or Registrar as appropriate, will be sent to the candidate by the HRD Personnel Administrator together with the contract.

9.3.10 The Appointment

A new staff has to be advised of specific joining instructions (e.g. venue, time, who to ask for etc.). Arrangements are to be made for receiving the new member of staff on the start date and for the provision of appropriate induction training as necessary. An arrangement to meet HRD Personnel Administrator has to be done as soon as possible to complete the Staff Registration form. All copies of the relevant paperwork from all panel members should be returned to the HRD Personnel Administrator prior to the start date. In order to comply with the requirements of the University, all such documents for unsuccessful candidates will be held centrally in a confidential file for six months or as the case may be following the completion of the recruitment process. This is necessary in the case of any legal proceedings if any. All relevant documentation for the appointed person will be placed in a confidential personnel file and retained centrally. These files can be accessed by the manager and the individual upon request, in accordance with the rules of the University.

9.3.11 Creation of Faculty Profile/Service Book

The rules governing the maintenance of service books in respect of University servants are contained in the Service Registers. Some important provisions of rules which should be kept in view while maintaining service books are mentioned in the ensuing paragraphs. A Service Book should be maintained by the Head of Office for every University Servant holding a substantive post on a permanent establishment or officiating in a post or holding a temporary post likely to last for more than one year. A service book shall be maintained for a University servant from the date of his first appointment to University service. It must be kept in the custody of the Head of the Office in which he is serving and transferred with him from office to office.

Every step in a University servant's official life should be recorded in his service book and each entry must be attested by the Head of Office or if he himself is the Head of Office, by his immediate superior. The Head of Office must see that all entries are duly made and attested and that the service book contains no erasure or over-writing, all corrections being neatly made and properly attested. The entries regarding increments, and fixation of pay should be based on the Increment Certificates, and Pay fixation statements. The declaration of the University servant electing the new scale of Pay and the statement showing the fixation of his initial pay in the relevant scale in support of the entry in the service book should be pasted in the service book. The Head of Office should show the service book to each University servant under his administrative control every year, and obtain his signature therein in token of his having inspected the service book. A certificate to the effect that he has done so in respect of the preceding financial year should be submitted by him to his next superior by the end of every September.

Proper entries regarding medical examination of the University servant at the time of appointment and attestation forms verifying antecedents and character etc. should be made at the appropriate places of the service book. Nowadays such paperwork is slowly getting eliminated. However all such entries are kept in the server and accessed. When needed the Registrar may provide to the individual. Any such decision before implementation is to be mailed to the individuals, so that any shortcomings can be brought to the notice of higher ups for the purpose of rectification.

9.4 EXAMINATION SYSTEM

The annual University Examinations will be held in the month of May/June for all the programmes. Supplementary examinations will be conducted in the month of November/December. Application forms for registration for the examinations will be sent in the month of February/March by the Controller of Examinations to all the students who have paid their tuition fees in full. Information regarding centers of examination, time-table, fees payable and other regulations governing the examination will be sent to the students along with that Application Form. The examination board should prepare comprehensive guidelines in detail with regard to the following aspects.

A. *Guideline Information for Students*

1. Information for Candidates about Special Exam Arrangements.
2. Undergraduate Examination Appeals.
3. Guidance note to students on examination concessions.
4. Information for Candidates regarding Plagiarism.
5. Rules for the Guidance of Candidates for the Prevention of Misconduct in Examinations
6. Information on Undergraduate Examination Warnings/Allowances for Students.
7. Guidance Note to invigilators on Examination Warnings.

B. *Guideline Information for Examiners*

1. Examiners' guide.
2. Guidance Notes on Examination Warnings and Examination Allowances to the Chairmen and Senior Examiners.
3. Guidance Notes for Preparation of Question Papers from 'Camera-Ready' Copy.
4. Guidance Notes for preparation of Question Papers wholly by Faculty members.
5. Good practice guidelines for the conduct and recording of Examiners' meetings.
6. Guidance Notes for drawing up the Class-list and Mark Book.
7. Plagiarism guide.
8. Dispensation for non-attendance at the final Examiners' meeting.

C. *Guidelines for Good Academic Practice and Avoiding Plagiarism*

These pages provide guidance about how to conform to the academic conventions used at the University and to raise awareness of plagiarism and how to avoid it. They also set out the policies and procedures to be followed if plagiarism or collusion is suspected in work submitted for examination.

For Students

1. University-wide statement on plagiarism.
2. Guidance from faculties and departments about local conventions.
3. Student's responsibilities, why plagiarism matters, usage of commercial organizations and essay banks, how the University detects and disciplines plagiarism.
4. Information about referencing and study skills.
5. Frequently asked questions and corresponding clarifications from the University side.
6. Resources and sources of support.

For Staff and Examiners

1. Policies and procedures to be followed if plagiarism or collusion is suspected in submitted work.
2. Policy on the use of text-matching software (For Example: Turnitin UK).

3. Forms of plagiarism and collusion with ideas for reducing the incidence of these transgressions.
4. Resources and contacts.

D. *Standing Committee on Applications*

The Standing Committee on Applications is a committee of the Council which may meet on a monthly basis throughout the year to consider applications for examination allowances (concessions) and related matters.

The Committee makes decisions on the following:

1. Examination allowances for Undergraduate students who as a consequence of illness or other grave cause have been unable to take their examinations or have under-performed as a consequence;
2. Exceptional permission to go out of residence (leave to degrade) and concession of term for the purpose of being in standing to take examinations.
3. Withholding names from class lists: an individual student's name may be withheld from the posted class list where there is demonstrable evidence that publication would endanger student's medical or mental well-being.
4. Fee remission or reduction of the University Composition Fees payable on the basis of severe hardship or other sufficient cause; and
5. Non-member leave to attend certain lectures or use the University's Language Centre.

All applications must be submitted by the relevant faculty advisor on behalf of the student concerned. Students should raise any queries relating to applications to their faculty advisor.

E. *Examination Entry Procedures*

The following links are intended to provide a reference point for dealing with all aspects of the examination entry procedures. The links are updated annually. Any comments may be submitted to the Board of Examinations:

1. Notes on examination entries.
2. Director of Studies Guide.
3. Examination Set-up templates (for examinations which adopt student self service enrolment).
4. Examination entry forms (for examinations which entail entry by submitted form).
5. Current Examination Entry Correction Form.

F. *Tables of Dates and Examinations*

The following tables provide details of examinations and dates for current year, including timetables which were previously published in a special edition of Reporter.

The Table of Dates provides information regarding the final dates for receiving examination entries; the last dates for receiving corrections to entries; the dates for publishing First and Final lists of Candidates; dates for issue of Entry Verification Forms and for Entry Confirmation Forms; and dates for the start of examinations. The Examination Start Date table is self explanatory for the next 5 years. The third table is a list of current examinations and their codes.

1. Table of Dates.
2. Examination start dates for various programmes.
3. Examination Codes.
4. Timetables.

G. *Appointment of Examiners and Assessors*

1. Guidelines for the nomination of Examiners and Chairman of Examiners for examinations.
2. Appointment of Internal Examiners/Assessors.
3. Appointment of External Examiner/Assessor.

9.4.1 Constitution of Examination Board

The Examination Board will invite a few examiners to sit for three/four years. The Board of Examinations is the statutory authority for conducting the Examinations and making policy decisions in regard to organizing and holding examinations, improving the systems of examinations. Appointing the Paper-setters, examiners, moderators and also prepare the schedule of dates of holding examinations and declaration of results.

The Board oversees and regulates the conduct of examinations in the colleges, institutions and university departments. It deals with all the matters in relation to Examinations. The Board hears and decides complaints received pertaining to any matter arising out of the conduct of examinations. It also deals with the preparation of the financial estimates of examination branch for incorporation in the budget of the University. The Hon'ble Vice-Chancellor is the Chairman of the Board of Examinations. The Vice-Chancellor may also designate any senior professor specifically for this purpose.

The Examination Board will also appoint the examiners and advise on curriculum and technical standards. The Examination Board will also provide an independent appeals committee on behalf of the Examination Council, should one be necessary.

9.4.2 Process of Examination

Functions related to the Pre-Examination work, Actual conduct of the Examinations and preparation of results and Post Examination work is carried out by different units of Examination Branch. These units and brief procedure of work is as follows.

Unit I: This Unit is related to Pre Examination work. Particularly it carries out:

1. The fixation of confidential printers for printing of question papers.
2. Receiving manuscript of Question Papers from Paper-setters.
3. Coding of manuscripts of Question Papers.
4. Printing of Question Papers and making arrangement for sending it to the various examination centres.
5. Solve the queries raised in the Question Papers during Examination period. Prepare sets of Question Papers for various reasons.
6. To get the expenditure of Confidential Printing of Question Papers audited from the approved Chartered Accountant.
7. To make the arrangement of payment to the Confidential Printers.

Unit II: It is also related to the Pre Examination Work; broadly it carries out the work as follows:

1. To convene the meetings for appointment of paper setters, examiners, moderators, referees.
2. To send the invitation letters to the paper-setters, examiners, moderators referees.
3. To prepare the schedule of examination at the end of the semester/the academic year.
4. To make arrangements for preparation of financial estimates of the examination branch.
5. To make substitute appointment of paper-setters, examiners and moderators if needed any.
6. Preparation of time-table for setting of question papers, and arrangements for setting of question papers.
7. Preparation of Programmes (Detailed Time-Table) of various examination and sending it to various colleges/institutions, University departments.
8. Making arrangements for appointments of Senior Supervisors, Vigilance Squads, Custodians, etc.
9. Making arrangements of furniture required at the examination centers during examination period.
10. Making arrangements of advances required for the conduct of examination.
11. Fixing venue for Central Assessment Programme and to appoint the Directors/Chiefs/Chairperson of the Central Assessment Programme.
12. Preparing list of examiners, moderators for the purpose of Central Assessment Programme.

Unit III: Scrutiny and Tabulation (S&T)

These units are mainly related to the work of Scrutiny and Tabulation of results of various examinations i.e. actual conductance of examinations and declaration of results. The works to be carried out by these units are given below:

Part (A)

1. Collection of examination forms from the colleges/institutes/university departments.
2. Scrutiny of Examination Forms.
3. Sending the Examination Forms to the Computer Section for further processing.
4. Collection of name lists, summary and admit cards of the students from the Computer Section.
5. Making arrangements for sending the name lists, summary and admit cards to the concerned Colleges/Institutions/University Departments.
6. Preparing a time-table for practical examinations and sending to the Colleges/Institutions/University Departments.
7. To issue instructions to the Colleges/Institutions for collection of answer-books from the examination centres to the venue of the Central Assessment Programme.

Part (B)

1. To remain present in the office one hour before the schedule time of the examinations to deal with the queries, if any, regarding the admit cards, seat numbers, etc.
2. To make arrangements for collection of answer-books from various examination centres to the venue of the Central Assessment Programme (CAP).
3. To make available the list of examiners, moderators to the CAP Directors/Chiefs/Chairperson.
4. To make funds available at the disposal of the CAP Directors/Chiefs/Chairperson.
5. To make available the question papers, model answers, scheme of marking etc to the CAP.
6. To keep liaison between the Director/Chiefs/Chairperson, CAP and the University.
7. To visit CAP Centres from time to time.

Part (C)

1. To receive mark-lists/C.D. of Marks-lists from the CAP/examiners as the case may be and to send the same to the computer section for further processing.
2. To receive discrepancies reports from the computer section, solving discrepancies and sending it to the computer section.
3. Checking of the results,
4. Collection of final results such as statements of marks, college result ledgers, office result ledger, and passing certificate and pass list.

5. Sorting of the statement of marks, college results ledger, passing certificates and pass list college wise/institution wise.
6. Making arrangement to distribute the examination results to concerned Colleges/ Institutions/University Departments.
7. To make the corrections if any in the examination result on the basis of revaluation, eligibility and unfair means, etc.

Unit IV: Certificate Section

Convocation: This Unit receives applications for conferment of degrees/diplomas for each year. The convocation is held once in a year. The work of convocation is assigned to an Assistant Section Officer and Assistants. This unit is required to make necessary arrangements for getting gold and silver medals ready from authorized Jewelers, to be awarded in the convocation.

1. Degree certificates are issued even after the convocation under the provisions of University.
2. *Duplicate Degree Certificates:* This Unit issues duplicate degree certificates under provisions in this regard.
3. *Special Certificates:* These certificates are issued to the passed out students on application.
4. *Verification of Documents:* Verification of Degree certificates, Duplicate degree certificates, Special certificates is done by this sub unit. This unit receives almost all certificates for verification, which are submitted abroad by the students of this university, to other Universities.
5. *Statement of Marks:* Under the Provisions of University bye laws, the statement of marks and passing certificates are issued to the students after collecting the prescribed fees.
6. *Duplicate Statement of Marks:* Under the Provisions of University bye laws, the duplicate statement of marks and passing certificates are issued to the students after collecting the prescribed fees.
7. *Transcripts and Rank Certificates:* Transcript is a special type of certificate, which shows all performances of the student for that particular course at a glance. Almost all the students who migrate for further studies abroad request this type of certificates. Rank certificates are issued to the rank holders for ranking either in whole examination or in particular subject as the case may be.

Medals and Prizes: Medals and Prizes are instituted under the provision of University bye-laws. The Medals are awarded at the Convocation.

Record Room: The original records related to all results of various examinations conducted by the University from it's establishment is preserved by this unit. In addition to this, record regarding original mark-lists so also unfair-means cases etc. for the last three years is also preserved in this unit.

Inward: The entire 'tapal' meant for examination section is received by this unit and whole procedure includes tapal marking, recording it in registers, distribution to concerned units/individuals.

Dispatch : The dispatch procedure includes sorting (district wise and pin code wise), franking, pasting of envelops and handing over these envelops/parcels etc. to the Courier/Post office before stipulated timing, maintenance of franking machine, keeping day to day accounts etc.

Unfair-means Committees: The cases of students who resort to unfair-means during the university examinations are received by this unit from Squads appointed by the university at the time of examinations, Senior Supervisors, Principals of the colleges, Director, Central assessment programs and various examination centres.

Lapses Committee: In order to investigate and take disciplinary action for malpractice and lapses on the part of candidate, paper setters, examiners, moderators, referees, teachers or any other person connected with the conduct of examinations, the committee is appointed under the provisions of University bye laws. This committee submits its report of recommendations to the Board of Examinations.

Unit V: Revaluation Section

Activities of this unit are given below:

1. To receive applications from students for verification and revaluation of answer books.
2. To register the applications faculty wise and examination wise.
3. To mask the answer-books before revaluation.
4. To make arrangements for Central Assessment Programme for revaluation.
5. To send the answer books for revaluation.
6. To collect the mark-lists after revaluation.
7. To communicate the revaluation results to the concerned students through colleges/ Institutes.

9.5 ACADEMIC INFORMATION SYSTEM

An Academic Info System (AIS) is a software application for education establishments to manage student data. Student information systems provide capabilities for entering student test and other assessment scores through an electronic grade book, building student schedules, tracking student attendance, and managing many other student-related data needs in a school, college or university. Also known as student information management system (SIMS, SIM), Student Records System (SRS), Student Management System (SMS), Campus Management System (CMS) or School Management System (SMS).

The Academic info system is equivalent to an Enterprise Resource Planning or ERP system for a corporate customer. As such, many of the issues with ERP System Selection Methodology, implementation, and operation of an ERP system apply to colleges and their Academic Information systems.

These systems vary in size, scope and capability, from packages that are implemented in relatively small organizations to cover student records alone, to enterprise-wide solutions that aim to cover most aspects of running large multi-campus organizations with significant local responsibility. Many systems can be scaled up to different levels of functionality by purchasing add-on "modules" and can typically be configured by their home institutions to meet local needs.

Until recently, the common functions of a student records system are to support the maintenance of personal and study information relating to:

1. Handling inquiries from prospective students.
2. Handling the admission process.
3. Enrolling new students and storing teaching option choices.
4. Automatically creating class and teacher schedules.
5. Handling records of examinations, assessments, marks, grades and academic progress.
6. Maintaining records of absence and attendance.
7. Recording communications with students.
8. Maintaining discipline records.
9. Providing statistical reports.
10. Maintenance of boarding house details.
11. Communicating student details to parents through a parent portal.
12. Special Education/Individual Education Plan (IEP) services.
13. Human resources services.
14. Accounting and budgeting services.
15. Student health records.

In larger enterprise solutions that have student data at their core, further functions include Student financial aid management and more may be customized by the developer. Where national or government systems exist for student finance or statistical return purposes, student records system often provide functionality that caters for this, by way of modules or core elements that handle the production of required files, or deal with the formatted transfer of information. With growing complexity in the business of educational establishments, most organizations now choose to buy customizable software, and increasing numbers are buying software as a service (SAAS).

Most student information systems in use today are server-based, with the application residing on a central computer server, and being accessed by clients at various places within and even outside the University.

9.6 PEOPLE IDENTIFICATION SYSTEM/MULTI-PURPOSE ELECTRONIC CARD

A multi-purpose system based on smart card technology designed for school/university campuses is preferable. The system takes advantage of the latest developments in smart-card technologies, covering most of university management tasks (ID card, access control, tests, exams, use of computers, printers and photocopiers, canteen or library management, etc.).

9.7 RESEARCH AND DEVELOPMENT CENTER (RDC)

The Centre for Research is functioning in University offering Ph.D./Other research programme in various branches. This centre should function with full commitment towards Research and Development of societal importance with the enthusiasm to serve the community. Research can be defined as the search for knowledge, or as any systematic investigation, with an open mind, to establish novel facts, usually using a scientific method. The primary purpose for basic research (as opposed to applied research) is discovering, interpreting, and the development of methods and systems for the advancement of human knowledge on a wide variety of scientific matters of our world and the universe.

9.7.1 Duties and Responsibilities of RDC

The role of a Research Centre Director should be determined using a proportionate approach based on the type of centre they lead. Specific duties and responsibilities should be negotiated with the appropriate Administrative Leader. Research centre Directors are responsible for providing research leadership, which normally includes:

1. Promoting and facilitating leading-edge research, including collaborative and interdisciplinary research, in areas related to the goals of the university.
2. Building, and providing sufficient support for, a community of innovative researchers to enhance research capacity at the university and to increase internal and external research opportunities for faculty, post-doctoral fellows, and graduate students.
3. Developing networks between the research centre and researchers in the field in the public and private sectors, locally, nationally and internationally.
4. Acting as the nexus between the university and the community with respect to research initiatives of mutual benefit.

5. Where applicable, developing mutually beneficial linkages with industry in order to develop partnerships and collaborative research.
6. Transferring knowledge to society through outreach (e.g. collaborative research; seminars; workshops; lectures; websites; publications) and, where applicable, through technology transfer (e.g. collaborative research; contract work; and commercialization of intellectual property).
7. Developing strong linkages with appropriate academic departments and units.
8. Leading strategic planning for the research centre to ensure that the centre's objectives are aligned with the university's Strategic Plan objectives.
9. Overseeing the proper discharge of administrative duties of the research centre including supervising personnel, financial management, and operations.
10. Working effectively with the research centre's governance committee(s).
11. Pursuing the equity goals of the university in the operations of the research centre.
12. Managing the research plan effectively and efficiently, ensuring that accepted standards of research and ethical behavior are met.
13. Managing the space needs of the research centre in cooperation with appropriate university authorities.
14. Representing the interests of the research centre internally with senior academic administrators.
15. Enhancing the reputation of the research centre and the university by undertaking quality research and communicating the essence of that research to the society.

Encouraging and supporting the raising of funds for research conducted by the research centre, capital and operating funds, including cooperation with the Alumni and development of Department's fundraising initiatives.

9.8 BOOK BANK

A book bank is an entity that works within a campus like a library except that it deals with educational text books and lends them to students for a semester. Though many libraries are available in the campuses, they are usually not stocked with enough books to cater to all the students enrolled. Book Bank claims to have cut its costs significantly by stocking its books outside the city to reduce its rental and operational costs if the University is functioning at a busy location.

It is a one place solution to get the entire books one needs for a course, to the choice of the student.

1. One can exchange books subject to availability.
2. One needs to pay only a small amount as caution deposit and can get books for the entire course on a semester basis.

3. One will be required to spend a large sum if purchase of new books is necessary.
4. Once the books are purchased from shops, one cannot exchange them after use.

9.9 FACULTY DEVELOPMENT CELL/CONTINUATION-EDUCATION PROGRAMME

In order to improve the Quality of Education, it is essential to improve the teaching skills and knowledge of the teachers in the subjects they teach. The Centre for Faculty Development should be started by each University and should conduct faculty development training programmes to cater to the needs of faculty members.

9.9.1 Assessment of Skill/Technology Requirement

Through assessment, faculty can better understand what types of course material will best help students achieve the level of success they desire. The Faculty Development Cell/Center, provides assessments that help teachers to understand the students as well as the present international requirements. Self-assessment tools have previously been used to assess the impact of a faculty development program on the teaching skills of educators. The Faculty Development Center offers both national and institutional self assessment and peer reviews.

9.9.2 Training Programme

The Centre trains the teachers to plan and prepare the lessons, understand the subject contents and improve the teaching quality. These programmes are conducted during the summer/Winter Vacation to enable the teachers to participate and benefit. The resource persons are experienced faculty members from University as well as experts from the industry/related establishments.

9.10 CURRICULUM DEVELOPMENT CELL

A Curriculum Development Cell (CDC) has to function at the University to create the curriculum, syllabi and identify new resources required to the various courses run by the University. The institution is to be geared to promote an ambience of creativity innovation and improving quality. The institution promotes inclusive practices for social justice and better stake holder relationships. The institution adopts quality management strategies in all academic and administrative aspects. The institution promotes value-based education for inculcating social responsibilities and good citizenry amongst its student community.

The curriculum development objectives can be outlined by taking care of the following activities:

1. To develop a Standard Curriculum
2. To maintain modular course structure
3. To have Choice based credit system
4. To keep Work Based Curriculum
5. To improve General Competencies and Skills
6. To have inter/multidisciplinary studies
7. To make provision for multi skill development and vocational skills
8. To maintain value based education
9. To keep pace with emerging areas and maintain global relevance
10. To include career orientation
11. To encompass Women empowerment and current concerns
12. To take care of continuing adult education/training
13. To inculcate the habit of faculty participation/initiative in curriculum development/ restructuring.

The activities of Curriculum Development Cell are coordinated by Faculty Development Centre and can be classified as follows:

9.10.1 Book Writing

One of the major objectives of the Curriculum Development Cell is the production of high quality text books and monographs. In addition, Curriculum Development Cell also encourages development of audio-visual aids and laboratory demonstration units, which supplement text books. Curriculum Development Cell provides financial assistance to authors to cover the costs involved in typing, drafting, and reproduction of a limited number of copies. The authors are encouraged to submit their manuscripts for publication.

9.10.2 Short Duration Programmes for Teachers

The Curriculum Development Cell has been encouraging short-term visits of faculty members from other colleges/Universities for collaborative work with the University faculty. During these visits, they conduct specific experiments or projects recommended by the parent institutions and prepare reports on their investigations. These visits have been found beneficial both to the parent institutions and to the teachers concerned. Curriculum Development Cell gives the visitors travelling and other allowances.

9.10.3 Developments Related to Educational Technology

In this programme, developments in multimedia technology, on-line instruction technology etc, will be incorporated into the field of higher education in engineering.

9.10.4 Development and Updating of Curriculum

University has to be continuously updating the curriculum as well as the course content of all of its post graduate/undergraduate degree programmes to incorporate the latest developments in the respective disciplines. It can be shared with the other institutions in the country offering post graduate programmes.

9.10.5 Development of Student Evaluation Procedures and Materials on Examination Reforms

A re-look at the student evaluation procedures has become necessary with the developments in educational technology, eg., on-line instruction, multimedia instruction etc. Curriculum Development Cell has to streamline this area also at least at the post graduate level.

9.10.6 Technical Education and Vocational Training of Physically Differently Abled Persons

Technical education and vocational training gives an additional qualification for persons with physical challenges who because of their impairment cannot easily secure employment. Hence at the Institute, programmes can be planned to give technical education and vocational training to physically differently abled persons.

9.11 PLACEMENT AND TRAINING CELL

Training and Placement Cell is an integral part of the University. The University has to provide complete infrastructure for effective functioning of the cell. Training activities are to be organized throughout the year in an effort towards preparing the prospective students for the campus selection programmes. The cell has to invite various industries and reputed firms for campus recruitment. The cell is to be sensitized to function all through the year towards generating placement and training opportunities for the students.

The cell has to make arrangements for visits of reputed industrial houses across the country regularly for the campus recruitment programmes. The placement cell has to coordinate quite well with the corporate sector and provide well-developed infrastructure to facilitate the campus selection programmes. The cell should maintain a very cordial relationship with all the recruiting industries and also prepares the recruited candidates to face the competitive world.

9.12 PLANNING AND DEVELOPMENT OFFICE (BUDGETING, LONG-TERM, SHORT-TERM)

The Office of University Planning and Development is responsible for the development of the university capital plan. The University is to be staffed with licensed professionals in the fields of architecture, landscape architecture, design and physical planning. The office is involved in the development of the initial scope, site selection and programming of major university capital projects.

The Office of University Planning and Development is charged with defining the long-range physical vision of each of the university campuses. The Office of University Planning and Development interfaces with state, county and municipal agencies regarding environmental and cultural resource stewardship, and coordination of long-range planning activities working closely with the Office of the Executive Vice President for Academic Affairs. Technical services and project support are provided to professional consultants and to the university community at large.

The Office of Planning and Development is responsible for reviewing all new Significant Project requests. Before a university building is designed and built the University Architect has the responsibility of developing the Feasibility Study. This document will provide all details including the Academic Program for future building. Once completed the Office of Planning and Development produces the Document. The Document is an official document that must be approved by the Buildings and Grounds Committee of the Board of Governors in order for a project to move forward. This document will allow for a project to move into the planning and development stage.

9.13 UNIVERSITY ENDOWMENT FUNDS

Endowments represent money or other financial assets that are donated to universities or colleges. The sole intention of the endowment is to invest it, so that the total asset value will yield an inflation-adjusted principal amount, along with additional income for further investments and supplementary expenditures. Typically, endowment funds follow a fairly strict policy of allocation, which is a set of long-term guidelines that dictates the asset allocation that will yield the targeted return requirement without taking on too much risk.

A financial endowment is a transfer of money or property donated to an institution. The total value of an institution's investments is often referred to as the institution's endowment and is typically organized as a public charity, private foundation, or trust. Among the institutions that commonly manage an endowment are: academic institutions (e.g., colleges, universities and private forums), cultural institutions (e.g., museums, libraries, theaters, hospitals) and religious establishments.

An endowment may come with stipulations regarding its usage. In some circumstances an endowment may be required to be spent in a certain way or alternatively invested, with the principal to remain intact in perpetuity or for a defined time period. This allows for the donation to have an impact over a longer period of time than if it were spent all at once.

Endowment donors can sometimes restrict Colleges/Departments on how they can spend this money. For example, donors can decide to use a portion of an endowment's scheduled income on a merit-based or need-based scholarship. Another standard restrictive use of an endowment's income is to provide funding for endowed professorships, which are used to attract world-class educators.

Other than these restrictions, universities can use the rest of the allotted spending amount as standard income. Decisions about whether it should be spent on hiring professors, upgrading/repairing facilities or funding more scholarships is left to University administrators. An endowment's investment income can also significantly lower tuition costs for students. For example, if a university's endowment yields a total of $150 million and has a 5% spending limit, this would provide $7.5 million of available income. If the university had originally budgeted $5.5 million in endowment funds, this would mean that the excess $2 million could be used to pay other debts/expenses—savings that could be passed on to students.

However, because universities depend on investment returns for supplementary income, there could be trouble if the investments do not yield a suitable amount of returns. Therefore, most endowments are run by professionals to ensure that the investments made are in line with the aforementioned policies.

9.13.1 Endowed Professorship

An endowed professorship (or endowed chair) is a position permanently paid for with the revenue from an endowment fund specifically set up for that purpose. Typically, the position is designated to be in a certain department. The donor is allowed to name the position, which typically takes the format: First-name Last-name Professor of Department-name. Endowed professorships aid the university by providing a faculty member who does not have to be paid entirely out of the operating budget, allowing the university to either reduce its student-to-faculty ratio, a statistic used for college rankings and other institutional evaluations, and/or direct money that would otherwise have been spent on salaries toward other university needs. In addition, holding such a professorship is considered to be an honor in the academic world, and the university can use them to reward its best faculty or to recruit top professors from other institutions.

9.13.2 Endowed Scholarship/Fellowship

An endowed scholarship is tuition (and possibly other cost) assistance that is permanently paid for with the revenue of an endowment fund specifically set up for that purpose. It can be either merit-based or need-based (which is only awarded to those students for whom the college expense would cause their family financial hardship) depending on university policy or donor preferences. Some universities will facilitate donors to meet the students they are helping. The amount that must be donated to start an endowed scholarship can vary greatly.

Fellowships are similar, although they are most commonly associated with graduate students. In addition to helping with tuition, they may also include a stipend. Fellowships with a stipend may encourage students to work on a doctorate. Frequently, teaching or working on research is a mandatory part of a fellowship.

9.14 CONCLUSION

It is needless to say that a University must institute the following systems such as:

1. Admission Process,
2. Recruitment Process,
3. Examination Process,
4. Research and Development Centre,
5. Faculty Development Cell,
6. Curriculum Development Cell,
7. Placement and Training Cell,
8. Planning and Development Process.

The creation of policy and handbook for functioning of all these system is very essential. It is also essential to disseminate the idea of this system to one and all concerned.

In general the process must be simple to be understood and followed by everyone concerned. Various forms that are used must be simple and requiring to make minimum entries. All such information has to be kept in a data base of the University for a very long period (May be even for more than 50 Years) for readily tracing required information. An overview of the systems and practices followed and how they got modified over the years and the consequences recorded can be of help in the formulation of new policies and practices.

CHAPTER 10

Checks and Balances of University System

10.1 INTRODUCTION

A good university system provides a secured and structured system to ensure the right functioning. This chapter explains the different types of checks and balances to improve the effective functioning of the University System.

10.2 ACADEMIC DISCIPLINE COMMITTEE

The mandate of the Committee on Discipline is to adjudicate cases of alleged misconduct by a student brought to its attention. In all cases, the Committee acts with power, including suspension, expulsion and revocation of a degree.

The University reserves the right to take any action that it deems as necessary or appropriate to protect the intellectual integrity, safety, and well being of the campus community. To that end, University students are expected to abide by the rules, regulations, and policies of the University, as well as city, state, and country laws. The MIT (Massachusetts Institute of Technology, USA) procedure is taken and is presented in this section as an example.

10.2.1 The Committee's Authority

The Committee on Discipline is a Standing Committee of the Faculty.

Each of the Standing Committees shall, in addition to the specific duties listed, be responsible for (1) formulating and reviewing educational policies and other policies which relate to its work, (2) requesting any needed clarification of such policies from the Faculty Policy Committee, (3) recommending to the Faculty Policy Committee any changes of such policies which it deems to be advisable, and (4) performing such other duties as may be delegated to it by the Faculty Policy Committee or by the Chairman of the Faculty.

The Committee on Discipline shall consist of six elected members of the Faculty, three undergraduate and two graduate students, and the Dean for Undergraduate Education, the Dean for Student Life, and the Dean for Graduate Students, ex officio, or representatives as designated by the respective Deans. Past members who have completed their terms may, for a period of three years thereafter, be called to fill out a quorum for a particular hearing, only one such member to serve in a given hearing.

The Committee shall consider such cases of alleged misconduct by students as shall be brought to its attention by any member of the University community. An accused student shall be given an opportunity to appear in person at a meeting of the Committee.

The Committee shall act with power in all circumstances, including, suspension or expulsion of a student from the Institute, or revocation of a degree. Appeals of a decision to suspend expel or revoke a degree will be made to the Chancellor on grounds that are described in the Rules and Regulations of the University.

The Committee adjudicates cases within the framework of Institute policies. Revisions to such policies are not of the Committee on Discipline, but of the office or committee that is responsible for considering changes in the policy. In connection with its consideration of a particular case, the Committee on Discipline may seek an interpretation or clarification of an Institute policy relevant to that case through the Faculty Policy Committee.

Except to the extent inconsistent with the Rules and Regulations of the Faculty, the Committee, after consultation with the Faculty Policy Committee, may from time to time amend these rules and regulations.

The Chair may appoint Associate Chairmen of the Committee for a period of time, usually an academic year, who will be empowered to chair hearings.

10.2.2 General Procedures

A. *Who May Bring Charges*

Anyone directly aggrieved, may file a complaint against a University student. Complaints against students by individuals who are not members of the University community (including persons who are not currently students, faculty, or staff but who participate in or are members of a University organization) will be reviewed by the Chair on a case-by-case basis to determine whether such complaints should be pursued in an University process, and, if so, how the complaint should be resolved. Moreover, charges of misconduct as related to a University function may originate from individuals responsible for such functions or for a department. For example, a Dean, a Director of a laboratory, the Chief of the Campus Police, the Chair of the Faculty, an Administrative Officer, an Officer of the Student Government, an officer of student residence, and a manager of facilities may initiate a complaint against a student. Complaints against non

University students, the University faculty, staff, or administration are not covered by these procedures.

B. *Steps to Filing a Complaint*

Usually those who have a complaint seek guidance from the Office of Student Mediation and Community Standards (OSMCS) regarding the options available to resolve the complaint and the steps to follow in each of them. Sometimes complainants decide in consultation with the OSMCS that a letter to the student, mediation, or other means of addressing concerns is sufficient. If a complainant decides to file a formal complaint, the OSMCS will provide guidance throughout the process. The complaint, information relevant to support the complaint, the names of any witnesses, and copies of any documents the complainant plans to present at a hearing in the event one is held are submitted to the OSMCS. As soon as a written complaint is received, the OSMCS staff member to the Committee will contact the student being charged.

The charge and its documentation are transmitted to the Chair of the Committee on Discipline. After a review of the documents, the Chair will decide whether or not a hearing by the Committee on Discipline is warranted, and, if so, if such hearing should be by the full Committee, a Committee on Discipline Panel, or an Administrative Review. The Chair may consult the Dean specified and/or the Chair of the Faculty in reaching this decision. However, the determination by the Chair whether or not to hear a case is final, and is not subject to appeal.

After a decision is reached, the complainant and the accused student are then notified of the Chair's decision and advised of their rights. Both the complainant and the accused student have the right to have an advisor and witnesses present at the hearing. Each advisor must be a member of the University Community (non-family, non-attorney, non-member of the media). If a hearing by the Committee on Discipline is not warranted, the Chair may recommend that the complainant seek a resolution through either the Office of the Dean for Student Life or other Institute processes for resolving disputes.

Off-campus misconduct may be a basis for University action if the University considers that such misconduct impinges on the well being or functioning of the University. The University reserves the right to determine its jurisdiction on a case by case basis.

C. *Committee Procedures*

The Committee typically observes the following procedures (the Committee reserves the right to adjust these procedures as it deems necessary in appropriate cases, and at all times to take prompt action outside these procedures in situations where there may be an imminent risk of serious harm):

The accused student will be provided with a written copy of the complaint with sufficient specificity to prepare for the hearing, including the names of any witnesses and copies of any documents that will be presented by the complainant.

The accused student is also provided with a copy of the Committee on Discipline Rules and Regulations and given ten official Institute working days in which to prepare a response to the charges. To expedite the scheduling of a hearing, the accused student may waive the right to this ten day period. The waiver must be submitted in writing to the DSL (Dean for Student Life) staff member to the Committee. The accused student should respond to the charge in writing. Included in the response should be the name of the advisor, the names of any witnesses who will be testifying at the hearing, and copies of any documents that will be presented at the hearing. The written response of the accused student should be received by DSL staff member to the Committee at least three Institute working days prior to the hearing. At the discretion of the Chair, supplemental submissions from the Complainant, the accused student, or both, may be accepted.

A student may not graduate if subject to a pending discipline case, defined as one where formal charges have been brought and the case is pending. The restriction of graduation is limited to cases that are sufficiently serious that disciplinary action, if taken, would likely bring a sanction of suspension or expulsion. This judgment of seriousness will be made by the Chair of the Committee on Discipline after consultation with the Chancellor and the specified Dean.

In the event that a case is brought after graduation, for actions that occurred before graduation, academic degrees may be revoked. The revocation may be for a specified period of time, after which the degree will be reinstated (the equivalent of suspension from the Institute), or it may be without limit of time (the equivalent of expulsion from the Institute).

The complainant and the accused student each have the right to an advisor in preparation of his/her response and to attend the hearing who is a member of the University Community (as long as non-family, non-attorney, non-member of the press). If the complainant or student decides to seek assistance from an individual who is not a member of the University community, they should be aware that such a person will not be allowed to be present at the hearing. Members of the University Community for this purpose are Faculty members, students, and employees. The student may ask the DSL staff member to the Committee for a referral to an adviser within the University Community. The DSL staff member to the Committee will maintain a list of faculty and experienced members of the senior staff in the offices of the Deans for Student Life, Undergraduate Education, and Graduate Students suitable for the role. The advisor may speak at the hearing with the permission of the Chair of the Committee.

If a complainant is unwilling or unable to gather the materials necessary to file a complaint or present the complaint at a hearing, the advisor who is a member of the University Community may carry out those responsibilities, with the permission of the Chair of the Committee.

Attorneys for either the accused student or the complainant will not be allowed to be present at a Committee hearing. The Chair may allow the presence of an attorney to the Committee itself in cases in which the Chair decides that the Committee would benefit from receiving legal advice during the hearing. When there is significant concern with respect to self-incrimination because of potential or pending criminal charges, the Chair may defer the Committee hearing until after any criminal charges have been resolved. When the Committee has deferred the hearing until court proceedings have been resolved, interim measures, including temporary suspension, may be taken by the Dean for Student Life.

The hearing is scheduled as soon as possible after the accused student's written response has been received by the OSMCS staff member. Once the hearing date has been established, any modification of the charge or additional charges must be submitted to the OSMCS staff member to the Committee and then to the accused at least three Institute working days prior to the scheduled hearing. However, the Chair may postpone a hearing or grant a continuance in any case for any reason deemed appropriate by the Chair.

The accused student has the right to be present at the hearing and to be heard by the Committee. However, refusal or failure by the student to participate in the hearing shall not prevent the Committee from proceeding with the hearing and adjudicating the complaint.

The accused student and the complainant may testify and present evidence in their behalf. They also may question witnesses presented by either party.

The Chair may call witnesses, including expert witnesses, to aid the Committee in its deliberations. Expert witnesses for the accused and the complainant will be allowed by the Chair only in unusual cases, and in such cases, the Chair should act to insure impartial expert testimony.

The Committee may hear cases in plenary session (a Committee on Discipline Hearing), a smaller Committee on Discipline Panel, or in an Administrative Review. Complaints of alleged misconduct that may lead to suspension or expulsion may only be heard by a Committee on Discipline Hearing. All other cases may be heard by a Committee on Discipline Panel, which shall consist of an Associate Chair of Committee (or in his or her absence, another faculty member of the Committee), an additional faculty member, two students, and a Dean who is a member of the Committee or his or her representative.

A Committee on Discipline Hearing may be held by a quorum of the Committee. A quorum consists of a majority of the members of the Committee, at least two of whom must be faculty members.

No member of the Committee who had any involvement in the events relating to a particular case will sit on a Committee on Discipline Hearing, Committee on Discipline Panel, or Administrative Review that considers that case.

The hearing will be chaired by the Committee Chair or Associate Chair in the case of a Committee on Discipline Hearing, by the Committee Chair or Associate Chair (or faculty member serving in his or her absence) in the case of Committee on Discipline Panel, and by the OSMCS staff member in the case of an Administrative Review.

Members who have finished their terms on the Committee may, for a period of three years after their service on the Committee, be called to fill out a quorum for a particular hearing by a Committee on Discipline Hearing or Committee on Discipline Panel, only one such member to be at a given hearing.

All hearings of the Committee are closed to individuals who are not directly involved as the complainant, the accused, advisors, and witnesses identified in advance by each party.

The Chair of the hearing may decide to permit witnesses to be present at the hearing only during their testimony. The Chair of the hearing may make an official tape recording of the testimony, but not of the deliberations, for the sole use of the Committee and then destroyed after the deliberations are completed. No other tape recording may be made.

The Chair of the hearing shall warn any participant that he or she deems to be disruptive or to be harassing or intimidating to any other participant and if he or she decides is appropriate, terminate that person's participation in the hearing, remove that person from the hearing, or take any other action deemed necessary by the Chair to ensure an orderly hearing.

The Committee's consideration and determination of complaints are confidential, and should not be discussed outside of the Committee process by members and staff of the Committee or by complainants, accused students, or witnesses. Confidential information includes the existence and substance of the complaint, the names of complainants, accused students, and witnesses, what is said at a hearing and by whom, and the findings made and sanctions imposed by the Committee. Any information regarding a complaint before the Committee or a decision by the Committee may only be communicated to other officials of University in order to permit them to fulfill their professional responsibilities, and only after consultation with the Chair of the Committee, to the extent it is feasible to do so.

The decision of the Committee is based on evidence introduced at the hearing. Formal rules of evidence that apply to civil or criminal judicial processes shall not be applicable.

The decision is made in executive session following the hearing, and based on a majority vote of the participating members. The standard for determining responsibility is the preponderance of the evidence.

The Committee's decision is final. The Chair of the Committee will usually meet with the accused student as soon as possible after the meeting. The decision will be transmitted to the accused student and the complainant in writing no later than ten days after the hearing.

A decision to suspend or expel a student may be appealed to the Chancellor, and a decision by a Committee on Discipline Panel may be appealed to a Committee on Discipline Hearing.

A record of the proceedings should be kept in the files of the Committee. This record should consist of: (1) the complaint and accused student's response, (2) all documents submitted at the hearing, and (3) the decision letter. This record does not summarize or otherwise attempt to preserve the testimony or deliberative discussions.

10.2.3 Specific Procedures for Conducting a Hearing

The hearing will typically follow the order described below; although the Chair at all times has the discretion to vary the order as the Chair may decide is appropriate:

Introductions and description of the hearing procedures to the parties.

The charges in the complaint are read and the Chair may ask the accused student to either admit or deny responsibility.

Opening statements by both the complainant and the accused student.

Complainant's testimony followed by the opportunity of the accused student to question the complainant.

Complainant's witnesses' testimony followed by the opportunity of the accused student and the Committee to question the complainant's witnesses.

Accused student's testimony followed by the opportunity of the complainant and the Committee to question the accused student.

Accused student's witnesses' testimony followed by opportunity of the complainant and the Committee to question the accused student's witnesses.

Chair may call witnesses to aid the Committee.

Closing statement by the Chair, including when decision is expected be made.

The Chair may call a brief recess at any time during the hearing.

Both parties are expected to offer their own testimony and the testimony of witnesses, if any, concerning the matters alleged in the complaint. Opening statements by the complainant and the accused student (#3) should normally not be interrupted with questions from the Committee. During actual testimony, questions should be limited to those asked for clarification purposes only. At any time, the Chair of the hearing can rule on the relevancy of any question or statement made or information provided by any party during the hearing.

After, all the testimony and statements have been completed and all questions asked, the hearing is concluded and the Committee meets in executive session to reach its decision. The Committee shall decide either to dismiss the complaint or to impose sanctions in accordance with the following Section.

10.2.4 Sanctions

The Committee has the authority to impose any sanction it deems appropriate. Possible sanctions include, by way of example, reprimand, informal probation, formal probation, suspension, and expulsion. Sanctions may also include requiring direct restitution and/or designated service to the Community.

Probation

A decision to place a student on probation must stipulate the time period for which probation is to be imposed. Only time during which the student is enrolled and attending classes at University counts toward the fulfillment of the probationary period.

Informal probation shall be noted only on the student's record within the OSMCS. Formal probation may be recorded on the student's official transcript.

Suspension

Suspension is imposed for a definite period of time. At the end of a suspension period, the student must apply for readmission through the Committee on Discipline.

If a student is suspended, the OSMCS staff shall notify the student's faculty advisor and Housemaster (if any) and the Registrar, who will have the appropriate disciplinary notation placed on the student's official transcript.

Expulsion

Expulsion implies that the student should not consider University for further education. However, to give the student the opportunity to have the decision reconsidered in light of the student's subsequent circumstances and accomplishments, the Committee decision to expel must include a time period after which the student may request the Committee to review the case. If a student is expelled, the OSMCS staff shall notify the student's faculty advisor and Housemaster (if applicable) and the Registrar, who will have the appropriate disciplinary notation placed on the student's official transcript.

If new evidence becomes available that substantially contradicts the evidence that a Committee on Discipline Hearing or a Committee on Discipline Panel relied on in making its decision, that evidence may form the basis for a petition to the Committee to reopen a case, although the length of time between the original decision and the petition may be a factor in denying the petition.

10.2.5 Disciplinary Notations

Formal probation, suspension, expulsion, and termination of expulsion are noted both on the student's official transcript and on the student's internal grade report, but not on end-of-term grade summaries except by request of the Committee. At the time the Committee imposes formal probation, suspension, or expulsion, it shall set two time limits:

The first time limit shall be established to indicate the earliest date on which a student may petition the Committee to remove the disciplinary notation from the official transcript and internal grade report. This time limit cannot be later than:

1. *For formal probation:* The limit is the end of the formal probation period.
2. *For suspension:* The limit is the end of the suspension period.
3. *For expulsion:* The limit is two years after the effective date of expulsion.

The second limit is the date on which the disciplinary notation shall be removed automatically. This date cannot be more than ten years for formal probation or suspension.

10.2.6 Appeals

All appeals must be submitted in writing to the OSMCS staff member to the Committee by the accused student within ten Institute working days of the date the accused student received the letter advising him or her of the decision of the Committee on Discipline Hearing or Committee on Discipline Panel. There is no appeal from the decision of an Administrative Review.

A Committee on Discipline Panel decision may be appealed to a Committee on Discipline Hearing. Such an appeal may only be made on one or more of the following grounds:

1. There was a substantial departure from the Committee rules and procedures that significantly affected the fairness of the process;
2. A material finding that formed a basis for the Committee's decision was substantially against the weight of the evidence that was before the Committee when it made the decision; or
3. The sanction substantially exceeds the range of sanctions appropriate in the situation.

The Chair of the Committee decides whether or not an appeal will be heard by a Committee on Discipline Hearing, based upon the accused student's written appeal, and so much of the record of the Committee on Discipline Panel's hearing of the case as the Chair determines it is appropriate for him or her to consider. If the Chair of the Committee decides that the case will be heard by a Committee on Discipline Hearing, the Committee on Discipline Hearing reviews the decision of the Committee on Discipline Panel based upon the accused student's written appeal, and so much of the record of the Committee on Discipline Panel's hearing of the case as the Committee on Discipline Hearing determines it is appropriate for them to consider.

A Committee on Discipline Hearing decision to suspend or expel a student may be appealed to the Chancellor. Such an appeal may only be made on one or more of the following grounds:

- There was a substantial departure from the Committee rules and procedures that significantly affected the fairness of the process;
- A material finding that formed a basis for the Committee's decision was substantially against the weight of the evidence that was before the Committee when it made the decision; or
- The sanction substantially exceeds the range of sanctions appropriate in the situation.

In all other cases, the Committee on Discipline Hearing decision is final.

The Chancellor decides an appeal on the basis of the accused student's written appeal providing the ground(s) the student is relying on for appeal, and so much of the record of the Committee on Discipline Hearing of the case as the Chancellor determines it is appropriate for him or her to consider. The Chancellor will consult with the Committee on Discipline Chair on all appeals. The Chancellor may also confer with other participants of the hearing, if necessary to consider a ground for appeal. Before modifying or overruling a decision of the Committee on Discipline, the Chancellor will meet, in person or telephonically, with available members of the Committee on Discipline who decided the case, and will make a final decision after consulting with them. The final decision will be communicated to the same people who received notice of the Committee on Discipline hearing decision, and to any other officials of University who need to be aware of it in order to permit them to fulfill their professional responsibilities. When it is reasonable, a member of the OSMCS staff shall meet with the parties regarding any appeal decision.

If the Committee on Discipline hearing decision imposes a sanction of suspension or expulsion to take effect before the time for the student to file an appeal has expired, or while an appeal is under consideration, the student may request in writing from the Chair of the Committee a postponement of the effective date of the sanction to permit the student to file the appeal and the Chancellor to decide the appeal. The

Chair may approve the request with or without conditions relating to the student's remaining at University while the appeal is pending. If the Chair denies the student's request for a postponement of the effective date, the student may request the postponement from the Chancellor, who may approve the postponement, with or without such conditions, after discussing with the Chair the student's request and the reasons the Chair denied the request.

10.2.7 Conditions for Early Removal of Disciplinary Note/Sanction

Early removal of disciplinary notations or sanctions may be considered by the Committee on Discipline. A student seeking early removal of a disciplinary notation or sanction may submit a petition to the Committee setting out the basis for the request. The Chair of the Committee will decide whether the Committee will consider the request, and if so, whether it will be considered by a Committee on Discipline Hearing or a Committee on Discipline Panel.

10.3 CAMPUS CRIME DIVISION

Campus security and safety are important issues in higher education today. Providing students with a safe environment in which to learn and keeping students, parents and employees well informed about campus security.

The Institution should adapt the following procedures to tackle the campus crimes.

1. Prepare the handbook on campus crimes
2. The handbook should give a policy disclosure about the crimes.
3. The handbook should give a complete guideline for campus police, crime reporting, crime alert, etc.
4. The complete procedure should be formulated as like the Academic Discipline Committee.

10.4 EXAM SQUAD

The University/College students are caught for indulging in malpractices in an exam; he/she will be barred from appearing in the subsequent three examinations. Not only that, scores in other subjects may also get annulled. The harsh deterrent is just one of the many measures that have been approved by the university's Executive Council. It is essential to constitute an Exam squad that will take care of inspecting the exam halls to avoid the malpractices. Also, the university should categorize the type of malpractices and punishments and make known to all concerned well in advance of examinations each time.

10.5 VISITORS' FEEDBACK SYSTEM/BOOK

It is essential to get the opinion of the outsider/visitor to improve the quality of service. The University should maintain a visitor's feedback system so as to get the opinion. This can be managed either in as a handbook or as a web-based feedback system. The feedback should be taken with a right-sprit and an appropriate measure should be initiated to implement/rectify/change the system.

10.6 STUDENT GRIEVANCE CELL

Student grievance cell offers the opportunity to students to air their grievances and valuable suggestions. Student Grievance redress cell is here to ensure effective solution to student grievances related to all the academic and administrative departments in an impartial and fair manner. Grievances related to hostel, sexual harassment, discrimination based on religion, race, or sex may be discussed with the respective teacher guardian/deputy director student affairs/warden/chief warden/associate deans or directly with the dean. Students are assured that every case will be dealt with the attention required. Grievances pertaining to the administrative delays may be brought to the notice of the management executive in the administrative office of the University. This must act as a separate cell in the University.

10.7 FACULTY/STAFF GRIEVANCE CELL

The centralized staff Grievance Cell is constituted in accordance with the System of University Administration. Separate grievances cell for the faculty and staff are functional. The grievances are screened by Dean Academics and the Director. They are discussed in detail every fortnight with the management. The grievances are accordingly settled. However, incase the grievances warrant immediate redressal, same are put up to the management and immediate action is taken to provide relief to aggrieved faculty members and staff.

10.8 VOTING SYSTEMS

The student society represents all undergraduate students at the University. The Society operates several businesses and provides services to students. The Society advocates on behalf of students on important issues such as increasing accessibility to education, racism, affordable public transportation and environmental sustainability. A petition was circulated among the membership to demand a referendum on continued membership and for the election of officials. Proponents of the petition cited nontransparent governance and accounting.

10.9 TECHNICAL/MAINTENANCE/SERVICE CELL/CENTRE

The technical maintenance/repair cell is offering various repair and maintenance services. This cell registers the complaints and does the maintenance. For example Electrical Maintenance Cell, Computer Maintenance Cell, Furniture Interior Cell, Equipments Maintenance, Air-Conditioner Maintenance Cell, Water Maintenance Cell, etc.

10.10 GENERAL INSPECTION COMMITTEE

A General Board Inspection Committee is constituted to look into the regular working of the University Systems. An important task of the Board Inspection Committee (BIC) is to ensure that all stakeholders concerned with the inspection process have appropriate access to information about the progress of an Inspection.

10.11 CONCLUSION

In this Chapter we have seen the checks and balances required to ensure the right functioning of any University System. The creation of policy and handbook for functioning of all these system and dissemination of idea of this system is very essential.

Some times if needed the University/Institute can go to the extent of handing over the student(s)/staff to the police if the situation warrants to maintain peace and tranquility of the campus and make life comfortable for all law abiding persons. Needless to state that the various punishments that are in store for commissions/omissions which are not in tune with good conduct are to be let known in detail in writing and specifying the same at various occasions and places, pasting posters, etc. Every one born is good until they are mislead by wrong notions like, enmass anything can be done by claiming "I was at the place of incidence but I don't know who did what exactly" and can escape. Such arguments will not hold water. One cannot get absolved of collective responsibility by individually disowning anything and everything. Students and staff do have a code of conduct and they are not to be found in wrong places. If so, they are also accountable and construed to be party for the wrong doing that has taken place in their midst.

CHAPTER 11

World Universities Ranking

11.1 INTRODUCTION

The international dimension of higher education is a topic of immense interest and debate in this second decade of the 21st century. The new realities facing the higher education sector are both domestic and global, presenting changes, introducing new trends and posing different challenges for internationalization of educational programmes. The mobility of people, programmes and institutions/providers has actually been increasing. Since the education service was treated as an object of trade in liberalization talks under the General Agreement on Trade in Services administered by the World Trade Organization, heated discussions have taken place over transnational higher education as well as the need for developing international frameworks in respect of quality assurance and appropriate information disclosure, from the perspectives of international validity, transferability and learners' protection.

The major reasons for internationalization are:

1. Mobility and Exchanges for Students and Teachers on account of lack of human resources in certain countries.
2. Importing Teaching and Research Collaboration.
3. Maintaining Academic Standards and Quality.
4. Involving Research Projects.
5. Getting Cooperation and Development Assistance.
6. Adopting Curriculum Development.
7. Making International and Inter-cultural Understanding.
8. Solving Regional Issues and Integrating.
9. International Student Recruitment.
10. Diversify Income Generation.

Normally it is inevitable to create competition among these institutions to achieve high quality and standards. This quality and standards can be motivated through ranking these Universities. At this juncture the big question before us is how to rank the world universities? What is the impact we are looking for? How it should direct or drive various communities to move forward? Is it just to asses the academic excellence or for any other purpose? What is the lesson we want to teach the whole society and educational community? By finding suitable answers we may be able to arrive at a solution useful to all.

What are all the parameters taken to rank the universities? Is it enough to put all the 500 universities under a category or different universities in the different ways? It is necessary to answer these questions before ranking the world universities. It is essential to think about the various new methods for evolving the quality attributes for higher learning institutes.

In this chapter, Section 11.2 outlines the survey of existing methods to rank Universities. Section 11.3 explains the aim and objective of ranking. Section 11.4 explains what types of universities are taken for the purpose of ranking. Section 11.5 explains who should rank the universities. Section 11.6 gives various parameters and attributes taken for ranking and Section 10.7 concludes this chapter.

The 2010 QS world university top 500 rankings can be had in the Annexure–A.

11.2 SURVEY OF EXISTING WORLD RANKING

In recent years, several rankings of world universities have been published by various organisations. These are I. Shanghai Jiao Tong University Ranking—SJTU, II. Times Higher Education Ranking—THES, III. Web metrics ranking, IV. The THE—QS World University Rankings, V. The Higher Education Evaluation and Accreditation Council of Taiwan, VI. The International Ranking Expert Group (IREG), VII. Global University City (GUC) Index, VIII. World Education News and Reviews, IX. Web Popularity ranking, X. CHE—Centre for Higher Education Development has" Ranking of Excellent European Graduate Programmes, etc.

The first (I) SJTU ranking is established using six parameters and with arbitrarily attributed weights.

- A - (20%) N&S. Number of articles published in Nature or Science;
- B - (20%) HiCi. Number of highly cited researchers in 21 broad subject categories;
- C - (10%) Size. Academic performance with respect to the size of the institution;
- D - (20%) Award. Number of staff of the institution winning Nobel Prize and Field Medals;
- E - (10%) Alumni. Number of alumni of the institution winning Nobel Prizes and Fields Medals;
- F - (20%) SCI. Articles in Science Citation Index-expanded, Social Science Citation Index, and Arts and Humanities Citation Index.

The SJTU considers the number of papers, scientists, prize and academic performance relative to size. This ranking considers various countries across the world. It is very complex to achieve these parameters in general for any of the universities. Most of these parameters support only the research organizations, the institutions in the developed nations.

The Second (II) is the THES ranking, of the Times Higher Education Supplement—THES adopted the following six parameters and respective weights:

- A - (40%) Peer review—opinion of 2,375 research-active academics;
- B - (20%) Citation/faculty;
- C - (10%) Recruiter's review—the opinion of employers;
- D - (20%) Faculty to student ratio;
- E - (5%) International student score—percentage of foreign students;
- F - (5%) International faculty score—percentage of foreign staff.

The THES ranking is based on relative numbers such as indices, ratios, academic performance, etc. The Web metrics ranking is established in terms of absolute numbers. It is important to notice that in one case it is essential to look at the relative performance, regardless of the size, while in the other case the size of the institution also impacts the ranking. In this case, larger institutions tend to be better ranked than smaller ones.

III. The third ranking is the Web Metrics Ranking measures the presence of the universities in the web, considering parameters such as size of the sites, files and visibility. It just measures the usage of the modern resource of the university.

The main objective is to find out which parameters are more and which are less important for the assessment of the academic performance of the world universities. The focus is to discuss methodology to establish new ranking parameters.

IV. The THE—QS World University Rankings were conceived to present a multi-faceted view of the relative strengths of the world's leading Universities. The research yields results on 600 on the whole and 300 in each of five broad faculty areas. The overall rankings are compiled based on six distinct indicators:

Table 1: The QS World University Ranking Indicators

Indicator	*Explanation*	*Weightage*
Academic Peer Review	Composite score drawn from peer review survey (which is divided into five subject areas). 6,354 responses in 2008.	40%
Employer Review	Score based on responses to employer survey. 2,339 responses in 2008.	10%
Faculty Student Ratio	Score based on student faculty ratio	20%
Citations per Faculty	Score based on research performance factored against the size of the research body	20%
International Faculty	Score based on proportion of international faculty	5%
International Students	Score based on proportion of international students	5%

In this method only six parameters are considered for ranking. It considers only the academic attributes for ranking. These indicators are then combined using standard statistical tools to yield the overall scores. Moreover, the first two attributes are based on the survey from the peer groups. Most of the time people have predetermined notion about a set of institutions and they may not accept new set of institutions which strive hard to achieve better status.

V. The Higher Education Evaluation and Accreditation Council of Taiwan takes into account three indicators each related to research. They are research productivity, *research impact*, and *research excellence*. It considers only research publication indicators alone. This approach is given in the following Table 2.

Table 2: The Criteria, Indicators and their Respective Weightings Used for the Overall Performance Ranking by Taiwan Higher Education Evaluation and Accreditation Council

Criteria	*2008 Overall Performance Indicators*	*Weight-age*	
Research Productivity	Number of articles of the last 11 years (1997–2007)	10	20
	Number of articles of the current year (2007)	10	
Research Impact	Number of citations of the last 11 years (1997–2007)	10	30
	Number of citations of the last 2 years (2006–2007)	10	
	Average number of citations of the last 11 years (1997–2007)	10	
Research Excellence	H-index of the last 2 years (2006–2007)	20	50
	Number of Highly Cited Papers (1997–2007)	15	
	Number of articles of the current year in high-impact journals (2007)	15	

VI. The International Ranking Expert Group (IREG), founded in 2004 by the UNESCO European Centre for Higher Education (UNESCO-CEPES) and the Institute for Higher Education Policy in Washington, DC, had the initiative to consider a set of principles of quality and good practice in HEI rankings—the Berlin Principles on Ranking of Higher Education Institutions. It is expected that this initiative has set a framework for the elaboration and dissemination of rankings—whether they are national, regional, or global in scope—that ultimately will lead to a system of continuous improvement and refinement of the methodologies used to conduct these rankings.

VII. The Global University City (GUC) Index was developed by RMIT (Royal Melbourne Institute of Technology) as a contribution to the work of the Committee for Melbourne Higher Education Taskforce. Firstly, global university cities are good places to live in. They combine factors such as affordability, safety, access to public transport, and cultural amenity with world class educational facilities. This approach weighted each of the factors that drive the GUC Index as follows: Size of city is an absolute threshold. Cities with a population less than 2 million are excluded. City liveability and amenity is weighted at 30%, the number of global universities and their degree of internationalisation is weighted at 30%, Educational inputs and performance is weighted at 20%, Research inputs and performance is weighted at 20%. This approach is likely to leave out the good but remotely located institutions.

VIII. World Education News and Reviews is the authoritative newsletter for professionals in international education, published every month by World Education Services, a non-profit organization specializing in the evaluation of foreign academic credentials. The growth in domestic and international rankings can be attributed to two major factors: the massifcation of tertiary education and globalization. This follows different approaches for different regions.

IX. The Web Popularity ranking is based upon an algorithm including three unbiased and independent web metrics extracted from three different search engines: Google Page Rank, Yahoo Inbound Links, Alexa Traffic Rank. The aim of this website is to provide an approximate popularity ranking of worldwide Universities and Colleges based upon the popularity of their websites. This can especially help international students to understand how popular a specific University/College is in a foreign country.

X. The CHE—Centre for Higher Education Development has developed a "Ranking of Excellent European Graduate Programmes" (CHE Excellence Ranking for short) for the disciplines of Biology, Chemistry, Physics and Mathematics. The ranking wants to highlight the research strengths European Higher Education Institutions have and to give ideas to further improve the programmes. Students can find the right Doctoral or Master programme as well as information on more than 1,000 research teams.

Apart from these there are also other approaches that are followed in different regions with different factors.

11.3 OBJECTIVES OF THE RANKING

Generally all nations are classified under one of the three categories. They are viz., developed, developing and underdeveloped nations. Most of the parameters chosen for existing ranking methods are good in the developed nations. It is not supporting the developing and underdeveloped nations. In an open economy, it should give the thrust for the over all development of the entire globe, motivate uniform growth among the nations. The chosen parameters should provide space for the developing, underdeveloped countries to improve themselves as well as enable the developed countries to help these countries to develop equally. This kind of direction of organizational setup will enable the uniform growth instead of creating a mere competition.

These parameters should consider the following objectives.

1. Increasing in productivity of the world economy
2. Increasing communal harmony

3. Enhancing the teaching, learning and research processes
4. Eliminate poverty
5. Contribution to the environmental protection
6. Contribution to avoid climate change/natural disaster management/mitigation facilities
7. Contribution to development of universities in developing and underdeveloped countries
8. Contribution to civilian technology transfer.

Every institution of higher learning in the world either directly or indirectly contributes to these objectives which is measurable.

11.4 TYPE OF UNIVERSITY RANKING

The universal ranking should not be a just on the 500 top university ranking. Because here is a disparity among different fields; a Science University cannot be equated with an Engineering University or Medical University can't be equated with a Science University.

Each is having its own credibility and can't be normalized with one another. In addition to this, the volume of growth of higher-education population and institutes, it is necessary to give equal opportunity to all states across the world. Increasing the volume will avoid the domination of the developed nations. It will motivate the institutes across the world to develop themselves to the international standards. So, apart from ranking world top most universities, there is also a need to find the top 500 universities in each specialization such as:

1. World's top 500 Engineering/Technological Institutes.
2. World's top 500 Science Institutes.
3. World's top 500 Medical Institutes.
4. World's top 500 Arts and Humanities Institutes.
5. World's top 500 Social Science Institutes.
6. World's top 500 Management/Economic Institutes/Schools.
7. World's top 500 Bio-Medicine Universities.

11.5 SURVEYING AUTHORITY

The UNESCO has to set up a universal representative like an International Association of Universities (IAU) across various countries and their agents should go into the details about the various organizations and collect the required data across the world. The data collected from these organizations needs to be analyzed and processed through an international body. Also, this process should be universally a transparent one. The authority should also asses the truthfulness and integrity of data before taking into account to avoid the falsification of data.

11.6 LIST OF PARAMETERS/ATTRIBUTES FOR ASSESSMENT SUGGESTED

There are a number of parameters/attributes which need to be considered for the assessment. The parameters need to be adapted after considering the various criteria. The following list of general parameters/attributes should be considered for quality assessment of institutes of higher-learning. This proposed new approach is given in Table 3.

Table 3: The Criteria, Indicators and their Respective Weights used for the Overall Performance Ranking for Proposed Method

S. No.	*Indicator*	*Explanation*	*Weighting*
1.	Quality Employability Ratio	Number of alumni employed at the executive levels of the fortune 500 companies.	4%
2.	Award Winners Ratio	Nobel/Field medals/Prizes given at various levels and received by Staff/student/alumni of the universities.	2%
3.	Graduation Ratio	Success of graduation percentage with in the stipulated period.	10%
4.	Faculty Student Ratio	Score based on student faculty ratio	10%
5.	Citations per Faculty/Students	Number of articles published in referred journals/conferences by the faculty and students.	4%
6.	IPRs and Patterns	Number of successful Patents/IPRs.	4%
7.	Social Peace Ratio	Number Alumni/Faculty received peace prizes on various subjects.	2%
8.	International Faculty	Score based on proportion of international faculty	4%
9.	International Students	Score based on proportion of international students	4%
10.	Fellow-ship/ Endowments	Availability of total number of registered fellowships/ Endowments/Scholarships (Internal/External/ National/International).	2%
11.	Joint Projects	Number of Successful Joint Projects with standard industries/institutes and a minimum limit of funding/ Number of National Projects with a certain amount of funding.	10%
12.	Social Publishing Ratio	Popular book writers/Other Publishing Prizes (Bookers prize award/Certain amount of selling).	4%
13.	Productivity Ratio	Employability/Placement/Entrepreneurship	10%
14.	Technology Adaptation Ratio	Level of Web Presence/Level of use of Modern Technology.	4%
15.	Provisions for differently abled	Development and usage of technology for persons with functional limitations or disabilities	2%

S. No.	*Indicator*	*Explanation*	*Weighting*
16.	Fellow Membership Ratio	Leadership in various fields'/Fellow Membership conferred at international bodies.	4%
17.	Leadership Ratio	Popular World Leaders graduated from the school/universities.	2%
18.	Academic Events Ratio	International level of invited Lectures/Conferences organized/Seminars organized.	4%
19.	Available Infrastructure Ratio	Infrastructure facilities available in the institution	4%
20.	Higher Degrees Growth Ratio	Number of Post-Doctoral/Doctoral awardees/Honorary Degrees.	4%
21.	Socio-Economic Commitment Ratio	Number of full-scholarship for graduation and post-graduation level	4%
22.	Environnement Protection and Disaster Management Commitment Ratio	Development of research for the environment protection and disaster management	2%

1. *Quality Employability Ratio:* This attribute accounts for the number of alumni employed at the executive levels of the fortune 500 companies. The Fortune Global 500 is a ranking of the top 500 corporations worldwide as measured by revenue. The list is compiled and published annually by *Fortune* magazine. It makes a huge contribution to the overall productivity in terms of quantitative and qualitative means to the entire world. It is an attribute to measure the industrial contribution of an institution.
2. *Award Winners Ratio:* Nobel/Field medals/Prizes given at various levels and received by Staff/Student/Alumni of the Universities. These awards are given to people who invent and contribute to the particular subject or felid. Every institution needs to encourage such people who invent. It is an attribute to measure the invention level of an institution.
3. *Graduation Ratio:* The successful graduation percentage within the stipulated period can speak about qualitative and quantitative growth. It is also an important attribute to be considered for the ranking.
4. *Faculty Student Ratio:* Student Faculty Ratio is, at present, the only globally comparable and available indicator that has been identified to address the stated objective of evaluating teaching quality. Clearly it is not a qualitative classroom evaluation as might be considered for a domestic teaching assessment, but it does speak to the notion of "commitment to teaching of an institution", which ought to correlate strongly, if not completely with the level of teaching quality.

5. *Citations per Faculty/Students:* Citations, evaluated in some fashion to take into account the size of institution, are the best understood and most widely accepted measure of research strength.
6. *IPRs and Patterns:* Intellectual property rights give creators exclusive rights to their creations, thereby providing an incentive for the author or inventor to develop and share the information rather than keep it secret. The legal protections granted by IP laws are credited with significant contributions toward economic growth. The successful IPR will definitely envisage the growth of the institution as well as will give a thrust for economic development.
7. *Social Peace Ratio:* The Peace Prize should be awarded "to the person who should have done the most or the best work for fraternity between nations, for the abolition or reduction of standing armies and for the holding and promotion of peace congresses." Institutions are the fundamental entities to create such persons. It is one of the important attribute that needs to be considered.
8. *International Faculty:* The international migration of students and faculty is a major trend in higher education and is inevitably driven both by the march of globalization and the pursuit of alternative higher education avenue streams by universities and governments. It neither be ignored nor denied. It is included largely because this is the world university ranking and set forth to track performance of institutions worldwide against indicators that are, like it or not, prerequisites to being heralded as a world class university.
9. *International Students:* How better to evaluate that than to assess the proportion of international students and faculty who are attracted to that institution. This enables a good friendship and relationship among the nations. It is an indirect way to improve the relationship among the nations such global Institutions are vital for development.
10. *Fellowship/Endowments:* This is financial aid for which financial need is not used to determine the recipient. The recipient may be determined by students' athletic, academic, artistic or other abilities. The actual monetary value of the scholarship may be negligible, the scholarship being meant to motivate the student and promote the study of the subject. However, this is not always the case and the largest scholarships are almost always merit-based. Such systems indicate the contribution of the institution to the socially backward poor society.
11. *Joint Projects:* Evaluated in some fashion to take into account the productivity of institution, is the best understood and most widely accepted measure of research strength.
12. *Social Publishing Ratio:* The winner of the Booker Prize is generally assured of international renown and success and, for this reason, the prize is of great significance for the book trade. It is also a mark of distinction for authors to be nominated for the Booker long list or selected for inclusion in the shortlist. Judges are selected from amongst leading literary critics, writers, academics and notable

public figures. It is these important facts that indicate academic strength and are the best understood and most widely accepted measures of societal strength.

13. *Productivity Ratio:* Refers to the employability ratio. Employability refers to a person's capability of gaining initial employment, maintaining employment, and obtaining new employment if required. For individuals, employability depends on, their assets in terms of the knowledge, skills and attitudes they possess, the way they use and deploy those assets, the way they present them to employers, crucially, the context within which they seek work.

    The prime objectives of modern universities are to produce best employable graduates. It is one of the important parameter that determines the productivity of an institute/university.
14. *Technology Adaptation Ratio:* It is a factor which decides the modern technology usage and development in an institution. Like for example, usage of Internet technology, etc.
15. *Provisions for Differently Abled:* Adaptive technology is the name for products which help people who cannot use regular versions of products, primarily people with physical disabilities such as limitations to vision, hearing, and mobility. Adaptive technology promotes greater effectiveness for persons with functional limitations or disabilities by enabling them to perform tasks that they were formerly unable to accomplish, or had great difficulty accomplishing. Adaptive technology provides changed methods of interacting with or enhancements to the technology.
16. *Fellow Membership Ratio:* A fellow in the broadest sense is someone who is an equal or a comrade. A fellow is often part of an elite group of learned people who work together as peers in the pursuit of knowledge or practice. Several academic societies and academic communities recognize learned people through fellow membership. It is an indirect measure that crosschecks the standards and quality of an education system.
17. *Leadership Ratio:* Influencing a group of people to move towards its goal setting or goal achievement. Institutions take credit for creating leaders such as state minister, governors, etc.
18. *Academic Events Ratio:* An academic conference is a conference for researchers to present and discuss their work. Together with academic or scientific journals, conferences provide an important channel for exchange of information between researchers. It indirectly paves the way for transfer of technology.
19. *Academic Infrastructure Ratio:* The Academic Infrastructure provides a means of describing academic standards in higher education. It allows for diversity and innovation within academic programmers offered by higher education. The Academic Infrastructure was developed by the Quality Assurance Agency (QAA-UK) to define clear and explicit standards, for public information and as nationally agreed reference points. It addresses the concerns of employers who wish to know what to expect from graduates who aspire for their jobs and openings.

20. *Higher Doctoral Degrees Growth Ratio:* It is a phenomenal attribute which decides the growth of the institution as well as the country. It is also an economic indicator for a country. This factor indicates the knowledge growth as well as the research and development of an institution.
21. *Socio-Economic Commitment Ratio:* Educational interest and intellectual commitment have a stronger relationship with the socio-economic relationship. Every institution needs a strong socio-economic commitment to improve the performance of the institution by having sufficient scholarships to the needy students.
22. *Environment Protection and Disaster Management Commitment Ratio:* The institutions are responsible for management of flora and fauna, promotion of environmentally sustainable consumption and production, protection of the state's cultural heritage, particularly aboriginal cultural heritage and regulation of air and water quality, noise, chemicals, radiation and waste disposal.

Emergency management (or disaster management) is the discipline of dealing with and avoiding risks. It is a discipline that involves preparing for disaster before it occurs, disaster response (e.g. emergency evacuation, quarantine, mass decontamination, etc.), as well as supporting, and rebuilding society after natural or human-made disasters have occurred. In general, any Emergency management is a continuous process by which all individuals, groups, and communities manage hazards in an effort to avoid or ameliorate the impact of disasters resulting from the hazards. The contributions of institutions in solving these problems are very significant. Institutions require to work towards the development of such parameter. The above 22 discussed parameters try to account for most of the aspects of an institution and satisfy the objective of global University ranking.

11.7 CONCLUSION

In this chapter an attempt has been made to propose a new set of attributes/parameters for ranking world universities after studying the existing university ranking system. It gives various objectives of the ranking, type of ranking for different universities, survey authority apart from the list of attributes. It just outlines only the general list of parameters for ranking with the objective of overall global development, cross-culture development, communal harmony, enhancement of teaching, learning and research; eliminating poverty, protecting the environment bettering disaster management and technology transfer. Further work may be done in this area to apply these specific parameters/attributes in each type of universities to present a new global ranking.

CHAPTER 12

University Financing and Cost Estimation

12.1 INTRODUCTION

The higher education systems play a major role in the nation's economy. It is essential to analyze the finance and cost estimation of a University System. This chapter explains the details about the finance of the higher education across the world and cost estimation of a University System and a mathematical model for this unit cost estimation.

12.2 FINANCING THE UNIVERSITY/HIGHER EDUCATION

The funding of higher education is a highly complex topic. It is complex in part because of its multiple sources of revenue and its multiple outputs, or products, which are only loosely connected to these different revenue sources. Furthermore, these revenue and expenditure patterns vary significantly between different types of institutions (university, four-year college, two year college), mode of governance (public or private), and the state policies. Within the private sector, expenditure levels as well as patterns of pricing and price discounting vary greatly according to institutional wealth and the depth, demographics, and family affluence of the applicant pool. In the public sector, these patterns also vary according to state funding levels, tuition policies, and enrollment limits that are set by state governments or public multi-campus governing boards or state higher education councils.

The topic is vast because finance underlies much of the three overarching themes of contemporary higher education policy; *quality* and the relationship between funding and quality in any of its several dimensions; *access,* or the search for social equity in that who benefits from, and who pays for, higher education; and *efficiency,* or the search for a cost-effective relationship between revenues (particularly those that come from students, parents, and taxpayers) and outputs (whether measured in enrollments, graduates, student learning, or the scholarly activity of the faculty).

12.2.1 The Economic, Social and Political Context

Higher education is recognized both as an engine of economic growth and as a gatekeeper to individual positions of high remuneration and status. Advanced education particularly in high technology, information processing, and sophisticated management and analysis is thought to be essential to maintain the countries' economic position in the increasingly competitive global economy. It follows that most jobs of high remuneration and status will require an advanced degree, probably beyond the bachelor degree. It further follows that the lack of post secondary education creates a lively hand of marginal income and status.

These propositions, however, do not mean that advanced education necessarily makes individuals more productive or that all recipients of advanced education will find remunerative, high-status employment. Higher education can make individuals more productive; but it can also simply screen, or select, for the kinds of intellectual, social, and personal characteristics required for the high-remuneration, high-status jobs that may be available. In short, higher education is essential for most good jobs, and the absence of education beyond high school will be an increasingly formidable barrier to obtaining them; but the mere possession of an advanced degree will guarantee neither good, nor lasting employment.

But these economic, social, and political themes, for all their complexity, provide a context for consideration of the three broad issues of higher education finance: (1) The size of the publicly funded higher educational enterprise (including the publicly funded portion of the private sector): How much publicly supported higher education do we need or will we choose to afford, measured either in total expenditures or as a percentage of our gross domestic product? (2) The efficiency and productivity of this enterprise. What should higher education, particularly public higher education, cost per unit (whether the unit is students enrolled, degrees granted, scholarship produced, service rendered, or combinations thereof)? (3) The sources of revenue to support this enterprise. Who pays (or who should pay) for the costs of higher education as among government or taxpayers, parents, students or philanthropists?

12.2.2 The Efficiency and Productivity of the Enterprise

Another issue within the financing of higher education is the efficiency, or expected productivity, with which all of these resources are employed in the higher educational enterprise. Productivity and efficiency look at both costs, and expenditures, and at benefits, or outputs. These costs can be dealt with, on the following bases: per student (which, of course, is not really an output but which has the advantage of being easily and unambiguously measured), or per unit of research, or per unit of learning (however measured), or per learning added by the institution. Because the real outputs of the university (the discovery, transmission, and promulgation of knowledge) are both multiple and difficult to measure, and because revenue, at least for the support of instructional expenditures, generally tracks student enrollment in both the public and the private sectors, the cost per student inevitably and overwhelmingly dominates approaches to questions of productivity and efficiency. But we ought not to forget that enrollment, however measured—and however sensitive to fields of study, levels of education, or methods of instruction—is still merely a proxy for the hard-to-measure real output, which is student learning.

12.2.3 Variation in Unit Costs

In the production of goods, there are usually multiple ways of combining productive inputs mainly different combinations of labor, capital, materials and managerial effectiveness to produce a unit of output. The most efficient combination of inputs is determined by the alternative manufacturing technologies and the relative costs of the inputs.

Given a set of input costs and a set of technologies for combining inputs into desired outputs, there generally is an unambiguously *most efficient way*: that is, a lowest cost per unit. The efficiency, then, of any alternative producer or production process can be measured by comparing with the most efficient way.

Higher education is not as fortunate as these goods-producing enterprises. The technology of university production (of learning and scholarship) is unclear and highly idiosyncratic to the institution, the department, and the individual professor. We know that per student costs vary significantly. Higher education is generally assumed to be more expensive at research universities than at undergraduate colleges due to the higher salaries, lower teaching loads, and more extensive academic support (e.g., libraries and computer facilities) accorded to the faculty of the research university. However, the direct instructional costs (especially at the margin) at least of freshmen at a typical public research university can be rather low due to the prevalence of low-cost teaching assistants and very large lecture courses—in contrast to the typical public four-year college, where more instruction may be carried out by regular faculty in moderate-sized classes, albeit with heavier average teaching loads. In the end, it is probably appropriate to claim that per student costs even for undergraduates are higher at most research universities than at four-year colleges; but it must not be forgotten that this is so at least partly because of certain assumptions and cost allocations that, while reasonable, are nonetheless judgmental and sometimes questionable.

12.2.4 Sources of Revenue for the University

The financing of higher education poses the question of how the costs should be apportioned among four parties: parents, students, taxpayers, and philanthropists. Parents would finance their children's education from current income, savings, or future income via increased indebtedness (such as a home mortgage/equity loan). Students would finance their own education from savings, summer earnings, term-time earnings, and future earnings via loans. Students if employed, do cover a part of fees that are from their earnings. Taxpayers at the federal, state, and local levels would finance students' education through taxes on income, sales, property, assets, business or manufacturing taxes (via the higher prices of the goods or services so taxed) or through the indirect "tax" of inflation brought about by public deficit spending. Philanthropists would finance students' education through endowments.

The sharing and song these parties can be a zero-sum game, in which a lessening of the burden upon, or revenue from, one party must be compensated either by a reduction of underlying costs or by a shift of the burden to another party. Thus, if state taxpayers' share of higher education costs is to be lessened, that reduced share must either lead to reduced institutional costs or be shifted, probably to students and parents via higher tuition. But if parents cannot pay or have enough political power to limit, by statute or regulation, a higher parental contribution, the burden would shift to students, principally through higher debt loads. This scenario—lower taxpayer contributions, reduced institutional budgets, higher tuitions, level parental contributions, and much higher debt burdens—is exactly what has happened in the last decades of the 20th and first decade of the 21st centuries.

12.3 WORLDWIDE TRENDS IN FINANCING HIGHER EDUCATION

Six trends in the latter years of the 20th and early years of the 21st centuries—each with economic, political, and social roots and consequences—are noteworthy for their impacts on the financing of higher education and in turn of higher educational participation and accessibility. These trends, while varying both among countries and within each country, form the context for higher education's currently widespread financial austerity as well as for the emerging policy solutions which, while again varying both among and within countries, exhibit some very similar patterns. In summary, these trends are:

1. Increasing unit, or per-student, costs of instruction.
2. Increasing enrollments.
3. The increasingly knowledge-based economies and the consequent additional expectations upon higher education as a major engine of economic development and individual betterment.
4. The failure of governmental, or public, revenues to maintain their *share* of the cost increases resulting from the aforementioned pressures on higher educational expenditures.
5. Increasing globalization (which contributes both to the increasing cost trajectories and to the faltering governmental revenues).
6. Increasing liberalization of economies and the resulting decentralization, devolution, and privatization of public and private systems and institutions of higher education.

We will look first at each of these trends, after which we will examine the dominant consequence—which is an increasing higher educational austerity—and conclude with an examination of some current policy solutions.

12.3.1 Increasing Unit, or Per-Student, Costs of Instruction

The fundamental financial problem of higher education all over the world, and the reason that even wealthy institutions can feel the pinch of austerity, begins with the fact that universities face a *trajectory* of annual cost increases, the natural and quite appropriate rate of increase of which is the rate of increase of their wages and salaries, which in turn tends to track the rate of increase of wages and salaries in the general economy—or, if there is any real growth in the economy, at *inflation plus*. This is the so-called *cost disease*, or the phenomenon of the *rising relative unit costs* in the labor intensive, productivity immune (or at least productivity resistant), sectors of the economy—which include symphony orchestras, schools, and universities, and which phenomenon was first articulated by Baumol and Bowen (1966). Accelerating this natural rate of unit (or perstudent) cost increase are other factors peculiar to many universities that further accelerate annual cost increases in varying degrees in different countries, depending mostly on available revenues.

12.3.2 Increasing Enrollments

The second trend, affecting national systems more than individual universities, is increasing enrollments. These increases, which accelerate the financial impact of the aforementioned increases in per-student costs, are a function of three forces, which vary greatly among countries. The first of these is demographics: specifically the change (generally the growth) over time in the number of youth within the conventional college or university age cohort (ages 18 through about 24). Some countries such as Italy, Germany, and other countries in Southern Europe, Russia, and Japan are experiencing demographic declines. Most countries, however—and nearly all low income countries, are experiencing increases in the traditional university age cohort (UNESCO-UIS/OECD 2005).

The second force affecting enrollments is the participation rate of this (generally increasing) university age cohort (UNESCO Institute for Statistics 2006). Increasing participation, in turn, is a function of: (a) increases in enrollments at secondary levels; (b) changing employment opportunities and a perception of increasing competition for these fewer "good" jobs which will be enhanced by higher education; and (c) an increasing regard for social and economic mobility and justice, leading to policies designed to increase higher educational participation, particularly among those traditionally less represented, such as ethnic and linguistic minorities, girls (in some cultures), or students from poor secondary schools or otherwise thought to be educationally disadvantaged.

A final factor affecting enrollments in some countries is the increasing amount, or final level, of higher education per entering student. This, too, is an *accelerating* factor as first degree graduates perceive a need for even higher levels of education to be competitive (e.g. the growth of MBAs and other professional master's degrees) and as professions (especially licensed professions such as teachers, and the non-physician health professions) endeavor to raise their stature and limit the numbers allowed to practice (thus limiting competition and enhancing status and remuneration).

The impact of increasing enrollments on the financing of higher education, at least in the first instance, is to increase the cost and thus to increase yearly the public resources required to maintain the quality of the educational product—the likely shortfalls of which are be the focus of much of this monograph. At the same time, increasing enrollments also makes more possible the kinds of management actions—for example, raising student-to-faculty ratios or implementing new and more cost-effective pedagogies—that are extremely difficult in a mode of stable or declining enrollments, where efficiency measures almost inevitably mean terminating jobs and incurring the extraordinary levels of resistance and demoralization that attend any downsizing of an institution.

12.3.3 The Increasingly Knowledge-Based Economy

The third factor affecting the financing of higher education in virtually all countries is the increasing share of world production, especially in the already industrialized countries, that is moving either into services or into the so-called knowledge-based economy of high tech, design, finance, management and the like (and even in manufacturing, moving into modes that are less labor- and more capital-intensive). The result is to increase the value, both to countries and to individuals, of at least some forms of higher education: especially management, finance, law, and the so-called STEM fields of science, mathematics, engineering, and technology (World Bank 2002). The financial impact of this increasingly knowledge-based economy on higher education is manifested by the new (and usually more expensive) educational programs offered and by a redistribution of faculty and students among these new programs (both effects tending to further accelerate the increase in per-student costs) and also by the increased premium to individuals who have the requisite higher education as well as to countries with higher education systems that are high in quality, oriented to needs of employers, and broadly inclusive.

This trend forms a third source for the increasing revenue needs of higher education every where and for the even greater austerity when these revenue needs are not forthcoming. At the same time, it also lays the groundwork for the possibility of increased higher educational investments both from governments (where such increases are possible and politically feasible) as well as from students or parents (also where such contributions are politically feasible and technically possible—as with student loan opportunities).

12.3.4 Faltering Governmental (Tax) Revenues

Governments everywhere struggle increasingly under escalating burdens of pensions and the rising costs of elementary and secondary education, health care, public infrastructure, security, and other social welfare costs. Electorates in many highly industrialized countries have been getting more conservative, particularly in their distaste for taxation and what they perceive to be wasteful government spending. Many European countries, with their high social welfare costs, and typically spending from one-third to more than one-half of national gross domestic products in the public sector, are trying to shift productive resources to the private sector and to reduce public deficits to comply with the requirements of the European Community and the Euro Zone. Russia, the rest of the countries that have emerged from the former Soviet Union, and the former Communist countries of Central and Eastern Europe all labor under the enormous costs of building an internationally-competitive productive infrastructure and weaning a labor force away from its deeply rooted dependence on state enterprises and governmental employment.

The United States struggles with an over-consuming, under-saving population that is unwilling to tax itself for the public benefits it demands. Taxation in the developing countries, where production and incomes often tend to be low anyway, is technically difficult. The financial challenge to governments is how to get a share of purchasing power when relatively little wealth comes from large, stable enterprises that can be taxed and that can also be counted upon to withhold taxes from their employees. Former Communist countries, once dependent on easy and extensive turnover taxes on state-owned enterprises, now need to tax personal or corporate incomes, retail or commercial transactions, and/or property—all of which are difficult to calculate, expensive to collect, and relatively easy to evade. Businesses and individuals in many countries seem increasingly able to hide incomes and the value of their taxable assets. And even in the wealthy highly industrialized countries with efficient tax systems, the increasing globalization of the world economy (see below) encourages productive enterprises and wealthy individuals to flee to countries with lower taxes.

Finally, governments everywhere are contending with politically and socially compelling competing needs for these increasingly scarce tax revenues. In much of the developing world and in many transitional countries, the competitors for public revenue include the replacement of decrepit public infrastructure, unfunded pension obligations, the need in most countries for a workable social safety net, and the cost of reversing generations of environmental degradation. In Sub-Saharan Africa, the competition for the extremely scarce public dollar is truly formidable and includes, in addition to the needs listed above, public health, the old scourge of malaria and new pandemic of HIV-AIDS, elementary secondary education, and assistance to a badly faltering economy. Finally, although the government (or taxpayer) in most developing countries as throughout the world will continue to be the principal revenue source for public higher education, most or even all of whatever limited additional revenue can be squeezed out of the public treasuries for higher education will be absorbed by the need to accommodate the inevitably expanding enrollments, leaving little or nothing to accommodate what ought to be the rising unit, or per-student, costs (much less allowing investment in new programs and pedagogies or in academic research).

12.3.5 Increasing Globalization

Globalization is not well-defined and is almost certainly an overused term in the discourse of higher education and of the economic, political, and social trends that form the backdrop for this review of worldwide trends in the financing of higher education. For the purpose of this chapter, however, globalization refers to the increasing *internationalization* (which implies a diminishing significance of national borders and even of nation states themselves) of: (a) *information and knowledge*, which is greatly facilitated by telecommunications that can send billions of digitized bits of information per second by optical fiber or microwave for fractions of pennies per mile; (b) *capital*, or the flows of claims on wealth between savers and borrowers (or investors), including students; and (c) *production*, which is increasingly sophisticated, technical, and capitalrich and which is therefore increasingly mobile and predisposed to locating where politics are stable, labor costs are low, contracts are enforceable, and tax and regulatory climates are benign. Thus in the globalized economy, wealth and power increasingly flow less from the location of natural resources (with the exception of oil and gas) and the production of goods, and more from the ownership of capital and knowledge, protected by enforceable contracts, patents, copyrights, and licensing agreements. Globalization further brings a *thinning* of the significance of that which is (or was) national and local, whether it be language, culture, traditions, or norms, and a correspondingly hegemonic flow of language and culture from the highly industrialized and technologically sophisticated countries represented by the members of the OECD (especially the United States and the other English-speaking members).

The impact of globalization on higher education finance is to further raise the stakes to both nations and individuals of having or obtaining high levels of knowledge and skills- and thus to increased levels of quality higher education. Globalization also applies directly to higher education in the increased ability of universities and other suppliers of knowledge to transmit this knowledge across borders electronically and without much, if any, control or even regulation by local or nation state governments. Finally, globalization has a profound impact on the financing of all publicly financed agencies, including universities (both public and private), in its limiting effect on the ability of governments to tax and thus to keep up with higher education's voracious and continuous revenue needs (and so underscoring the imperative of increasing nongovernmental revenues).

12.3.6 Increasing Liberalization of Economies

A final trend or set of related trends in most countries (most wrenchingly in the former Communist countries) is a movement in the direction of increasing liberalization of economies. This trend conveys a greater reliance on (or acceptance of) market forces and a commensurately lesser dependence on government to allocate resources, set prices, determine production technologies, and compensate individuals for their contributions to output. Along with this increasing liberalization comes increased decentralization, devolution, and privatization of the productive economy—including institutions such as public universities that may remain publicly owned and ultimately publicly controlled, but that are increasingly *privatized* in their reliance on non-governmental revenues, responsiveness to market forces, and incorporation of managerial norm associated with private enterprise. Although large public sectors, generous economic safety nets, and redistributive taxes remain in many countries (e.g. the Nordic countries), and public ownership and heavy regulation of factories and financial institutions remain in most formerly communist countries (e.g. Russia and China), the governmental ownership of all means of production and the *dirigisme* of governmental bureaucracies in most countries are giving way to governmental *steering* and to the policies and procedures associated with the *New Public Management* (Barzeley 2001 and Almaral 2003).

Two complementary effects of this liberalization on higher education are, first, the encouragement of private higher education (both for-profit and not-for-profit) and second and equally important, the *privatization* of *public* higher education. Regardless of the legal *publicness* or *privateness* of their ownership or the seeming *publicness* or *privateness* of their missions or their degree of dependence on public revenue, universities around the world, including both public and private institutions, are moving (or being forced to move) from a status very much like all other state agencies—that is, with clear governmental ownership, substantial governmental or ministerial control, and governmental or civil service employment of faculty and staff—toward the status of *public corporations*, empowered to raise and keep supplemental revenue, employ and compensate staff, make contracts, incur debt, and sue and be sued in courts of law.

12.3.7 Higher Educational Finance and Accessibility

The costs of higher education, including the per-student costs of instruction, the institutionally-borne costs of research (that is, research costs that are not externally supported), the capital and operating costs of accommodating increased enrollments, and the expenses of student maintenance, are increasing rapidly and continuously throughout the world—in most countries are greatly exceeding the possible increases in governmental, or tax-generated, revenues. The resulting divergence in the trajectories of total higher educational costs (or revenue needs) and the total available public revenues is leading in most countries toward increasing higher educational austerity. This austerity is especially acute in developing countries that face the most financially devastating combination of: (a) pressures to accommodate the greatly increasing demand for additional higher educational places; (b) very limited availability of public revenues; and (c) extreme competition for these limited available public revenues. This financial austerity is being met with a variety of so-called *solutions.* The most obvious solution on the cost-side is to constrain the budgets of the existing universities and to constrain also the student numbers, primarily by academic entrance requirements that hold capacity to the number that the scarce governmental funds can (barely) accommodate. Of course, this kind of rationing, while clearly superior to rationing purely by the market or by the ability of parents to bribe their children into universities, still favors those aspiring secondary school graduates who have had the advantages of the best preparation and who are, unsurprisingly, disproportionately from the most advantaged classes. Although the principal barriers to increasing higher educational accessibility in the poorest countries will continue to lie at the middle and secondary levels of education, and while the combination of living expenses and fees can also constitute barriers to higher educational entry, the biggest single barrier to access in low income countries is this public university capacity constraint, the solution to which requires new revenue from somewhere to build the lecture theatres, laboratory space, and dormitory rooms able to accommodate the rising numbers of higher educational aspirants from low income, rural, and ethnically- and linguistically-minority families.

This cost-revenue squeeze is also leading to attempts at revenue-side solutions, the most financially promising of which are the various forms of *cost-sharing,* or measures that require parents and/or students to bear an increasing share of these higher educational expenses. But imposing or increasing tuition and other fees, although a proven source of additional revenue best exemplified, by the financial success of the dual track tuition fee policies of Uganda, Kenya, and other East African countries, also imposes barriers on both access and completion. As in the United States and elsewhere in the OECD countries, these financial barriers are increasingly being met most cost-effectively with a combination of moderate tuition and other fees, targeted, or means-tested, grants, and student loans, the additional public costs of which, at least in theory, can be met with the additional fee revenue from the parents and students who can and will assume some of the costs of their higher education.

The *higher educational finance-access linkage,* therefore, is essentially circular: rising costs lead to capacity constraints, which limit higher education either to those academically prepared enough to be accepted into the low tuition public universities or to the sons and daughters of families with sufficient resources to get into the much higher fee private alternatives or into the high tuition fee tracks in the public universities. The shortage of revenue is forcing higher fees at private and public colleges and universities throughout the world—which then demands technically difficult and sometimes costly policies and programs of means-testing and student loans.

These very broad brushstrokes of conceptual overview lead to several conclusions regarding the higher educational finance-access linkage:

1. Raising higher educational participation and access in the poorest countries needs to begin at the level of basic education by increasing the numbers of low income and other traditionally underrepresented students through a quality academic secondary education.
2. The necessary rationing of higher educational places at the low-cost public higher educational alternatives must be sensitive to the social class, regional, and ethnic/linguistic differences in middle and secondary school preparation and should resist excessive reliance on those forms of screens that simply select for socioeconomic class or for the level and cost of the secondary school preparation.
3. In most countries, where distances and the absence of accessible public transportation are such that attending a college or university while commuting from home is not possible, financially accessible (preferably means-tested) lodging and food must be made available. (This does not mean that it must be provided by the government or the public institution of higher education itself.)
4. A combination of moderate tuition fees, means-tested grants, and moderately subsidized student loans is necessary for the cost-effective use of public higher educational revenue in the policy pursuit of expanding accessibility.
5. In most countries, revenue supplementation, especially including tuition fees and other forms of cost-sharing, while necessary, should not be used to substitute for public revenues, but to supplement them. Student should be able to perceive benefits to them of any newly imposed tuition or other fees.
6. Private alternatives should be encouraged; but governments should not restrict public attention and public resources to only the elite public universities and assume that the inevitable enrollment expansion can be handled only by a perpetually expanding private higher educational sector.
7. A mix of higher or postsecondary educational alternatives (e.g. research Universities, polytechnics, and other short cycle institutions) should be offered, with attention to the assurance of quality facilities, appropriate programs and curricula, and competent faculty at the non-university alternatives.
8. Cost-sharing is usually politically contested when first implemented, but will be more acceptable when: (a) financial assistance is in place and has been made understandable, (b) the university management is perceived to be doing (or to have

done) its share of difficult economizing, and (c) the government that is imposing the cost-sharing is perceived as generally efficient and free from corruption.

In these and other ways, governmental policies can pursue affordable, quality higher education for the inevitably growing numbers of traditional and non-traditional age students.

12.4 UNIVERSITY COST ESTIMATION

In considering the importance of higher education, there is a growing sentiment worldwide that higher education institutions must reduce their cost. The literature on higher education in the last two decades documents an increasing global trend to shift part of the financing burden for higher education from the public to the private sector. Many countries have adopted a policy of reduced direct public spending for higher education. The rationale for such a move is principally economic. It is essential to compute the unit of cost programs. In order that these studies are more useful, it is necessary that these be conducted on a uniform pattern based on agreed concepts and definitions.

Actually, the problem of unit costs and efficiency (or inefficiency) in higher education is less a function of unit costs, per se, and more a function of the seemingly inexorable increase of such costs and of the resulting tuition increases at rates considerably in excess of the rate of inflation. This is the cost disease described as characteristic of the so-called productivity-immune sectors of the economy, which are generally labor-intensive, with few opportunities for substitution of capital or new production technologies for labor. Because workers in such enterprises typically get the same wage and salary increases as those in the productivity-sensitive, goods-producing sectors of the economy, in which constant infusions of capital and technology produce real productivity gains and allow unit cost increases to be less than compensation increases, the unit costs in productivity-immune sectors will inevitably exceed those in goods-producing sectors. Thus, unit-cost increases in higher education will be "above average." And since the rate of inflation is nothing more than a weighted average of many price increases, it is inevitable that unit costs—and thus tuitions—in higher education will rise in normal years faster than the rate of inflation.

This, then, is the normal, or default, condition in higher education: unit costs that increase slightly in excess of the prevailing rate of inflation. Tuitions, however, tend to increase at even higher rates, substantially exceeding the prevailing rates of inflation, resulting from the following practices:

1. State governments that continue year after year to shift the cost burden from taxpayers to students and families through very high percentage tuition increases in the public sector.

2. Private colleges that year after year have to put more of their marginal tuition dollars back into student aid, thus requiring even larger tuition increases to keep up with rising costs.
3. Faculty compensation increases-many institutions exceed compensation increases prevailing in the economy generally.
4. Higher education that becomes more and more "input rich" in the form, say, of more technology per student, higher faculty and staff to student ratios, or more costly physical plant per student.

All of these factors have been at work for most of the past several decades, resulting in very substantial tuition increases in both the private and the public sectors.

12.5 MODEL FOR UNIT COST ESTIMATION

The university's three main functions are instruction, research, and extension. Consequently, all costs of the university can be classified under any of these three groupings. Activities that contribute to the completion of a student's program of study are considered as related to instruction. Thus, the cost of research laboratories that a student uses to complete a project that is required by his/her program is part of cost of instruction. The compensation of personnel who reproduce classroom materials, handle the students' academic records, maintain the classrooms and laboratories, and undertake similar activities is also considered part of the cost of instruction. If a resource is used for two or more functions, an allocation procedure is undertaken to distribute the cost of the resource.

In this study and as defined in management accounting textbooks, direct costs are costs that can be traced in a feasible manner to an identified cost object. All other costs related to the cost object but cannot be traced feasibly to it are considered indirect. Thus, if one can determine the amount of resources consumed for a cost object in a feasible manner, then this cost is direct with respect to the said cost object.

The classification of costs as direct or indirect is a dynamic process. If information collection and processing costs decline, or if the benefits of more accurate cost estimates are large enough, then a cost may be reclassified as direct because now the effort to trace the cost object's consumption of that particular resource has become worth it.

The cost object of specific interest in this study is instruction at each academic unit. The University's accounting and budgeting system accumulates the costs of each academic unit. Since the University also collects faculty load data that can be used to allocate an academic unit's costs among the three functions, then the costs of an academic unit can be argued to be traceable in a feasible manner to each of the three functions, including instruction. Once a cost of instruction for each academic unit is determined, it is a simple matter, again using the methodology proposed by Tan (2003), to calculate the direct costs of a degree program.

Thus, all costs presently reported by the university's accounting and budgeting system as incurred by an academic unit are direct costs of instruction, research or extension. These direct costs are personnel services (faculty, administrative and research staff), MOOE (Maintenance and Other Operating Expenses Attributable to Graduate Instruction), and laboratory and library expenditures. The share of undergraduate instruction in these costs is determined using the ratio of undergraduate instruction to the total load (i.e., instruction + research + extension) of the faculty.

Direct costs also include the cost of facilities used for undergraduate instruction. Facilities are fixed assets such as libraries, computer and research laboratories that a university needs to make available to students as these are used by the latter to comply with and complete certain requirements of their programs of study. As these facilities have useful lives beyond one year, an allocation procedure will be undertaken in order to determine the facilities' annual cost.

Representation of Conceptual Framework

Total Cost of Instruction	*Indirect*	*Direct*
University System Cost	Administrative Costs	–
Campus Cost	Costs of Student Services (e.g., Sports, Medical, Admission, Registration) + Costs of Campus-Level Research and Extension Activities + Campus Administration Costs	
Academic Unit Cost	Costs of Unit-Level Research and Extension Activities	Costs of Instruction Personnel Services + MOOE + Annualized Cost of Facilities Laboratory and Library
	Total Annual Indirect Cost of Instruction	**Total Annual Direct Cost of Instruction/Total SCU per Year**

The Estimation Model and Procedures

The estimation model is as follows:

$$DC(I)_{i,t} = \frac{PS(I)_{i,t} + MOOE(I)_{i,t} + AFC_{i,t} + LLE(I)_{i,t}}{TSCU_{i,t}}$$

Where: i = Academic Unit i in an Autonomous Campus

t = Year

and

DC (I) = Direct Cost of Graduate Instruction

PS (I) = Cost of Personnel Services Attributable to Graduate Instruction
= Annual Personnel Services Cost × Ratio of Graduate Instruction to Total Faculty Load, Excluding Administration

MOOE (I) = Maintenance and Other Operating Expenses Attributable to Graduate Instruction
= MOOE × ratio of Graduate Instruction Load to Total Faculty Load, Excluding Administration

AFC = Annualized Cost of Facilities used for Graduate Instruction

LLE (I) = Laboratory and Library Expenses Attributable to Graduate Instruction
= Laboratory and Library Expenses × Ratio of Graduate Instruction Load to Total

Instruction Load

TSCU = Total Student Credit Units of the Academic Unit for the Year

$$= \sum_{a=1}^{n} x_a u_a$$

x = Number of Students Enrolled in Class
u = Number of Credit Units of Class a
n = Number of Classes Offered by the Campus.

In Tan Formula for the Estimation of Cost of Degree Program at University

$$\text{Program Cost}_i = \sum_{c=1}^{C} p_c(CSC_{i,c}) + n(AOS_I) + n(AOCU_{I,c})$$

Where i = Program i in CU
c = College/Unit where a prescribed course originates
p = Number of credits required from college c
n = Number of Years of Complete Program i.

The variables in the formula are measured as follows:

CSC = Cost per Student Credit
= Total Cost of Instruction (TCI) divided by Total Student Credits (TSC)

TCI = Total Cost of Instruction = DCI + IDC

DCI = Direct Cost of Instruction = Expenditures for Faculty Personnel Services (FPS) × Faculty Load for Instruction/Total Faculty Load or (FLI/FLT) + Maintenance, Operating and Other Expenses (MOOE) for Library and Laboratory × Ratio of FLI/(FLI+FLRE). Recall research extension (RE) are taken to be separate outputs of the University.

IDC = Indirect Cost of Instruction is all other costs of the college or its budget minus DCI and minus the cost of research and extension (RE). The Share of

RE in FPS is RE share in faculty load multiplied by FPS and the share of RE in MOOE = FLRE (FLI + FLRE) × MORE for library and laboratory.

TSC = The Weighted sum of Student Credits of all Courses Offered by a College. It is the Divisor DC and IDC or TCI. Student credits for a course are the number of Academic Credits Assigned to it multiplied by the number of Students enrolled in it. Graduate courses are assigned 1.5 the weight of Graduate Courses.

$AOCU_{I,c}$ = Administrative and other overhead cost of Constituent University (CU). This is directly obtained from the internal operating budget of each CU. The budget document gives the budget for the chancellor's office, medical services and other support services, advanced higher education, research and extension and others. AOCU is simply the CU administrative and the two support services' budgets of the University. $AOCU_I$ is divided by the weighted enrollment of the CU with .75, 1.0 and 1.5 weights given respectively for basic education.

AOS_I = Share of Instruction per Student of the AOS_I is the product of the share of instruction in the budget for programs multiplied by the budget of the Office of the Chancellor. AOS_I is divided by the total enrollment of the UP System weighted as above.

Estimate of Replacement Cost of Buildings and Classrooms Used in Graduate Instruction in University

S. No.	*Title*	*Cost*
1.	Construction cost of a classroom	X
2.	Construction cost of toilets, common area and administrative offices (Relative to one Classroom)	Y
3.	Cost of furniture and fixures (e.g., Chairs, Whiteboard)	Z
4.	Total cost	T = X+Y+Z
5.	Divided by useful life in years	N
6.	Annualized cost	T/N
7.	Divided by number of classes to be held in the classroom per year	A
8.	Annualized cost per class subject (Say for Example B)	C = A * B
9.	Divided by number of units per class	5
10.	Annualized cost per unit	C/5

12.6 PARENT STUDENT TOTAL COST ESTIMATION AMONG NATIONS

The higher education cost sharing is a very important factor to be understood by all stake holders. This cost sharing differs from Public to Private Universities in different countries. This section gives the comparative details about education cost sharing in

India, China, Australia, USA, Canada, France, Russia and Japan. This is shown in the following tables.

12.6.1 Estimated Expenses of Higher Education in India

India Higher Education Expenses Borne by Parents and Students
First Degree, Academic Year 2001–2002

[National currency (Rupees) converted to $US by [2001]
purchasing power parity estimate $1 =India rupees 46.948]

		Public				***Private College (aided)***
		Central University[6]	***State University***[7]	***University College***	***Gov't College***	
	Special "One-Time" or "Up Front" Fees	141 $3	799 $17	564 $12	799 $17	789 $17
Instructional Expenses	Tuition	940 $20	3995 $85	1739 $37	1739 $37	1739 $37
	Other Fees	423 $9	2350 $50	3196 $68	2350 $50	2350 $50
	Books and Other Educational Expenses[8]	3431 $73	2068 $44	1786 $38	893 $19	2397 $51
	Subtotal Expenses of Instruction	4935 $105	9212 $196	7285 $155	5781 $123	7285 $155
Student Living Expenses	Lodging	1739 $37	7990 $170	7802 $166	376 $8	11985 $255
	Food	25944 $552	23923 $509	25994 $552	29939 $637	47893 $1019
	Transportation	5452 $116	4230 $90	1974 $42	1692 $36	1833 $39
	Other Personal Expenses[10]	1175 $25	846 $18	658 $14	282 $6	893 $19
	Subtotal Expenses of Student Living	34310 $730	36989 $787	36378 $775	32289 $687	62604 $1332
	Total Cost to Parent and Student	39201 $835	46201 $983	43663 $929	38070 $810	69889 $1487

12.6.2 Estimated Expenses of Higher Education in China

Higher Education Expenses Borne by Parents and Students First Degree, Academic Year 2009
[National currency RMB Yuan (¥) converted to $US by 2009 Purchasing Power Parity $1 = ¥3.45]

		Public			*Private*	
		Low Public	*Moderate Public*	*High Public*	*Low Private*	*High Private*
Instructional Expenses	Tuition	¥2,500 $724	¥5,000 $1,449	¥10,000 $2,899	¥5,000 $1,449	¥10,000 $2,899
	Books and Other Educational Expenses	¥250 $72	¥500 $145	¥1,000 $290	¥500 $145	¥1,500 $435
	Subtotal Costs of Instruction	¥2,750 $797	¥5,500 $1,594	¥11,000 $3,188	¥5,500 $1,594	¥11,500 $3,333
Student Living Expenses	Lodging	¥500 $145	¥800 $232	¥1,200 $348	¥500 $145	¥1,200 $348
	Food	¥3,500 $1,014	¥6,000 $1,739	¥6,000 $1,739	¥3,500 $1,014	¥6,000 $1,739
	Transportation	¥300 $87	¥600 $174	¥1,000 $290	¥300 $87	¥1,000 $290
	Other Personal Expenses	¥1,000 $290	¥1,500 $435	¥2,000 $580	¥1,000 $290	¥2,000 $580
	Subtotal Cost of Student Living	¥5,300 $1,536	¥8,900 $2,580	¥10,200 $2,958	¥5,300 $1,536	¥10,200 $2,957
	Total	¥ 8,050 **$2,333**	¥14,400 **$4,174**	¥21,200 **$6,145**	¥10,800 **$3,130**	¥21,700 **$6,290**

12.6.3 Estimated Expenses of Higher Education in Australia

Australia Higher Education Expenses Borne by Parents and Students
First Degree, Academic Year 2006–07 (9 months 3)
[National currency (Australian dollar) converted to $US by 2005 purchasing power parity estimate $1 -= A$1.38]

		Public			*Private*
		Low Public	*High Public*	*Fee Paying*	
Instructional Expenses	Special "one-time" or "up-front" fees	N/A	N/A	N/A	N/A
	Tuition	A$4,204 US$3,550	$7,035 US$5,940	$18,000 US$13,000	$34,000 US$24,640
	Other Fees	A$600 US$435	A$600 US$435	A$600 US$435	A$88 US$65

		Public			*Private*
		Low Public	*High Public*	*Fee Paying*	
	Books and Other Expenses	A$220 US$160	$660 US$480	A$500 US$362	A$900 US$652
	Subtotal Expenses of Instruction	A$5,720 US$4,145	A$9,460 US$6,855	A$19,100 US$13,840	A$34,990 US$25,355
Student Living Expenses	Lodging	A$0	A$5,000 US$3,623	A$8,600 US$6,230	A$6,000 US$4,350
	Food	A$1,800 US1,300	A$4,000 US$2,900	A$4,000 US$2,900	A$8,500 US$6,160
	Transportation	A$900 US$650	A$1,500 US$1,090	A$1,500 US$1,090	A$1,500 US$1,090
	Other Personal Expenses	A$1,200 US$870	A$3,000 US$2,175	A$3,000 US$2,175	A$2,700 US$1,960
	Subtotal Expenses of Student Living	A$3900 US$2,825	A$13,500 US$9,780	A$17,100 US$12,390	A$18,700 US$13,551
	Total Cost to Parent and	A$9,620 US$6970	A$22,960 US$16,638	A$36,200 US$26,230	A$53,690 US$38,900

12.6.4 Estimated Expenses of Higher Education in US

Higher Education Expenses Borne by Parents and Students in the United States Academic Year 2009–10

		Public Universities		*Private Universities*	
		Low	*High*	*Low*	*High*
Instructional Expenses	Special "one-time" or "up-front" fees	$40	$40	$75	$75
	Tuition	$7,000	$15,000	$26,000	$38,045
	Other Fees	$2,000	$2,000	$1,000	$1,000
	Books and Other Expenses	$1,000	$1,000	$900	$1,200
	Subtotal Expenses of Instruction	$10,040	$18,040	$27,975	$40,320
Student Living	Lodging	0	$6,000	$6,000	$9,000
	Food	$1,100	$4,100	$3,120	$3,920
	Transportation	$1,300	$800	$800	
	Other Personal Expenses	$1,200	$1,200	$1,200	$1,600
	Subtotal Expenses of Student Living	$3,600	$12,100	$11,120	$14,520
	Total Cost to Parent and	$13,640	$30,140	$39,095	$54,840

12.6.5 Estimated Expenses of Higher Education in Canada

Higher Education Expenses Borne by Parents and Students, Canadian Colleges and Universities First Degree, [Academic] Year 2009–10
(National currency (CA Dollar) converted to $US by 2005 PPP estimate $1 = CA$1.20)

		Public Universities		*Private Universities*	
		Low Public (Degree Granting College)	***High Public (University)***	***Low Private***	***High Private***
Instructional Expenses	Special "one-time" or "up-front" fees	0	0	0	0
	Tuition	CA$4,300 (US$3,554)	CA$9,350 (US$7,727)	CA$6,000 (US$4,959)	CA$17,460 (US$14,430)
	Other Fees	CA$800 (US$661)	CA$1,190 (US$983)	CA$600 (US$496)	CA$600 (US$496)
	Books and Other Expenses	CA$1,200 (US$992)	CA$1,200 (US$992)	CA$1,200 (US$992)	CA$1,200 (US992)
	Subtotal Expenses of Instruction	CA$6,300 (US$5,207)	CA$11,740 (US$9.702)	CA$7,800 (US$6,446)	CA$19,260 (US$15,917)
Student Living	Lodging	CA$0 (US$)	CA$6,560 (US$5,421)	CA$8,000 (US$6,612)	CA$8,000 (US$6,612)
	Food	CA$1,000 (US$826)	CA$4,090 ($3,380)		
	Transportation	CA$900 (US$744)	CA$1,000 (US$826)	CA$1,100 (US$909)	CA$1,100 (US$909)
	Other Personal Expenses	CA$1,800 (US$1,488)	CA$2,000 (US$1,653)	CA$1,800 (US$1,487)	CA$2,000 (US$1,653)
	Subtotal Expenses of Student Living	CA$3,700 (US$3,057)	CA$13,650 (US11,280)	CA$10,900 (US$9,008)	CA$11,100 (US$9,174)
	Total Cost to Parent and	CA$10,000 (US$8,264)	CA$25,390 (US$20,983)	CA$18,700 (US$15,455)	CA$20,360 (US$25,091)

12.6.6 Estimated Expenses of Higher Education in France

Higher Education Expenses Borne by Parents and Students

First Degree, Academic Year 2006–07 (9 months) [National currency, Euros, converted to $US by 2005 International Comparison Program PPP of $1 = Euro 0.9225]

		Public Universities			*Private Universities*	
		Low Public	*Medium Public*	*High Public*	*Private*	*High Private*
Instructional Expenses	Fees	150 [US$138]	270 [US$249]	0	0	0
	Tuition	0	0	5,300 [US$4,889]	4,500 [$4,151]	7,500 [$6,919]
	Other Fees	50 [$46]	350 [$323]	350 [$323]	350 [$323]	350 [$323]
	Health Insurance	350 [$323]	450 [$415]	450 [$415]	450 [$415]	450 [$415]
	Books and Other Educ Expenses	450 [$415]	450 [$415]	450 [$415]	450 [$415]	450 [$415]
	Subtotal Expenses of Instruction	1,000 [$923]	1,120 [$1,033]	6,150 [$5,673]	5,350 [$4,935]	8,350 [$7,703]
Student Living Expenses	Lodging	0	2,660 [$2,454]	3,000 [$2,768]	3,500 [$3,229]	4,200 [$3,875]
	Food	900 [$830]	1,800 [$1,661]	1,800 [$1,661]	1,800 [$1,661]	2,000 [$1,845]
	Local Transportation	405 [$374]	780 [$720]	780 [$720]	780 [$720]	1000 [$923]
	Other Personal Expenses	1,800 [$1,661]	1,800 [$1,661]	2,000 [$1,845]	1,800 [$1,661]	2,000 [$1,845]
	Subtotal Expenses of Student Living	3,105 [$2,864]	7,040 [$6,494]	7,580 [$6,992]	7,880 [$7,269]	9,200 [$8,487]
	Total Cost to Parent and Student	4,105 [$3,787]	8,160 [$7,528]	13,730 [$12,665]	13,230 [$12,205]	17,500 [$16,190]

12.6.7 Estimated Expenses of Higher Education in England and Northern Ireland

Expenses Borne by Parents and Students First Degree, Academic Year 2007–08
[National currency (English Pound) converted to $US by 2007 purchasing power parity estimate $1 = £ 0.656**]

		Public (outside London)	*Public (London)*	*Northern Ireland*
Instructional Expenses	Tuition	£2,900 US$4,420	£2,900 US$4,420	£2,900 US$4,420
	Other Fees	N/A	N/A	N/A
	Books and Other Ed. Expenses	£320 US$490	£320 US$490	£447 US$680
	Subtotal Costs of Instruction	£3,220 US$4,910	£3,220 US$4,910	£3,350 US$5,100
Student Living Expenses	Lodging	£3,500 US$5,335	£4,000 US$6,100	£2,500 US$3,810
	Food	£800 US$1,220	£1,460 US$2,225	£1,400 US$2,135
	Transportation	£320 US$490	£400 US$610	£400 US$610
	Other Personal Expenses	£1,500 US$2,285	£1,500 US$2,285	£2,500 US $3,810
	Subtotal Cost of Student Living	£6,120 US$9,330	£7,360 US$11,220	£6,800 US $10,365
	Total Cost to Parent and Student	£9,340 US$14,240	£10,580 US$16,130	£10,150 US$15,480

12.6.8 Estimated Expenses of Higher Education in the Russian Federation

Higher Education Expenses Borne by Parents and Students First Degree, Academic Year 2009–10

Ruble (RUB) converted to $US based on World Bank ICP 2005 PPP of $1 = 12.74 rubles

		Public			*Private*	
		State-supported	*Low Fee-paying*	*High Fee-paying*	*Low Private*	*High Private*
Instructional Expenses	Application Fee and One-Time Fees	RUB1,443 US$113	RUB1,500 US$118	RUB14,330 US$1125	–	–
	Tuition	0	RUB30,000 US$2355	RUB300,000 US$23548	RUB 26,000 US$2041	RUB 36,600 US$2873
	Other Fees	0	RUB 144 US$11	RUB 1,000 US$78	RUB 1,445 US$113	RUB2,880 US$226
	Books and Other Expenses	0	RUB 570 US$45	RUB 1,445 US$113	RUB 1,445 US$113	RUB5,700 US$447
	Subtotal Instruction	RUB1,443 US$113	RUB32214 US$2,529	RUB316775 US$24,865	RUB 28890 US$2,268	RUB 45 US$3,546
Student Living Expenses	Lodging	0 0	RUB 432 US$392	5,000 RUB US$3454	44,000 RUB US$34	RUB34,560 US$ 2,713
	Food	RUB5800 US$455	RUB10,000 US$785	RUB 17,280 US$1356	RUB 5800 US$455	RUB 17280 US$1356
	Transportation	RUB 432 US$34	RUB 864 US$68	RUB8,655 US$679	RUB 864 US$68	RUB 8,655 US$679
	Other Personal Expenses	RUB 5,184 US$407	RUB 10,370 US$814	RUB10,370 US$814	RUB10,370 US$814	RUB 10,370 US$814
	Subtotal Student Living	RUB11,416 US$896	RUB26,234 US$2,059	RUB 80,305 US$ 6,303	RUB17,466 US$ 1,371	RUB70,865 US$5,562
	Total Cost to Parent and Student	RUB12,859 US$ 1,009	RUB58,448 US$ 4,588	RUB397,080 US$ 31,168	RUB 46,356 US$ 3,639	RUB116,045 US$ 9,109

12.6.9 Estimated Expenses of Higher Education in Japan

Higher Education Expenses Borne by Parents and Students
Undergraduate, Academic Year 2002–2003
National Currency (Japanese Yen) converted to $US by 2003
purchasing power parity estimate $1=JY139

		National	*Public*	*Private*
Instructional Expenses	Tuition	JY468,400 ($3,370)	JY474,100 ($3,411)	JY886,600 ($6,378)
	Books and Other Educational Expenses	JY108,300 ($779)	JY100,200 ($721)	JY352,900 ($2,539)
	Subtotal Expenses of Instruction	JY576,700 ($4,149)	JY574,300 ($4,132)	JY1,239,500 ($8,917)
Student Living Expenses	Transportation	JY50,300 ($362)	JY63,600 ($458)	JY77,500 ($558)
	Food	JY254,400 ($1,830)	JY225,500 ($1,622)	JY207,900 ($1,496)
	Lodging	JY353,000 ($2,540)	JY300,300 ($2,160)	JY244,200 ($1,757)
	Other Personal Expenses	JY355,500 ($2,558)	JY380,100 ($2,735)	JY376,200 ($2,706)
	Subtotal Expenses of Student Living	JY1,013,200 ($7,290)	JY969,500 ($6,975)	JY905,800 ($6,517)
	Total Cost to Parent and Student	JY1,589,900 ($11,439)	JY1,543,800 ($11,107)	JY2,145,300 ($15,434)

12.7 CONCLUSION

This chapter presents the analysis of various issues of financing the higher education. It presents the different cost estimation technique for the institutions. It also presents the total cost expense to parent and students in various countries. This gives a rough idea about of the total cost expense for the parents and students in many countries. These costs are indicative only. Due to lapse of time (in Years) and consequent cost escalation and variations in money exchange rates it is expected to vary. A person interested can always contact the embassy or login to the web pages of the concerned Institute to have latest information.

ANNEXURE–A

World University Rankings 2010

The QS World University Rankings is a ranking of the world's top 500 universities by Quacquarelli Symonds using a methodology that is published annually since 2004.

The QS World University Rankings is not to be confused with the THE World University Rankings. The QS rankings were originally published in collaboration with Times Higher Education, and known as the THE-QS World University Rankings. QS assumed sole publication of the existing methodology when Times Higher Education got split in order to create a new ranking methodology in 2010, which became the THE World University Rankings.

METHODOLOGY

QS tried to design its rankings based on a broad range of university activities. The six indicators are used.

Academic Peer Review (40%)

The most controversial part of the QS World University Rankings is their use of an opinion survey referred to as the Academic Peer Review. Using a combination of purchased mailing lists and applications and suggestions, this survey asks active academics across the world about the top universities in fields they know about. QS has published the job titles and geographical distribution of the participants.

The 2010 rankings included results from 15,050 people in its Academic Peer Review, including votes from the previous two years rolled forward provided there was no more recent information available from the same individual. Participants can nominate up to 30 universities but are not able to vote for their own. They tend to nominate a median of about 20, which means that over 170,000 data points make up this survey. QS regards this as a statistically robust total as even the 500th institution in its ranking has a valid number of votes.

In 2004 when the rankings first appeared, academic peer review accounted for half of a university's possible score. In 2005, its share was cut to 40 per cent because of the introduction of the Recruiter Review.

Recruiter Review (10%)

This part of the ranking is obtained by a similar method to the Academic Peer Review, except that it samples recruiters who hire graduates on a global scale. The numbers are smaller—5007 responses in 2010—and are used to produce 10 per cent of any university's possible score. This survey was introduced in the belief that employers can accurately track graduate quality and because students are bound to be interested in which universities their potential employers regard as the best.

Faculty Student Ratio (20%)

These two indicators account for 50 per cent of a university's possible score in the rankings. A further 20 per cent comes from a university's ratio of faculty to students. These indicators attempt to measure teaching commitment, but QS has admitted these are less than satisfactory.

Citations per Faculty (20%)

Citations of published research are among the most widely-used inputs to national and global university rankings. The QS World University Rankings used citations data from Thomson (now Thomson Reuters) from 2004 to 2007, and since then uses data from Scopus, part of Elsevier. The total number of citations for a five-year period is divided by the number of academic staff in a university to yield the score for this measure, which accounts for 20 per cent of a university's possible score in the Rankings.

QS has explained that it uses this approach, rather than the citations per paper preferred by other systems, because it reduces the effect of biomedical science on the overall picture—biomedicine has a ferocious "publish or perish" culture. Instead it attempts to measure the density of research-active staff at each institution. But issues still remain about the use of citations in ranking systems, especially the fact that the arts and humanities generate comparatively few citations.

QS has produced some data collection errors regarding citations per faculty, but not for several years. Like other ranking organizations, QS is interested in possible ways of assessing academic outputs other than papers in refereed journals, such as books, monographs and conference proceedings.

One interesting issue is the difference between the Scopus and Thomson Reuters databases. For major world universities, the two systems capture more or less the same publications and citations. For less mainstream institutions, Scopus has more non-English language and smaller-circulation journals in its database. This can result in fewer citations per paper on average.

International Orientation (10%)

The final ten per cent of a university's possible score is derived from measures intended to capture their internationalism: 5 per cent from their percentage of international students, and another 5 per cent from their percentage of international staff.

Data Sources

The information used to compile the World University Ranking comes partly from the online surveys carried out by QS, partly from Scopus, and partly from an annual information-gathering exercise carried out by QS itself. QS collects data from universities directly and from their web sites and publications, and from national bodies such as education ministries and the National Center for Education Statistics in the US and the Higher Education Statistics Agency in the UK.

Aggregation

The data is aggregated into columns according to its Z score, an indicator of how far removed any institution is from the average. Between 2004 and 2007 a different system was used whereby the top university for any measure was scaled as 100 and the others received a score reflecting their comparative performance. According to QS, this method was dropped because it gives too much weight to some exceptional outliers, such as the very high faculty/student ratio of the California Institute of Technology.

Classifications

In 2009, a column of classifications was introduced to provide additional context to the *rankings* tables. Universities are classified by size, defined by the size of the student body; comprehensive or specialist status, defined by the range of faculty areas in which programs are offered; and research activity, defined by the number of papers published in a five-year period.

Results

QS makes the point that its rankings are intended to assess large, general research institutions, not specialist ones. To be included in the QS World University Rankings, institutions must teach in at least two of the five main areas of academic life (the social sciences, the arts and humanities, biomedicine, engineering and the physical sciences), and must teach undergraduates.

Faculty-Level Analysis

QS also publishes a simple analysis of the top 100 institutions in each of the five faculty-level areas mentioned above: natural sciences, technology, biology and medicine, social sciences and the arts and humanities. These five tables list universities in order of their Academic Peer Review score. They also give the citations per paper for each institution.

QS does not aggregate these scores and has said that doing so would not produce a meaningful result. It uses citations per paper rather than per person partly because it does not hold details of the academic staff in each subject area, and partly because the number of citations per paper should be a consistent indicator of impact within a specific field. The 2010 QS World University Top 500 Rankings is presented in the following table.

The universities are arranged in the alphabetical order of the countries in which they are for the convenience of aspiring students.

2010 QS WORLD UNIVERSITY TOP 500 RANKINGS

Rank	*School Name*	*Country*	*Size*	*Research*	*Focus*	*Score*
326	Universidad de Buenos Aires	Argentina	XL	HI	FC	34.67
358	Universidad Austral	Argentina	S	VH	FO	32.06
20	Australian National University	Australia	M	VH	CO	88.58
37	The University of Sydney	Australia	XL	VH	FC	81.31
38	The University of Melbourne	Australia	XL	VH	FC	80.64
43	The University of Queensland	Australia	XL	VH	FC	77.56
46	The University of New South Wales	Australia	XL	VH	FC	76.66
61	Monash University	Australia	XL	VH	FC	72.54
89	The University of Western Australia	Australia	L	VH	FC	66.95
103	The University of Adelaide	Australia	L	VH	FC	63.87
220	Macquarie University	Australia	L	HI	FC	45
224	RMIT University	Australia	XL	VH	CO	44.77
251	Flinders University	Australia	L	MD	FC	41.87
256	University of Newcastle	Australia	L	HI	FC	41.45
257	University of Technology, Sydney	Australia	L	VH	CO	41.43
268	University of Wollongong	Australia	L	HI	FC	40.66
274	Curtin University of Technology	Australia	L	VH	CO	39.23
281	University of South Australia	Australia	L	VH	CO	38.75
287	La Trobe University	Australia	L	VH	CO	38.25
289	Queensland University of Technology	Australia	L	VH	CO	38.12
320	University of Tasmania	Australia	L	VH	CO	35.48
323	Griffith University	Australia	L	HI	FC	35.03
355	James Cook University	Australia	M	VH	FC	32.29

Rank	*School Name*	*Country*	*Size*	*Research*	*Focus*	*Score*
362	Deakin University	Australia	L	MD	FC	31.87
426	Swinburne University of Technology	Australia	L	HI	CO	28.63
477	Murdoch University	Australia	M	VH	CO	24.31
143	University of Vienna	Austria	XL	HI	FC	55.27
240	Vienna University of Technology	Austria	M	VH	FO	42.68
278	Universität Innsbruck	Austria	L	MD	FC	38.95
349	Karl-Franzens-Universitaet Graz	Austria	L	VH	FO	32.74
463	Johannes Kepler University Linz	Austria	M	VH	CO	24.28
86	Katholieke Universiteit Leuven	Belgium	XL	VH	FC	67.56
124	Université Catholique de Louvain (UCL)	Belgium	L	HI	FC	59.08
179	University of Antwerp	Belgium	M	VH	FC	50.26
192	University of Ghent	Belgium	L	VH	FC	48.38
209	Universite Libre de Bruxelles (ULB)	Belgium	L	HI	FC	46.73
238	Vrije Universiteit Brussel (VUB)	Belgium	M	VH	FC	42.77
248	University of Liege	Belgium	L	VH	FC	41.98
253	Universidade de São Paulo	Brazil	XL	VH	FC	41.67
292	Universidade Estadual de Campinas (Unicamp)	Brazil	L	VH	FC	37.89
381	Universidade Federal do Rio de Janeiro	Brazil	XL	VH	FC	30.49
19	McGill University	Canada	L	VH	FC	89.25
29	University of Toronto	Canada	XL	VH	FC	84.29
44	University of British Columbia	Canada	XL	VH	FC	77.41
78	University of Alberta	Canada	XL	VH	FC	69.3
132	Queen's University	Canada	L	VH	FC	58.17
136	Universite de Montreal	Canada	XL	VH	FC	56.87
145	University of Waterloo	Canada	L	VH	CO	54.73
162	McMaster University	Canada	L	VH	FC	51.85
164	The University of Western Ontario	Canada	L	VH	FC	51.83
165	University of Calgary	Canada	L	VH	FC	51.74
212	Dalhousie University	Canada	L	VH	FC	46.4
214	Simon Fraser University	Canada	L	VH	CO	45.88
231	University of Ottawa	Canada	XL	VH	FC	43.54
241	University of Victoria	Canada	L	VH	CO	42.64
271	Laval University	Canada	L	VH	FC	39.77
333	York University	Canada	XL	VH	CO	34.17

Rank	School Name	Country	Size	Research	Focus	Score
357	University of Manitoba	Canada	L	VH	FC	32.1
413	Carleton University	Canada	L	VH	CO	25.62
422	Concordia University	Canada	L	VH	CO	25.56
479	Université du Québec	Canada	XL	HI	FC	23.91
331	Pontificia Universidad Católica de Chile	Chile	L	HI	FC	34.23
367	Universidad de Chile	Chile	XL	HI	FC	31.54
47	Peking University	China	L	VH	FC	76.35
54	Tsinghua University	China	L	VH	FC	74.18
105	Fudan University	China	L	VH	FC	63.44
151	Shanghai Jiao Tong University	China	L	VH	FC	53.68
154	University of Science and Technology of China	China	L	VH	CO	53.25
177	Nanjing University	China	L	VH	FC	50.63
218	Zhejiang University	China	XL	VH	FC	45.51
388	Tongji University	China	XL	VH	FC	29.65
406	Tianjin University	China	L	VH	CO	26.82
450	Xi'an Jiaotong University	China	L	VH	FC	28.13
267	Charles University	Czech Republic	XL	VH	FC	40.66
440	Czech Technical University In Prague	Czech Republic	L	VH	SP	27.41
45	University of Copenhagen	Denmark	L	VH	FC	76.71
84	Aarhus University	Denmark	L	VH	FC	68.55
141	Technical University of Denmark	Denmark	M	VH	FO	55.63
298	University of Southern Denmark	Denmark	M	VH	FO	37.43
497	Aaiborg University	Denmark	M	HI	FC	24.12
478	Cairo University	Egypt	XL	VH	CO	23.8
76	University of Helsinki	Finland	L	VH	CO	69.64
211	University of Turku	Finland	M	VH	FC	46.43
250	Aalto University	Finland	L	VH	SP	41.9
303	University of Jyväskylä	Finland	M	VH	CO	37.01
308	University of Eastern Finland	Finland	M	VH	CO	36.32
313	University of Oulu	Finland	M	VH	FC	35.93
369	University of Tampere	Finland	M	VH	FO	31.5
33	École Normale Supérieure, Paris	France	S	VH	SP	82.09
36	École Polytechnique	France	S	VH	CO	81.33

Rank	*School Name*	*Country*	*Size*	*Research*	*Focus*	*Score*
118	Université Pierre et Marie Curie (UPMC)	France	XL	VH	FO	60.5
139	École Normale Supérieure de Lyon	France	S	VH	CO	56.2
186	Université Paris Sorbonne, Paris IV	France	L	VH	SP	49.03
203	Sciences Po Paris	France	M	VH	SP	47.38
226	Université Paris-Sud 11	France	L	VH	FO	44.22
229	Université Paris 1, Panthéon-Sorbonne	France	XL	VH	FO	43.69
246	Université de Strasbourg	France	XL	MD	FC	42.13
273	Université Grenoble, Joseph Fourier	France	L	VH	FO	39.24
279	École des Ponts, ParisTech	France	S	VH	FO	38.8
282	Université Paris Diderot—Paris 7	France	L	HI	FC	38.52
288	Université Montpellier 2, Sciences et Techniques	France	M	VH	FO	38.21
329	Université Paris Descartes	France	L	VH	FC	34.39
346	Université Lille 1, Sciences et Technologie	France	L	VH	FO	33.1
382	Université Toulouse III, Paul Sabatier	France	L	VH	FO	30.31
390	Université Claude Bernard Lyon 1	France	L	VH	FC	29.54
403	Université Paris Dauphine	France	M	VH	SP	27.14
404	Université Henri Poincaré Nancy 1	France	L	VH	FO	25.93
468	Université de Rennes 1	France	L	VH	FO	23.8
475	Université Paris 2, Panthéon-Assas	France	L	VH	SP	22.37
51	Ruprecht-Karls-Universität Heidelberg	Germany	L	VH	FC	75.89
58	Technische Universität München	Germany	L	VH	FO	72.99
66	Ludwig-Maximilians-Universität München	Germany	XL	VH	FC	71.25
70	Freie Universität Berlin	Germany	XL	VH	FC	70.55
97	Universität Freiburg	Germany	L	VH	FC	65.11
123	Humboldt-Universität zu Berlin	Germany	L	HI	FC	59.3
131	Eberhard Karls Universität Tübingen	Germany	L	VH	FC	58.19
158	Rheinisch-Westfälische Technische Hochschule Aachen	Germany	XL	HI	FC	52.58
167	Universität Karlsruhe	Germany	L	VH	CO	51.67
174	Georg-August-Universität Göttingen	Germany	L	VH	FC	51.23
195	Universität Frankfurt am Main	Germany	XL	VH	FC	48.15
200	Rheinische Friedrich-Wilhelms-Universität Bonn	Germany	L	VH	FC	47.51

Rank	*School Name*	*Country*	*Size*	*Research*	*Focus*	*Score*
205	Universität Stuttgart	Germany	L	VH	CO	47.23
215	Julius-Maximilians-Universität Würzburg	Germany	M	VH	FC	45.87
217	Technische Universität Berlin	Germany	L	VH	CO	45.53
242	Universität Hamburg	Germany	XL	HI	FC	42.56
244	Universität Mannheim	Germany	M	VH	FO	42.36
245	Universität Köln	Germany	XL	HI	FC	42.29
247	Universität Ulm	Germany	M	VH	FO	42.12
260	Universität Erlangen-Nürnberg	Germany	L	VH	FC	41.01
266	Technische Universität Darmstadt	Germany	L	VH	FO	40.71
294	Universität Leipzig	Germany	L	VH	FC	37.78
310	Ruhr-Universität Bochum	Germany	XL	HI	FC	36.14
312	Universität Konstanz	Germany	S	VH	CO	36.12
315	Universität des Saarlandes	Germany	L	HI	FC	35.82
317	Universität Bielefeld	Germany	L	VH	CO	35.66
322	Technische Universität Dresden	Germany	XL	HI	FC	35.22
324	Universität Düsseldorf	Germany	L	VH	FC	34.97
325	Westfälische Wilhelms-Universitat Münster	Germany	L	VH	FC	34.94
339	Universität Bremen	Germany	L	VH	CO	33.75
344	Johannes Gutenberg Universität Mainz	Germany	XL	HI	FC	33.33
373	Universität Bayreuth	Germany	M	VH	CO	31.12
378	Philipps-Universität Marburg	Germany	L	HI	FC	30.67
379	Universität Regensburg	Germany	L	VH	FO	30.58
399	Universität Jena	Germany	L	VH	FC	28.86
400	Christian-Albrechts-Universität zu Kiel	Germany	L	VH	FC	28.76
410	Technische Universität Braunschweig	Germany	L	VH	CO	25.75
438	Universität Dortmund	Germany	L	VH	CO	26.63
455	Universität Duisburg-Essen	Germany	XL	HI	FC	24.36
456	Leibniz Universität Hannover	Germany	L	VH	CO	23.91
460	Justus-Liebig-Universität Gießen	Germany	L	HI	FC	22.32
470	Martin-Luther-Universität Halle-Wittenberg	Germany	L	HI	FC	23.47
286	University of Athens	Greece	XL	VH	FC	38.25
412	University of Crete	Greece	L	MD	FC	26.35
415	Aristotle University of Thessaloniki	Greece	XL	VH	FC	28.29
472	National Technical University of Athens	Greece	L	VH	FO	23.94

Rank	*School Name*	*Country*	*Size*	*Research*	*Focus*	*Score*
496	University of Patras	Greece	L	HI	FC	24.08
23	University of Hong Kong	Hong Kong	L	VH	FC	87.28
40	The Hong Kong University of Science and Technology	Hong Kong	M	VH	CO	78.67
42	The Chinese University of Hong Kong	Hong Kong	L	VH	FC	77.94
129	City University of Hong Kong	Hong Kong	M	VH	CO	58.38
166	The Hong Kong Polytechnic University	Hong Kong	L	VH	CO	51.67
342	Hong Kong Baptist University	Hong Kong	M	VH	CO	33.36
418	Eötvös Loránd University	Hungary	L	VH	CO	26.43
462	University of Szeged	Hungary	L	HI	FC	23.24
187	Indian Institute of Technology Bombay (IITB)	India	M	VH	CO	48.79
202	Indian Institute of Technology Delhi (IITD)	India	M	VH	CO	47.39
249	Indian Institute of Technology Kanpur (IITK)	India	S	VH	CO	41.95
262	Indian Institute of Technology Madras (IITM)	India	S	VH	CO	40.87
311	Indian Institute of Technology Kharagpur (IITKGP)	India	M	VH	FO	36.13
371	University of Delhi	India	XL	MD	FC	31.21
448	Indian Institute of Technology Roorkee (IITR)	India	S	VH	FO	26.2
476	University of Mumbai	India	XL	LO	FC	22.38
236	University of Indonesia	Indonesia	XL	LO	FC	42.9
321	Universitas Gadjah Mada	Indonesia	XL	LO	FC	35.25
445	Bandung Institute of Technology (ITB)	Indonesia	L	LO	CO	28.6
461	Airlangga University	Indonesia	L	LO	FC	22.6
419	University of Tehran	Iran	XL	VH	CO	25.91
52	Trinity College Dublin	Ireland	L	HI	FC	75.04
114	University College Dublin	Ireland	L	HI	FC	62.42
184	University College Cork	Ireland	L	HI	FC	50.07
232	National University of Ireland, Galway	Ireland	M	HI	FC	43.46
330	Dublin City University	Ireland	M	VH	FO	34.38
395	Dublin Institute of Technology	Ireland	M	HI	CO	29.04
433	National University of Ireland Maynooth	Ireland	M	VH	FO	24.9

Rank	*School Name*	*Country*	*Size*	*Research*	*Focus*	*Score*
493	University of Limerick	Ireland	M	HI	FC	24.36
109	Hebrew University of Jerusalem	Israel	L	VH	FC	63.11
138	Tel Aviv University	Israel	L	VH	FC	56.44
159	Technion—Israel Institute of Technology	Israel	M	VH	FC	52.38
337	Ben Gurion University of The Negev	Israel	L	VH	FC	33.91
176	University of Bologna	Italy	XL	VH	FC	50.85
190	Sapienza University of Rome	Italy	XL	VH	FC	48.41
261	University of Padua	Italy	XL	VH	FC	40.91
295	Politecnico di Milano	Italy	L	VH	SP	37.73
301	University of Pisa	Italy	XL	VH	FC	37.16
328	University of Florence	Italy	XL	VH	FC	34.45
363	Università degli Studi di Pavia	Italy	L	HI	FC	31.82
407	University of Trieste	Italy	L	HI	FC	26.16
428	Università degli Studi di Roma—Tor Vergata	Italy	XL	VH	CO	25.12
432	University of Trento	Italy	L	VH	CO	26.31
447	University of Naples—Federico Ii	Italy	XL	VH	FC	24.92
453	University of Milano	Italy	XL	LO	FC	22.02
458	Politecnico di Torino	Italy	L	VH	FO	24.8
467	University of Turin	Italy	XL	VH	FC	22.69
488	University of Siena	Italy	L	HI	FC	23.44
24	The University of Tokyo	Japan	L	VH	FC	86.74
25	Kyoto University	Japan	L	VH	FC	85.89
49	Osaka University	Japan	L	VH	FC	76.21
60	Tokyo Institute of Technology	Japan	M	VH	FO	72.59
91	Nagoya University	Japan	L	VH	FC	66.41
102	Tohoku University	Japan	L	VH	FC	63.96
153	Kyushu University	Japan	L	VH	FC	53.32
172	University of Tsukuba	Japan	L	VH	FC	51.42
175	Hokkaido University	Japan	L	VH	FC	51.06
182	Waseda University	Japan	XL	VH	CO	50.12
206	Keio University	Japan	XL	VH	FC	47.22
234	Kobe University	Japan	L	VH	FC	43.04
254	Hiroshima University	Japan	L	VH	FC	41.66
300	Tokyo Medical and Dental University	Japan	S	VH	FO	37.16

Rank	*School Name*	*Country*	*Size*	*Research*	*Focus*	*Score*
318	Chiba University	Japan	L	VH	FC	35.62
414	Yokohama City University	Japan	S	VH	FO	27.71
420	Tokyo Metropolitan University	Japan	M	VH	CO	26.64
421	Okayama University	Japan	L	VH	FC	27.78
423	Nagasaki University	Japan	M	VH	FO	28.39
429	Kumamoto University	Japan	M	VH	FC	26.73
454	Gifu University	Japan	M	VH	FC	23.68
485	Osaka City University	Japan	M	VH	FC	24.41
486	Kanazawa University	Japan	M	VH	FC	24.48
494	Tokyo University of Science (TUS)	Japan	L	VH	CO	23.16
499	Yokohama National University	Japan	M	VH	FO	24.24
495	L.N. Gumilyov Eurasian National University	Kazakhstan	M	LO	CO	24.73
50	Seoul National University	Korea, South	L	VH	FC	76.06
79	KAIST—Korea Advanced Institute of Science and Technology	Korea, South	M	VH	CO	69.05
112	Pohang University of Science And Technology (POSTECH)	Korea, South	S	VH	FO	62.75
142	Yonsei University	Korea, South	XL	VH	FC	55.51
191	Korea University	Korea, South	XL	VH	FC	48.4
343	Sungkyunkwan University	Korea, South	L	VH	FC	33.35
345	Kyung Hee University	Korea, South	L	HI	FC	33.12
348	Ewha Womans University	Korea, South	L	MD	FC	32.77
354	Hanyang University	Korea, South	L	VH	FC	32.29
392	Pusan National University	Korea, South	L	HI	FC	29.41
397	Sogang University	Korea, South	M	VH	CO	29
465	Kyungpook National University	Korea, South	L	HI	FC	22.69
341	American University of Beirut (AUB)	Lebanon	M	HI	FC	33.4
207	Universiti Malaya (UM)	Malaysia	L	HI	FC	47.09
263	Universiti Kebangsaan Malaysia (UKM)	Malaysia	L	MD	FC	40.84
309	Universiti Sains Malaysia (USM)	Malaysia	L	HI	FC	36.16
319	Universiti Putra Malaysia (UPM)	Malaysia	L	HI	FC	35.49
365	Universiti Teknologi Malaysia (UTM)	Malaysia	L	HI	CO	31.58
222	Universidad Nacional Autónoma de México (UNAM)	Mexico	XL	VH	FC	44.86
387	Tecnológico de Monterrey (ITESM)	Mexico	L	LO	FC	29.68
56	University of Amsterdam	Netherlands	XL	VH	FC	73.45

Rank	School Name	Country	Size	Research	Focus	Score
82	Leiden University	Netherlands	L	VH	FC	68.81
83	Utrecht University	Netherlands	L	VH	FC	68.77
99	Erasmus University Rotterdam	Netherlands	L	VH	FO	64.48
108	Delft University of Technology	Netherlands	L	VH	FO	63.14
111	Maastricht University	Netherlands	L	VH	FO	62.77
120	University of Groningen	Netherlands	L	VH	FC	60.34
126	Eindhoven University of Technology	Netherlands	M	VH	FO	58.52
149	Radboud University Nijmegen	Netherlands	L	VH	FC	54.2
171	VU University Amsterdam	Netherlands	L	VH	FC	51.43
178	Wageningen University	Netherlands	M	VH	FO	50.35
199	University of Twente	Netherlands	M	VH	FO	47.66
68	The University of Auckland	New Zealand	L	VH	FC	71.13
135	University of Otago	New Zealand	L	VH	FC	57.08
189	University of Canterbury	New Zealand	L	VH	CO	48.51
225	Victoria University of Wellington	New Zealand	L	VH	CO	44.37
302	Massey University	New Zealand	L	VH	CO	37.02
316	University of Waikato	New Zealand	M	VH	CO	35.66
100	University of Oslo	Norway	L	VH	FC	64.21
133	University of Bergen	Norway	M	VH	FC	57.92
237	Norwegian University of Science And Technology	Norway	L	VH	FC	42.79
293	University of Tromso	Norway	S	VH	FC	37.83
366	National University of Sciences and Technology (NUST) Islamabad	Pakistan	M	LO	FC	31.56
307	Ateneo de Manila University	Philippines	M	LO	FC	36.38
314	University of the Philippines	Philippines	XL	LO	FC	35.9
471	De La Salle University	Philippines	M	LO	CO	24.66
304	Jagiellonian University	Poland	XL	VH	CO	36.87
364	Warsaw University	Poland	XL	VH	CO	31.64
384	Universidade Nova de Lisboa	Portugal	L	MD	FC	30.23
396	University of Coimbra	Portugal	L	HI	FC	29.03
469	University of Porto	Portugal	XL	HI	FC	22.09
93	Lomonosov Moscow State University	Russia	XL	VH	FC	66.12
210	Saint-Petersburg State University	Russia	L	HI	FC	46.68
375	Novosibirsk State University	Russia	M	MD	FC	30.93
408	Tomsk State University	Russia	M	HI	CO	24.9

Rank	*School Name*	*Country*	*Size*	*Research*	*Focus*	*Score*
466	State University Higher School of Economics (HSE)	Russia	L	LO	FO	22.52
221	King Saud University	Saudi Arabia	XL	LO	FC	44.89
255	King Fahd University of Petroleum and Minerals	Saudi Arabia	M	VH	FO	41.51
439	King Abdul Aziz University (KAU)	Saudi Arabia	XL	LO	FC	26.1
31	National University of Singapore (NUS)	Singapore	XL	VH	FC	82.78
74	Nanyang Technological University (NTU)	Singapore	L	VH	CO	69.77
161	University of Cape Town	South Africa	L	HI	FC	51.98
360	University of The Witwatersrand	South Africa	L	HI	FC	31.9
459	University of Pretoria	South Africa	XL	MD	FC	22.77
148	University of Barcelona	Spain	XL	VH	FC	54.28
173	Universitat Autònoma de Barcelona	Spain	L	VH	FC	51.26
213	Universidad Autónoma de Madrid	Spain	L	VH	FC	46.05
269	University Complutense Madrid	Spain	XL	HI	FC	40.61
336	Universitat Pompeu Fabra	Spain	M	VH	FO	33.97
353	University of Navarra	Spain	M	VH	FC	32.39
427	Universitat de Valencia	Spain	XL	HI	FC	27.23
473	University of Granada	Spain	XL	HI	FC	23.48
489	Universidade de Santiago de Compostela	Spain	L	VH	CO	24.08
492	University of Salamanca	Spain	XL	MD	FC	23.2
62	Uppsala University	Sweden	L	VH	FC	72.16
72	Lund University	Sweden	L	VH	FC	70.38
150	KTH, Royal Institute of Technology	Sweden	L	VH	CO	53.73
168	Stockholm University	Sweden	L	VH	CO	51.51
183	University of Gothenburg	Sweden	L	VH	FC	50.1
204	Chalmers University of Technology	Sweden	M	VH	CO	47.34
297	Umeå University	Sweden	L	HI	FC	37.45
389	Linköping University	Sweden	L	VH	CO	29.56
18	ETH Zurich (Swiss Federal Institute of Technology)	Switzerland	L	VH	FO	89.28
32	Ecole Polytechnique Fédérale de Lausanne	Switzerland	M	VH	FO	82.27
71	University of Geneva	Switzerland	L	VH	FC	70.53
101	University of Zurich	Switzerland	L	VH	FC	64.04

Rank	*School Name*	*Country*	*Size*	*Research*	*Focus*	*Score*
137	University of Basel	Switzerland	M	VH	FC	56.68
152	University of Lausanne	Switzerland	M	VH	FO	53.37
163	University of Bern	Switzerland	L	VH	FO	51.85
383	University of St Gallen (HSG)	Switzerland	M	VH	SP	30.25
94	National Taiwan University (NTU)	Taiwan	XL	VH	FC	66.03
196	National Tsing Hua University	Taiwan	M	VH	CO	47.94
283	National Cheng Kung University	Taiwan	L	VH	FC	38.47
290	National Yang Ming University	Taiwan	S	VH	FC	38.04
327	National Chiao Tung University	Taiwan	M	VH	CO	34.46
370	National Taiwan University of Science And Technology (formerly National Taiwan Institute of Technology)	Taiwan	M	VH	FO	31.46
398	National Central University	Taiwan	M	VH	CO	28.95
443	National Sun Yat-sen University	Taiwan	M	VH	CO	26.95
484	National Taiwan Normal University	Taiwan	L	HI	CO	22.12
180	Chulalongkorn University	Thailand	XL	HI	FC	50.21
228	Mahidol University	Thailand	L	HI	FC	43.74
444	Chiang Mai University	Thailand	XL	MD	FC	25.16
474	Thammasat University	Thailand	XL	LO	FC	23.4
332	Bilkent University	Turkey	M	VH	CO	34.2
417	KoÃ§ University	Turkey	S	MD	FC	24.92
430	Sabanci University	Turkey	S	VH	CO	25.41
441	Istanbul University	Turkey	XL	MD	FC	26.31
452	KoÃ§ University	Turkey	S	MD	FC	24.92
500	Istanbul Technical University	Turkey	L	VH	CO	23.09
372	United Arab Emirates University	UAE	L	MD	FC	31.18
1	University of Cambridge	UK	L	VH	FC	100
4	UCL (University College London)	UK	L	VH	FC	98.54
6	University of Oxford	UK	L	VH	FC	98.16
7	Imperial College London	UK	L	VH	FC	97.78
21	King's College London (University of London)	UK	L	VH	FC	88.45
22	University of Edinburgh	UK	L	VH	FC	88.01
27	University of Bristol	UK	L	VH	FC	85.22
30	The University of Manchester	UK	XL	VH	FC	83.33
53	The University of Warwick	UK	L	HI	FC	74.28
59	University of Birmingham	UK	L	VH	FC	72.68

Rank	*School Name*	*Country*	*Size*	*Research*	*Focus*	*Score*
69	The University of Sheffield	UK	L	VH	FC	70.76
73	The University of Nottingham	UK	L	VH	FC	69.95
77	University of Glasgow	UK	L	VH	FC	69.54
80	London School of Economics and Political Science (LSE)	UK	M	VH	SP	68.86
81	University of Southampton	UK	L	VH	FC	68.85
85	University of Leeds	UK	L	VH	FC	68.08
88	University of York	UK	M	VH	FC	67.37
92	Durham University	UK	L	HI	FC	66.29
95	University of St Andrews	UK	M	VH	FC	65.69
117	University of Aberdeen	UK	L	HI	FC	61.3
121	University of Liverpool	UK	L	VH	FC	59.5
122	Cardiff University	UK	L	VH	FC	59.47
140	Newcastle University	UK	L	VH	FC	56.06
144	University of Bath	UK	L	VH	CO	55.25
147	Queen Mary, University of London (QMUL)	UK	L	HI	FC	54.47
156	University of Sussex	UK	M	VH	FC	53.08
169	University of Leicester	UK	L	HI	FC	51.5
181	Lancaster University	UK	M	VH	FC	50.2
185	University of Reading	UK	L	VH	CO	50
197	Queen's University of Belfast	UK	L	HI	FC	47.9
201	University of Dundee	UK	M	VH	FC	47.46
243	University of Surrey	UK	M	VH	CO	42.42
258	SOAS—School of Oriental and African Studies, University of London	UK	S	VH	SP	41.27
259	University of Exeter	UK	L	HI	FC	41.13
265	University of Strathclyde	UK	L	VH	CO	40.74
270	Loughborough University	UK	L	VH	FO	40.28
291	Royal Holloway University of London	UK	M	VH	CO	37.97
296	Aston University	UK	M	VH	CO	37.66
299	University of East Anglia (UEA)	UK	L	HI	FC	37.27
305	University of Essex	UK	M	VH	CO	36.7
356	Heriot-watt University	UK	M	VH	CO	32.13
361	Brunel University	UK	L	VH	CO	31.89
368	Bangor University	UK	M	HI	FC	31.52
376	Swansea University	UK	M	HI	FC	30.72

Rank	School Name	Country	Size	Research	Focus	Score
380	Aberystwyth University	UK	M	VH	CO	30.55
386	Goldsmiths, University of London	UK	M	VH	FO	29.92
394	University of Bradford	UK	M	VH	CO	29.11
435	University of Kent	UK	L	VH	CO	26.47
480	The Open University	UK	XL	VH	CO	23.07
483	University of Hull	UK	L	MD	FC	23.82
490	City University London	UK	L	HI	CO	22.91
2	Harvard University	United States	L	VH	FC	99.18
3	Yale University	United States	M	VH	FC	98.68
5	Massachusetts Institute of Technology (MIT)	United States	M	VH	CO	98.19
8	University of Chicago	United States	M	VH	FC	97.52
9	California Institute of Technology (Caltech)	United States	S	VH	CO	96.46
10	Princeton University	United States	M	VH	CO	96.03
11	Columbia University	United States	L	VH	FC	95.99
12	University of Pennsylvania	United States	L	VH	FC	95.97
13	Stanford University	United States	L	VH	FC	93.62
14	Duke University	United States	L	VH	FC	92.29
15	University of Michigan	United States	XL	VH	FC	92.2
16	Cornell University	United States	L	VH	FC	90.44
17	Johns Hopkins University	United States	L	VH	FC	89.67
26	Northwestern University	United States	L	VH	FC	85.4
28	University of California, Berkeley (UCB)	United States	XL	VH	FC	85.18
34	Carnegie Mellon University	United States	M	VH	FC	81.8
35	University of California, Los Angeles (UCLA)	United States	XL	VH	FC	81.49
39	Brown University	United States	M	VH	FC	80.54
41	New York University (NYU)	United States	XL	VH	FC	78.41
48	University of Wisconsin-Madison	United States	XL	VH	FC	76.28
55	University of Washington	United States	XL	VH	FC	73.75
57	University of North Carolina, Chapel Hill	United States	L	VH	FC	73.22
63	University of Illinois at Urbana-Champaign	United States	XL	VH	FC	71.75
64	Boston University	United States	L	VH	FC	71.73

Rank	*School Name*	*Country*	*Size*	*Research*	*Focus*	*Score*
65	University of California, San Diego (UCSD)	United States	L	VH	FC	71.55
67	University of Texas at Austin	United States	XL	VH	FC	71.24
75	Washington University in St. Louis	United States	L	VH	FC	69.64
87	Purdue University	United States	XL	VH	FC	67.54
90	Dartmouth College	United States	M	VH	FC	66.86
96	University of Minnesota	United States	XL	VH	FC	65.58
98	Pennsylvania State University	United States	XL	VH	FC	64.91
104	University of Maryland, College Park	United States	XL	VH	FC	63.72
106	Georgia Institute of Technology	United States	L	VH	CO	63.34
107	Emory University	United States	L	VH	FC	63.15
110	University of California, Davis	United States	L	VH	FC	62.85
113	University of Southern California	United States	XL	VH	FC	62.66
115	Rice University	United States	M	VH	FC	61.52
116	University of California, Santa Barbara (UCSB)	United States	L	VH	CO	61.37
119	University of Pittsburgh	United States	L	VH	FC	60.37
125	Ohio State University	United States	XL	VH	FC	59.05
127	Case Western Reserve University	United States	M	VH	FC	58.42
128	University of Rochester	United States	M	VH	FC	58.42
130	University of Virginia	United States	L	VH	FC	58.3
134	Vanderbilt University	United States	M	VH	FC	57.24
146	University of California, Irvine	United States	L	VH	FC	54.68
155	Georgetown University	United States	L	HI	FC	53.11
157	Tufts University	United States	M	VH	FC	52.69
160	University of Arizona	United States	XL	VH	FC	52.35
170	University of Colorado at Boulder	United States	L	VH	CO	51.47
188	University of Iowa	United States	L	VH	FC	48.74
193	University of Florida	United States	XL	VH	FC	48.25
194	Stony Brook University	United States	L	VH	FC	48.19
198	Texas A&M University	United States	XL	VH	FC	47.87
208	Michigan State University	United States	XL	VH	FC	47.05
216	Rutgers, The State University of New Jersey, New Brunswick	United States	XL	VH	CO	45.6
219	University of Notre Dame	United States	M	VH	CO	45.03
223	Rensselaer Polytechnic Institute	United States	M	VH	CO	44.81
227	Indiana University Bloomington	United States	XL	VH	FC	44.09

Rank	*School Name*	*Country*	*Size*	*Research*	*Focus*	*Score*
230	University of Massachusetts, Amherst	United States	L	VH	CO	43.57
233	Wake Forest University	United States	M	VH	FC	43.21
235	University of Miami	United States	L	VH	FC	42.97
239	Tulane University	United States	M	VH	FC	42.71
252	University of Illinois, Chicago (UIC)	United States	L	VH	FC	41.86
264	George Washington University	United States	L	HI	FC	40.76
272	North Carolina State University	United States	L	VH	CO	39.52
275	Iowa State University	United States	L	VH	CO	39.13
276	University of Cincinnati	United States	L	VH	FC	39.13
277	University of Hawaii at MÄ•noa	United States	L	VH	FC	39.06
280	Brandeis University	United States	M	VH	CO	38.78
284	University of California, Santa Cruz	United States	L	VH	CO	38.46
285	University of California, Riverside	United States	L	HI	FC	38.35
306	University of Utah	United States	L	VH	FC	36.52
334	Colorado State University	United States	L	VH	CO	34.08
335	Arizona State University	United States	XL	VH	CO	34
338	University of Connecticut	United States	L	VH	FC	33.88
340	Virginia Polytechnic Institute (Virginia Tech)	United States	XL	VH	FC	33.63
347	The University of Georgia	United States	XL	VH	FC	33.06
350	University of Kentucky	United States	L	VH	FC	32.69
351	University of Alabama	United States	L	VH	CO	32.61
352	Washington State University	United States	L	HI	FC	32.61
359	Boston College	United States	L	VH	CO	31.94
374	Illinois Institute of Technology	United States	M	VH	CO	31.08
377	University of Kansas	United States	L	VH	FC	30.7
385	University of Tennessee	United States	XL	VH	FC	29.95
391	Howard University	United States	M	HI	FC	29.45
393	University at Buffalo SUNY	United States	L	VH	FC	29.31
401	University of Delaware	United States	L	VH	CO	25.53
402	Yeshiva University	United States	S	MD	FC	24.9
405	University of Vermont	United States	M	VH	FC	26.01
409	University of Houston	United States	L	VH	CO	25.96
411	Drexel University	United States	L	HI	FC	27.79
416	City University of New York	United States	XL	VH	CO	25.86
424	Oregon State University	United States	L	VH	CO	25.31

Rank	*School Name*	*Country*	*Size*	*Research*	*Focus*	*Score*
425	University of South Carolina	United States	L	HI	FC	25.4
431	University of Missouri, Columbia	United States	L	VH	FC	28.71
434	College of William and Mary	United States	M	VH	CO	26.64
436	University of Oklahoma	United States	L	VH	FC	27.71
437	Florida State University	United States	L	HI	FC	28.55
442	University of New Mexico	United States	L	VH	FC	27.74
446	Lehigh University	United States	M	VH	CO	26.07
449	University of Oregon	United States	L	VH	CO	26.21
451	City University of New York	United States	XL	VH	CO	25.86
457	Worcester Polytechnic Institute	United States	S	VH	CO	22.98
464	Syracuse University	United States	L	VH	CO	22.19
482	University of Nebraska	United States	L	VH	CO	24.08
487	American University	United States	M	VH	CO	22.98
491	Virginia Commonwealth University	United States	L	HI	FC	22.82
498	Temple University	United States	XL	HI	FC	22.19
481	Universidad ORT Uruguay	Uruguay	S	HI	FO	23.95

ANNEXURE–B

In Indian Context

UGC Academic Performance Indicators—2010

Table 1: Proposed Scores for Academic Performance Indicators (APIS) in Recruitments and Career Advancement Scheme (CAS) Promotions of University/College Teachers

Category I: Teaching, Learning and Evaluation Related Activities

Brief Explanation: Based on the teacher's self-assessment, API scores are proposed for (a) teaching related activities; (b) domain knowledge; (c) participation in examination and evaluation; (d) contribution to innovative teaching, new courses etc. The minimum API score required by teachers from this category is 75. The self-assessment score should be based on objectively verifiable criteria wherever possible and will be finalized by the screening/selection committee.

Universities will be required to detail the activities and in case institutional specificities require, adjust the weightages, without changing the minimum total API scores required under this category.

S. No.	*Nature of Activity*	*Maximum Score*
1.	Lectures, seminars, tutorials, practicals, contact hours undertaken taken as percentage of lectures allocated[a]	50
2.	Lectures or other teaching duties in excess of the UGC norms	10
3.	Preparation and Imparting of knowledge/instruction as per curriculum; syllabus enrichment by providing additional resources to students	20
4.	Use of participatory and innovative teaching-learning methodologies; updating of subject content, course improvement etc.	20
5.	Examination duties (Invigilation; question paper setting, evaluation/assessment of answer scripts) as per allotment.	25
	Total Score	**125**
	Minimum API Score Required	**75**

Note: [a]Lectures and tutorials allocation to add up to the UGC norm for particular category of teacher. University may prescribe minimum cut-off (net of due leave), say 80%, for 1 and 5 above, below which no scores may be assigned in these sub-categories.

Category II: Co-Curricular, Extension and Professional Development Related Activities

Brief Explanation: Based on the teacher's self-assessment, category II API scores are proposed for both co-curricular and extension activities; and Professional development related contributions. The minimum API required by teachers for eligibility for promotion is 15. A list of items and proposed scores is given below. It is evident that all teachers can earn scores from a number of items, whereas some activities will be carried out only be one or a few teachers. The list of activities is however; broad enough for the minimum API score required (15) in this category to accrue to all teachers. As before, the self-assessment score should be based on objectively verifiable criteria and will be finalized by the screening/selection committee.

The model table below gives groups of activities and API scores. Universities may detail the activities or, in case institutional specificities require, adjust the weightages, without changing the minimum total API scores required under this category.

S. No.	*Nature of Activity*	*Maximum Score*
1.	Student related co-curricular, extension and field based activities (such as extension work through NSS/NCC and other channels, cultural activities, subject related events, advisement and counseling)	20
2.	Contribution to Corporate life and management of the department and institution through participation in academic and administrative committees and responsibilities.	15
3.	Professional Development activities (such as participation in seminars, conferences, short term, training courses, talks, lectures, membership of associations, dissemination and general articles, not covered in Category III below)	15
	Minimum API Score Required	15

Category-III: Research and Academic Contributions

Brief Explanation: Based on the teacher's self-assessment, API scores are proposed for research and academic contributions. The minimum API score required by teachers from this category is different for different levels of promotion and varies from university to university, college to college. The self-assessment score will be based on verifiable criteria and will be finalized by the screening/selection committee.

S. No.	*APIs*	*Engineering/Agriculture/ Veterinary Science/Sciences/Medical Sciences*	*Faculties of Languages Arts/Humanities/ Social Sciences/Library/ Physical education/ Management*	*Max. Points for University and College Teacher Position*
Research Papers		Refereed Journals*	Refereed Journals* 15/publication	
III (A)	Published in:	Non-refereed but recognized and reputable journals and periodicals, having ISBN/ISSN numbers.	Non-refereed but recognized and reputable journals and periodicals, having ISBN/ISSN numbers.	10/ Publication
		Conference proceedings as full papers, etc. (Abstracts not to be included)	Conference proceedings as full papers, etc. (Abstracts not to be included)	10/ Publication
III (B)	Research Publications (books, chapters in books, other than refereed journal articles)	Text or Reference Books Published by International Publishers with an established peer review system	Text or Reference Books Published by International Publishers with an established peer review system	50/sole author; 10/chapter in an edited book
		Subjects Books by National level publishers/State and Central Govt. Publications with ISBN/ISSN numbers	Subject Books by/national level publishers/State and Central Govt. Publications with ISBN/ISSN numbers.	25/sole author, and 5/chapter in edited books
		Subject Books by Other local publishers with ISBN/ISSN numbers	Subject Books by Other local publishers with ISBN/ISSN numbers.	15/sole author, and 3/chapter in edited books
		Chapters contributed to edited knowledge based volumes published by International Publishers	Chapters contributed to edited knowledge based volumes published by International Publishers	10/Chapter
		Chapters in knowledge based volumes by Indian/National level publishers with ISBN/ISSN numbers and with numbers of national and international directories	Chapters in knowledge based volumes in Indian/National level publishers with ISBN/ISSN numbers and with numbers of national and international directories	5/Chapter
III (C):	**Research Projects**			
III (C) (i)	Sponsored Projects carried out/ongoing	(a) Major Projects amount mobilized with grants above 30.0 lakhs	Major Projects amount mobilized with grants above 5.0 lakhs	20/each Project

S. No.	*APIs*	*Engineering/Agriculture/ Veterinary Science/Sciences/Medical Sciences*	*Faculties of Languages Arts/Humanities/ Social Sciences/Library/ Physical education/ Management*	*Max. Points for University and College Teacher Position*
		(b) Major Projects amount mobilized with grants above 5.0 lakhs up to 30.00 lakhs	Major Projects Amount mobilized with minimum of ₹ 3.00 lakhs up to ₹ 5.00 lakhs	15/each Project
		(c) Minor Projects (Amount mobilized with grants above ₹ 50,000 up to ₹ 5 lakh)	Minor Projects (Amount mobilized with grants above ₹ 25,000 up to ₹ 3 lakh)	10/each Project
III (C) (ii)	Consultancy Projects carried out/ongoing	Amount mobilized with minimum of ₹ 10.00 lakh	Amount mobilized with minimum of ₹ 2.0 lakhs	10 per every ₹ 10/2 respectively
III (C) (iii)	Completed projects: Quality Evaluation	Completed project Report (Acceptance from funding agency)	Completed project report (Accepted by funding agency)	20/each major project and 10/each minor project
III (C) (iv)	Projects Outcome/Outputs	Patent/Technology transfer/Product/Process	Major Policy document of Govt. Bodies at Central and State level	30/each national level output or patent/50/ each for International level
III (D):	**Research Guidance**			
III (D) (i)	M.Phil.	Degree awarded only	Degree awarded only	3/each candidate
III (D) (ii)	Ph.D.	Degree awarded Thesis submitted	Degree awarded Thesis submitted	10/each candidate 7/each candidate
III (E):	**Training Courses and Conference/Seminar/Workshop Papers**			
III(E) (i)	Refresher courses, Methodology workshops, Training, Teaching-Learning-Evaluation Technology Programmes, Soft Skills development Programmes, Faculty Development Programmes (Max: 30 points)	(a) Not less than two weeks duration (b) One week duration	(a) Not less than two weeks duration (b) One week duration	20/each 10/each

S. No.	*APIs*	*Engineering/Agriculture/ Veterinary Science/Sciences/Medical Sciences*	*Faculties of Languages Arts/Humanities/ Social Sciences/Library/ Physical education/ Management*	*Max. Points for University and College Teacher Position*
III(E) (ii)	Papers in Conferences/Seminars/ workshops etc.**	Participation and Presentation of research papers (oral/poster) in	Participation and Presentation of research papers (oral/poster) in	
		(a) International conference	(a) International conference	10 each
		(b) National	(b) National	7.5/each
		(c) Regional/State level	(c) Regional/State level	5/each
		(d) Local –University/College level	(d) Local-University/ College level	3/each
III(E) (iv)	Invited lectures or presentations for conferences//symposia	(a) International	(a) International	10/each
		(b) National level	(b) National level	5

Notes:

1. It is incumbent on the Coordination Committee proposed in these Regulations and the University to prepare and publicize within six months subject-wise lists of journals, periodicals and publishers under categories IIIA and B. Till such time, screening/selection committees will assess and verify the categorization and scores of publications.
2. The API for joint publications will have to be calculated in the following manner: Of the total score for the relevant category of publication by the concerned teacher, the first/Principal author and the corresponding author/supervisor/mentor of the teacher would share equally 60% of the total points and the remaining 40% would be shared equally by all other authors.

Table 2(A): Minimum APIS as Provided in Table 1 to be Applied for the Promotion of Teachers under Career

Advancement Scheme (CAS) in University Departments, and Weightages for Expert Assessment

		Assistant Professor/ Equivalent Cadres: (Stage 1 to Stage 2)	*Assistant Professor/Equivalent Cadres: (Stage 2 to Stage 3)*	*Assistant Professor (Stage 3) to Associate Professor/Equivalent Cadres (Stage 4)*	*Associate Professor (Stage 4) to Professor/ Equivalent Cadres (Stage 5)*	*Professor (Stage 5) to Professor (Stage 6)*
I	Teaching-learning, Evaluation Related Activities (category I)	75/Year	75/year	75/year	75/year	75/year
II	Co-curricular, Extension and Profession related activities (Category II)	15/year	15/year	15/year	15/year	15/year

Contd...

Table 2(A) contd...

		Assistant Professor/ Equivalent Cadres: (Stage 1 to Stage 2)	*Assistant Professor/Equivalent Cadres: (Stage 2 to Stage 3)*	*Assistant Professor (Stage 3) to Associate Professor/Equivalent Cadres (Stage 4)*	*Associate Professor (Stage 4) to Professor/ Equivalent Cadres (Stage 5)*	*Professor (Stage 5) to Professor (Stage 6)*
III	Minimum total average annual Score under Categories I and II*	100/year	100/year	100/year	100/year	100/Year
IV	Research and Academic Contribution (Category III)	10/Year (40/assessment period)	20/Year(100/ assessment Period)	30/Year (90/assessment period)	40/Year (120/assessment period)	50/Year (500/. assessment period)
	Expert Assessment System	Screening Committee	Screening Committee	Selection Committee	Selection Committee	Expert Committee
V	Percentage Distribution of Weightage Points in the Expert Assessment (Total weightage = 100. Minimum required for promotion is 50)	No separate points. Screening committee to verify API scores	No separate points. Screening committee to verify API scores	30% - Contribution to Research 50% Assessment of domain knowledge and teaching practices. 20% - Interview performance	50% - Contribution to Research. 30% - Assessment of domain knowledge and teaching practices. 20% - Interview performance	50% - research. 50% - Performance evaluation and other credential by referral procedure

* Teachers may score up to 10 points from either Category I or Category II to achieve the minimum score required under Category I + II.

Note: For universities for which Sixth PRC Awards are applicable, Stages 1, 2, 3, 4, 5 and 6 correspond to scales with AGP of ₹ 6000, 7000, 8000, 9000, 10000 and 12000 respectively.

Table 2(B): Minimum Point Norms of the APIS as Provided in Table 1 and Weightages for Expert Assessment to be Applied for the Promotion of Teachers, in Colleges (UG and PG) Under Career Advancement Scheme (CAS)

		Assistant Professor/Equivalent Cadres Stage 1 to Stage 2:	*Assistant Professor/Equivalent Cadres: Stage 2 to Stage 3*	*Assistant Professor (Stage 3) to Associate Professor/Equivalent Cadre (Stage 4)*	*Associate Professor to Professor Promotion in Colleges (Stage 5) as Per Assigned Posts*
I	Teaching-learning, Evaluation Related Activities (Category – I)	75/year	75/year	75/year	75/year

Contd...

Table 2(B) contd...

		Assistant Professor/Equivalent Cadres Stage 1 to Stage 2:	*Assistant Professor/Equivalent Cadres: Stage 2 to Stage 3*	*Assistant Professor (Stage 3) to Associate Professor/Equivalent Cadre (Stage 4)*	*Associate Professor to Professor Promotion in Colleges (Stage 5) as Per Assigned Posts*
II	Co-curricular, Extension and Profession related activities (Category – II)	15/year	15/year	15/year	15/year
III	Minimum total average annual Score under Categories I and II*	100/year	100/year	100/year	100/year
IV	Research and Academic Contribution (Category III)	5/Year (20/assessment period)	10/Year (50/assessment period)	15/Year (45/assessment period)	20/Year (60/assessment period)
	Expert Assessment System	Screening Committee	Screening Committee	Selection Committee	Selection Committee
V	Percentage Distribution of Weightage Points in the Expert Assessment (Total weightage = 100. Minimum required for promotion is 50)	No separate points. Screening committee to verify API scores	No separate points. Screening committee to verify API scores	20% - Contribution to Research 60% - Assessment of domain knowledge and teaching practices. 20% - Interview performance	30% - Contribution to Research. 50% - Assessment of domain knowledge and teaching practices. 20% - Interview performance

* Teachers may score up to 10 points from either Category I or Category II to achieve the minimum score required under Category I + II. Note: For universities for which Sixth PRC Awards are applicable, Stages 1, 2, 3, 4 and 5 correspond to scales with AGP of ₹ 6000, 7000, 8000, 9000 and 10000 respectively.

Explanatory Note for Tables 2(A) and 2(B)

1. All universities/colleges will set up verifiable systems for the API related information required in these tables within THREE months of notification of these regulations. They will have to be documented and collated annually by the Internal Quality Assessment cells (IQACs) of the universities/colleges for follow up by the universities/college authorities. In order to facilitate this process, all teachers shall submit the duly filled-in Performance Based Appraisal System (PBAS) proforma to the IQAC annually.
2. However, in order to remedy the difficulties of collecting retrospective information and to facilitate the implementation of these regulations from 31–12–2008 in the CAS Promotion, the API based PBAS will be progressively and prospectively rolled out.
3. Accordingly, the PBAS based on the API scores of categories I and II as mentioned in these tables is to be implemented for one year, initially based on the existing systems in universities/colleges for one year only with the minimum average scores as depicted in Table 2(A) and (B) in rows I to III. This annualized API scores can then be compounded progressively as and when the teacher becomes eligible for CAS promotion to the next cadre. Thus, if a teacher is considered for CAS promotion in 2010, one year API scores for 2009-10 alone will be required for assessment. In case of a teacher being considered for CAS promotion in 2011, two years average of API scores for these categories will be required for assessment and so on leading progressively for the complete assessment period.
4. As shown in Table 2, the aggregate minimum API score required (given in row III) can be earned from any of the two broad categories, subject to the minimum prescribed in each category. This will provide for due

weightage to teachers who contribute additionally through any of the components given in Categories I and II also, for the differing nature of contributions possible in different institutional settings

5. For Category III (research and academic contributions), maintenance of past record is done on a normal basis by teachers and hence no difficulty is envisaged in applying the API scores for this category for the entire assessment period. In this category, an aggregate minimum score is required for promotion over each stage. Alternatively, a teacher should acquire the required minimum aggregate score over two previous stages, taken together. In the case of promotion to Professor, the publication requirement shall be met over the two previous stages.
6. Candidates should offer themselves for assessment for promotion, if they fulfill the minimum API scores indicated in Tables 1 and 2, by submitting an application and the required proforma. They can do so three months before the due date if they consider themselves eligible. Candidates, who do not consider themselves eligible, can also apply at a later date.
7. If however, on final assessment, candidates do not either fulfill the minimum criteria under Rows III and IV of Tables 2(A) and 2(B) or obtain less than 50% in the expert assessment, they will be reassessed only after a minimum period of one year.
8. (a) If a candidate applies for promotion on completion of the minimum eligibility period and is successful, the date of promotion will be deemed to be the minimum period of eligibility.
   (b) If however, the candidate finds that she/he fulfills the eligibility conditions at a later date and applies on that date and is successful, her/his promotion will be deemed to be from that date of application
   (c) If the candidate does not succeed in the first assessment, but succeeds in an eventual assessment, her/his promotion will be deemed to be from the later date.

Table 2(C): Minimum Scores for APIs for Direct Recruitment of Teachers in University Departments/Colleges, Librarian/Physical Education Cadres in Universities/Colleges and Weightages in Selection Committees to be Considered along with Other Specified Eligibility Qualifications Stipulated in the Regulation

	Assistant Professor/Equivalent Cadres (Stage 1)	*Associate Professor/Equivalent Cadres (Stage 4)*	*Professor/Equivalent Cadres (Stage 5)*
Minimum API Scores	Minimum Qualification as stipulated in these regulations	Consolidated API score requirement of 300 points from category III of APIs	Consolidated API score requirement of 400 points from category III of APIs
Selection Committee criteria/ weightages (Total Weightages = 100)	(a) *Academic Record and Research Performance (50%)* (b) *Assessment* of Domain Knowledge and Teaching Skills (30%) (c) Interview performance (20%)	(a) Academic Background (20%) (b) Research performance based on API score and quality of publications (40%). (c) Assessment of Domain Knowledge and Teaching Skills (20%) (d) Interview performance: (20%)	(a) Academic Background (20%) (b) Research performance based on API score and quality of publications (40%). (c) Assessment of Domain Knowledge and Teaching Skills (20%) (d) Interview performance: (20%)

Note: For universities/colleges for which Sixth PRC Awards are applicable, Stages 1, 4 and 5 correspond to scales with AGP of ₹ 6000, 9000 and 10000 respectively.

Table 3: Minimum Academic Performance and Service Requirements for Promotion of Teachers in Universities and Colleges

S. No.	Promotion of Teachers through CAS	Service Requirement	Minimum Academic Performance Requirements and Screening/ Selection Criteria
1.	Assistant Professor/equivalent cadres from Stage 1 to Stage 2	Assistant Professor in Stage 1 and completed four years of service with Ph.D. or five years of service who are with M.Phil/PG Degree in Professional Courses such as LLM, M.Tech, M.V.Sc., M.D., or six years of service who are without Ph.D/M.Phil/PG Degree in Professional Courses	1. Minimum API scores using PBAS scoring proforma developed by the concerned university as per the norms provided in Table 2(A)/2(B). 2. One Orientation and one Refresher/Research Methodology Course of 2/3 weeks duration. 3. Screening cum Verification process for recommending promotion.
2.	Assistant Professor/equivalent cadres from Stage 2 to Stage 3	Assistant Professor with completed service of five years in Stage 2.	1. Minimum API scores using the PBAS scoring proforma developed by the concerned university as per the norms provided in Table 2(A)/II(B) 2. One course/programme from among the categories of refresher courses, methodology workshops, Training, Teaching-Learning-Evaluation Technology Programmes, Soft Skills development Programmes and Faculty Development Programmes of 2/3 week duration. 3. Screening cum Verification process for recommending promotion.
3.	Assistant Professor (Stage 3) to Associate Professor (Stage 4)	Assistant Professors with three years of completed service in Stage 3.	1. Minimum API scores using the PBAS scoring proforma developed by the concerned university as per the norms provided in Table 2A/2(B. 2. At least three publications in the entire period as Assistant Professor (twelve years). However, in the case of College teachers, an exemption of one publication will be given to M. Phil. holders and an exemption of two publications will be given to Ph.D. holders. 3. One course/programme from among the categories of methodology workshops, Training, Teaching-Learning-Evaluation Technology Programmes, Soft Skills development Programmes and Faculty

Contd...

Table 3 contd...

S. No.	*Promotion of Teachers through CAS*	*Service Requirement*	*Minimum Academic Performance Requirements and Screening/ Selection Criteria*
			Development Programmes of minimum one week duration. 4. A selection committee process as stipulated in this regulation and in Tables 2(A) and 2(B).
4.	Associate Professor (Stage 4) Professor/equivalent cadres (Stage 5)	Associate Professor with three years of completed service in Stage 4.	1. Minimum yearly/cumulative API scores using the PBAS scoring proforma developed by the concerned university as per the norms provided in Table 2(A)/II(B). Teachers may combine two assessment periods (in Stages 2 and 3) to achieve minimum API scores, if required. 2. A minimum of five publications since the period that the teacher is placed in Stage 3. 3. A selection committee process as stipulated in this regulation and in Tables 2(A) and 2(B).
5.	Professor (Stage 5) to Professor (Stage 6).	Professor with ten years of completed service (universities only)	1. Minimum yearly/cumulative API scores for the assessment period as per the norms provided in Table 2(A). 2. Additional credentials are to be evidenced by: (a) post doctoral research outputs of high standard; (b) awards/honours/recognitions/patents and IPR on products and processes developed/technology transfer achieved; and Additional research degrees like D.Sc., D.Litt., LL.B., etc., 3. A review process by an Expert Committee as stipulated in this regulation and in Tables 2(A) and 2(B).

* For teachers seeking promotion under CAS to Associate Professor, for those who on the date of this notification are Assistant Professors in Stage 2, the requirement of publications may be adjusted pro rata. For all others who enter Stage 2, subsequent to this notification, the requirement of three publications, as defined in these regulations, will be applicable.

Note: For universities/colleges for which Sixth PRC Awards are applicable, Stages 1, 2, 3, 4, 5 and 6 correspond to scales with AGP of ₹ 6000, 7000, 8000, 9000, 10000 and 12000 respectively.

Table 4: Academic Performance Indicators (APIS) and Proposed Scores Developed by UGC for Adoption of Performance Based Appraisal System (PBAS) for Career Advancement Scheme (CAS) Promotions of University/Director/Deputy Director, Assistant Director of Physical Education/College Director of Physical Education

Category I: Teaching, Training, Coaching, Sports Person Development and Sports Management Activities

S. No.	*Nature of Activity*	*Maximum Score*
Category -I		
1.	Management of Physical Education and Sports Programme for students (Planning, executing and evaluating the policies in Physical Education and Sports) (20 Points) Lecture cum practice based athlete/sports classes, seminars undertaken as percentage of allotted hours (20 Points).	40
2.	Extending services, sports facilities and training on holidays to the institutions and organizations.	10
3.	Organizing and conducting sports and games competitions at the International/National/State/Inter University/Inter Zonal Levels (25 Points). Organizing and conducting coaching camps/sports person development/training programmes (15 Points).	40
4.	Upgradation of scientific and technological knowledge in Physical Education and Sports (5 Points). Identifying sports talents and Mentoring sports excellence among students (10 Points).	20
5.	Development and maintenance of play fields, purchase and maintenance of the other sports facilities.	15
	Total Score	**125**
	Minimum API Score Required	75

Category II: Co-Curricular, Extension and Professional Development Related Activities

S. No.	*Nature of Activity*	*Maximum Score*
1.	Student related co-curricular, extension and field based activities (such as Cultural exchange and Sports Programmes (Various level of extramurals and intramural programmes); extension work through NSS/NCC and other channels	20
2.	Contribution to Corporate life and management of the sports units and institution through participation in sports and administrative committees and responsibilities	15
3.	Professional Development activities (such as participation in seminars, conferences, short term, training courses, camps and events, talks, lectures, membership of associations, dissemination and general articles, not covered in Category III below)	15
	Minimum API Score Required	15

Category-III: Research and Academic Contributions

S. No.	*APIs*	*Faculties of Physical Education*	*Max. Points for University and College Teacher Position*
III(a)	Research Publication (Journals)	Refereed Journals*	15/publication
		Non-referred but recognized and reputable journals and periodicals, having ISBN/ISSN numbers.	10/publication
		Full papers in Conference proceedings, etc.* (Abstracts not to be included)	10/publication
III(b)	Research Publications (books, chapters in books, other than refereed journal articles)	Text or Reference Books Published by International Publishers**	50/sole author 10/chapter in an edited book
		Text or Reference Books Published by National/Central/State Government/Societies**	25/sole author, 5/chapter in edited books
		Subject Books by Other local publishers with ISBN/ISSN numbers**	15/sole author, 3/chapter in edited books
		Chapters in knowledge based volumes in Indian/National level publishers with ISBN/ISSN numbers and with numbers of national and international directories.**	5/Chapter

* For Joint Research papers, the First/Principal author will share 60%, while the rest joint authors will share the 40% of API scores.

** Scores (50/25/10/03 whatever the case may be) to be shared equally by all authors.

III(C)	**Research Project**		
III (C) (i)	Sponsored Projects carried out/ongoing	Major Projects/Events amount mobilized with grants above 5.0 lakhs	20 each Project
		Major Projects/Events Amount mobilized with minimum of ₹ 4.00 lakhs up to ₹ 5.00 lakhs	15 each major project
		Minor projects from central/state funding agencies with grants below 4.00 lakhs	10 each minor Project
III (C) (ii)	Consultancy Projects carried out/ongoing	Amount mobilized with minimum of ₹ 1.0 lakh	10 per every ₹ 5.0 lakhs 2 per every ₹ 1.0 lakhs
III (C) (iii)	Completed projects : Quality Evaluation	Completed project report (Accepted by funding agency)	20/each major project and 10/ each minor project
III (C) (iv)	Projects Outcome/Outputs	Policy document of Govt. Bodies at Central and State level	30/each output or outcome for National patents etc/50/each for International patents.
III (D)	**Research Guidance**		
III (D)(i)	M.Phil.	Degree awarded only	3/each candidate
III (D) (ii)	Ph.D	Degree awarded	10/each candidate
		Thesis submitted	7/each candidate
III(E)	**Training Courses and Conference/Seminar/Workshop Papers**		
III(E)(i)	Research Methodology/ Training/ Coaching Workshops	Research methodology/Training/ Coaching programme (not less than three weeks)/ workshops of not less than one week	20
III(E)(ii)	Papers in Conferences/ Seminars/ workshops etc.	Participation and Presentation of research papers (oral/poster) in:	
		(a) International conference	10/each
		(b) National	7.5/each
		(c) Regional/State level (d) Local – University/ College level	5/each 3/each
III(E) (iv)	Invitations for conferences/seminars/ workshops/ symposia to deliver lectures/chair sessions	(a) International	10/each
		(b) National	7.5/each
		(c) State level/Regional	5/each
		(d) University/College level Endowment lectures	5/each

Table 5(A): Minimum Norms of APIS as Provided in Table 4 to be Applied for the Career Advancement Scheme (CAS) Promotion of University Director/Deputy Director/Assistant Director of Physical Education, and Weightages for Expert Assessment in Selection Committees

		Assistant Director of Physical Education (Stage 1 to Stage 2 (Senior Scale)	*Assistant Director of Physical Education (Senior Scale) (Stage 2) to Deputy Director of Physical Education/Assistant Director Physical Education (Selection Grade) (Stage 3)*	*Deputy Director Physical Education/Assistant Director Physical Education (Selection Grade), Stage 3 to Stage 4*	*Deputy Director Physical Education/Assistant Director Physical Education (Selection Grade), (Stage 4) to Director of Physical Education (Stage 5) (university only)*
1.	Teaching, training coaching, sports person development and sports management activities (Category – I)	75/year	75/year	75/year	75/year
2.	Extension and Profession related activities (Category II)	15/year	15/year	15/year	15/year
3.	Minimum total average API annual score under Categories I and II*	100/year	100/year	100/year	100/year
4.	Research and Academic Contributions (Category III) – Minimum Annual score required – to be assessed cumulatively	10/year (40/assessment period)	20/year (100/assessment Period)	30/year (90/assessment period)	40/year (120/assessment period)
	Expert Assessment System	Screening Committee	Screening Committee	Selection Committee	Selection Committee
5.	Percentage Distribution of Weightage Points in the Expert Assessment (Total weightage = 100. Minimum required 50)	No separate points. Screening committee to verify API scores	No separate points. Screening committee to verify API scores	30% - Research evaluation 50% - Assessment of domain knowledge and skills in sports 20% - Interview performance	50% - Research evaluation. 30% - Assessment of domain knowledge contribution and organisation track record with vision plan. 20% - Interview performance

* Candidates may score 10 points from either Category I or Category II to achieve the minimum score required under Category I + II.

Note: For universities for which Sixth PRC Awards are applicable, Stages 1, 2, 3, 4 and 5 correspond to scales as provided, and AGP of ₹ 6000, 7000, 8000, 9000 and 10000 respectively.

Table 5(B): Minimum APIS as Provided in Table 4 to be Applied for the Career Advancement Scheme (CAS) Promotion of College Director of Physical Education (Senior Scale)/College Director of Physical Education (Selection Grade), and Weightages for Expert Assessment in Selection Committees

S. No	*Categories of Criteria*	*Minimum Average, yearly or cumulative, API score required during the assessment period of each level as evaluated under the Performance Based Appraisal System (PBAS) with weightages for Expert Assessment*		
		College Director of Physical Education to College Director of Physical Education (Senior Scale) (Stage 1 to Stage 2)	*College Director of Physical Education Senior Scale to Selection Grade (Stage 2 to Stage 3).*	*College Director of Physical Education (Selection Grade) (Stage 3 to Stage 4).*
1.	Teaching-learning, Evaluation Related Activities (Category – I)	75/year	75/year	75/year
2.	Co-curricular, Extension and Profession related activities (Category – II)	15/year	15/year	15/year
3.	Minimum total average annual Score under Categories I and II*	100/year	100/year	100/year
4.	Research and Academic Contribution (Category III) – Minimum Annual Score Required-to assessed cumulatively	5/Year (20/assessment period)	10/Year (50/assessment period)	15/Year (45/assessment period)
	Expert Assessment System	Screening Committee	Screening Committee	Selection Committee
5.	Percentage Distribution of Weightage Points in the Expert Assessment (Total weightage = 100. Minimum required 50)	No separate points. Screening committee to verify API scores	No separate points. Screening committee to verify API scores	30% - Research evaluation 50% - Assessment of domain knowledge and skills in sports. 20% - Interview performance

* Teachers may score 10 points from either Category I or Category II to achieve the minimum score required under Category I + II.

Note: For colleges in which Sixth PRC Awards are applicable, Stages 1, 2, 3 and 4 correspond to scales as provided, and AGP of ₹ 6000, 7000, 8000 and 9000 respectively.

Table 5(C): Minimum APIS and Other Norms for the Direct Recruitment of Physical Education Personnel in University Departments/Colleges

(To be considered along with other specified eligibility qualifications stipulated in this UGC regulation)

S. No. of Category	*Minimum Norm/Criteria*	*Assistant Director of Physical Education/College Director of Physical Education (Entry Stage – Stage 1)*	*Deputy Director of Physical Education in university (Stage 4)*	*Director of Physical Education in university (Stage 5)*
1.	API score (Research and Academic Contribution – Category III)		Consolidated API score requirement of 300 points	Consolidated API score requirement of 400 points
2.	Selection Committee criteria/weightages (Total weightage = 100)	(d) Track Record of championship won (30%) (e) Sports and athletic skills (40%) (f) Interview performance (30%)	(h) Research papers (3 nos) evaluation: (40%) (i) Organizational skills/Plans of sports: (30%) (j) Interview performance: (30%)	(a) Research papers (5 nos) evaluation: (50%) (b) Organisational track vision plan: (25%) (c) Interview performance: (25%)

Note: For universities/colleges in which Sixth PRC Awards are applicable, Stages 1, 4 and 5 correspond to scales as provided, and AGP of ₹ 6000, 9000 and 10000 respectively

Table 6: Minimum Academic Performance and Service Requirements for Promotion of Physical Education Cadres in Universities and Colleges

S. No.	*Promotion of Physical Education Cadres through CAS*	*Service (as prescribed by the MHRD Notification) requirement*	*Minimum Academic Performance Requirements and Screening/ Selection Criteria*
1.	Assistant DPE/College DPE to Assistant DPE (Senior Scale)/College DPE (Senior Scale) (Stage 1 to Stage 2)	Assistant DPE/College DPE completed four years of service in Stage 1 with Ph.D. or five years of service who are with M.Phil. or six years of service who are without Ph.D/M.Phil	1. Minimum API scores using PBAS scoring proforma developed by the concerned university as per the norms provided in Table 5(A) of for university DPEs cadres in Universities and in Table 5(B) of for cadres in Colleges. 2. One Orientation and one Refresher Course of ¾ weeks duration. 3. No separate interview points for the Screening cum Evaluation process of recommending promotion.
2.	Assistant DPE (senior scale)/College DPE (senior scale) to Deputy DPE/Assistant DPE (selection grade)/College DPE (selection grade) (Stage 2 to Stage 3)	Assistant DPE (senior scale) College DPE (senior scale) with completed service of five years in Stage 2	1. Minimum API scores using the PBAS scoring proforma developed by the concerned university as per the norms provided in Table 5(A) of for university DPEs cadres in Universities and in Table 5(B) of for DPEs cadres in Colleges. 2. Additionally, two refresher courses of 3–4 weeks duration to have been undergone during the assessment period. 3. No separate interview points for the Screening cum Evaluation process of recommending promotion.
3.	Deputy DPE/Assistant DPE (Selection Grade)/College DPE (Selection Grade) to Deputy DPE/Assistant DPE (Selection Grade)/College DPE (Selection Grade) (Stage 3 to Stage 4).	Deputy DPE/Assistant DPE (Selection Grade)/College DPE (Selection Grade) with three years of completed service in Stage 3.	1. Minimum API scores using the PBAS scoring proforma developed by the concerned university as per the norms provided in Table 5(A) of for university DPEs cadres in Universities and in Table 5(B) of for cadres in Colleges. 2. Minimum three publications over twelve years. For promotion in Colleges an

Contd...

Table 4 contd...

S. No.	*Promotion of Physical Education Cadres through CAS*	*Service (as prescribed by the MHRD Notification) requirement*	*Minimum Academic Performance Requirements and Screening/ Selection Criteria*
			exemption of one publication for M. Phil. holders and exemption of two publications for Ph. D. holders. 3. Evidence of having produced teams/athletes 4. A selection committee process as stipulated in this regulation and in Table 5(A) of for the university DPE cadres in universities and in Table 5(B) of for cadres in colleges.
4.	University DPE (Stage 5) (For universities only)	Deputy DPE in universities with three years of completed service in Stage 4.	1. Minimum API scores using the PBAS scoring proforma developed by the concerned university as per the norms provided in Table 5(A) for DPEs in university. These may be achieved over two assessment periods, if required. 2. A minimum of five publications over two assessment periods (six years). 3. Evidence of having produced teams/athletes. 4. A selection committee process as stipulated in this regulation and in Table 5(A) for DPEs in the university.

Note: The explanatory note provided for Tables 2(A) and (B) for CAS for teachers is also applicable for the Physical Director cadres as per the API score specified for this cadre.

Note: For universities/colleges for which Sixth PRC Awards are applicable, Stages 1, 2, 3, 4 and 5 correspond to scales with AGP of ₹ 6000, 7000, 8000, 9000 and 10000 respectively.

Table 7: Academic Performance Indicators (APIS) and Proposed Scores Developed by UGC for Adoption of Performance Based Appraisal System (PBAS) for Direct Appointment/Career Advancement Scheme (CAS) Promotions Applicable to Librarian (University) Deputy Librarian and Asst. Librarian/College Librarian

Category – I: Procurement, organization, and delivery of knowledge and information through Library services

S. No.	*Nature of Activity*	*Maximum Score*
1.	Library resources organization and maintenance of books, journals, reports; Provision of library reader-services, literature retrieval services to researchers and analysis of reports; Provision of assistance to the departments of University/College with the required inputs for preparing reports, manuals and related documents; Assistance towards updating institutional website with activity related information and for bringing out institutional Newsletters, etc.	40
2.	ICT and other new technologies' application for up gradation of library services such as automation of catalogue, learning resources procurement functions, circulation operations including membership records, serial subscription system, reference and information services, library security (technology based methods such as RFID, CCTV), development of library management tools (software), Intranet management.	30
3.	Development, organization and management of e-resources including their accessibility over Intranet/Internet, digitization of library resources, e-delivery of information, etc.	25
4	User awareness and instruction programmes (Orientation lectures, users' training in the use of library services as e-resources, OPAC; knowledge resources user promotion programmes like organizing book exhibitions, other interactive latest learning resources, etc.	20
5.	Additional services such as extending library facilities on holidays, shelf order maintenance, library user manual, building and extending institutional library facilities to outsiders through external membership norms	10
	Total Score	125
	Minimum API score required	75

Category-II: Co-Curricular, Extension and Professional Development Related Activities

S. No.	*Nature of Activity*	*Maximum Score*
1.	Student related co-curricular, extension and field based activities (such Cultural exchange and Library service Programmes (various level of extramural and intramural programmes); extension, library-literary work through different channels,	20
2.	Contribution to Corporate life and management of the library units and institution through participation in library and administrative committees and responsibilities.	15
3.	Professional Development activities (such as participation in seminars, conferences, short term, e-library training courses, workshops and events, talks, lectures, membership of associations, dissemination and general articles, not covered in Category III below)	15
	Minimum API Score Required	15

Category –III : Research and Academic Contributions

S. No.	*APIs*	*Activity*	*Maximum Point*
III A	Research Papers published in:	Refereed Journals	15/publication
		Non-refereed but recognized and reputable journals and periodicals, having ISBN/ISSN numbers.	10/publication
		Conference proceedings as full papers, etc. (Abstracts not to be included)	10/publication
III (B)	Research Publications (books, chapters in books, other than refereed journal articles)	Text or Reference Books Published by International Publishers with an established peer review system	50/sole author; 10/chapter in an edited book
		Subjects Books by National level publishers/State and Central Govt. Publications with ISBN/ISSN numbers.	25/sole author, and 5/chapter in edited books
		Subject Books by Other local publishers with ISBN/ISSN numbers.	15/sole author, and 3/chapter in edited books

S. No.	*APIs*	*Activity*	*Maximum Point*
		Chapters contributed to edited knowledge based volumes published by International Publishers	10/Chapter
		Chapters in knowledge based volumes by Indian/National level publishers with ISBN/ISSN numbers and with numbers of national and international directories	5/Chapter
III (C)			
III (C) (i)	Sponsored Projects carried out/ongoing	(d) Major Projects amount mobilized with grants above 30.0 lakhs	20/Project
		(e) Major Projects amount mobilized with grants above 5.0 lakhs up to 30.00 lakhs	15/Project
		(f) Minor Projects (Amount mobilized with grants above ₹ 50,000 up to ₹ 5.0 lakh)	10/Project
III (C) (ii)	Consultancy Projects carried out/ongoing	Amount mobilized with minimum of ₹ 10.00 lakhs	10 per every ₹ 10.0 lakhs and ₹ 2.0 lakhs, respectively
III (C) (iii)	Completed projects : Quality Evaluation	Completed project Report (Acceptance from funding agency)	20/each major project and 10/each minor project
III (C) (iv)	Projects Outcome/Outputs	Patent/Technology transfer/Product/Process	30/each national level output or patent/50/ each for International level
III (D)			
III (D) (i)	M.Phil.	Degree awarded only	3/each candidate
III (D) (ii)	Ph.D	Degree awarded	10/each candidate
		Thesis submitted	7/each candidate

S. No.	*APIs*	*Activity*	*Maximum Point*
III(E)			
III(E) (i)	Refresher courses, Methodology workshops, Training, Teaching-Learning- Evaluation Technology Programmes, Soft Skills development Programmes, Faculty Development Programmes (Max: 30 points)	Not less than two weeks duration	20/each
		One week duration	10/each
III(E) (ii)	Papers in Conferences/ Seminars/workshops etc. *	Participation and Presentation of research papers (oral/poster) in	
		International conference	10/each
		(b) National	6/each
		(c) Regional/State level	5/each
		Local –University/College level	3/each
III(E) (iv)	Invited lectures or presentations for conferences/symposia	International	10/each
		National level	5

*If a paper presented in Conference/Seminar is published in the form of Proceedings, the points would accrue for the publication (III (A)) and not under presentation (III (E)(ii)).

Notes:

1. The API for joint publications will have to be calculated in the following manner: Of the total score for the relevant category of publication by the concerned teacher, the first/Principal author and the corresponding author/supervisor/mentor of the teacher would share equally 60% of the total points and the remaining 40% would be shared equally by all other authors.

Table 8(A): Minimum APIs as provided in Table 7 to be applied for the Promotion of Library staff of universities and Weightages for Expert Assessment Under Career Advancement Scheme (CAS)

		Assistant Librarian to Assistant Librarian (senior scale) (Stage 1 to Stage 2)	*Deputy Librarian/Assistant Librarian (Selection Grade) (Stage 2 to Stage 3)*	*Deputy Librarian/Assistant Librarian (selection Grade) (Stage 3 to Stage 4)*	*Librarian (university only) (Stage 4 to Stage 5)*
1.	Procurement, organization and delivery of knowledge and information thro' library services (category I)	75/year	75/year	75/year	75/year
2.	Extension and Profession related activities (Category II)	15/year	15/year	15/year	15/year
3.	Minimum total average annual Score under Categories I and II*	100/year	100/year	100/year	100/year
4.	Research and Academic Contribution (Category III) – Minimum Annual Score Required – to be assessed cumulatively	10/Year (40/assessment period)	20/Year (100/assessment period)	30/Year (90/assessment period)	40/Year (120/assessment period)
	Expert Assessment System	Screening Committee	Screening Committee	Selection Committee	
5.	Percentage Distribution of Weightage Points in the Expert Assessment (Total weightage = 100. Minimum required 50))	No separate points. Screening committee to verify API scores	No separate points. Screening committee to verify API scores	30% - Library related research papers evaluation 50% - Assessment of domain knowledge on Library automation and Organizational skills 20% - Interview performance	50% Library publication work 30% Assessment of innovative Library service and organization of digital library services 20% Interview performance

* Candidates may score 10 points from either Category I or Category II to achieve the minimum score required under Category I + II.

Note: For universities/colleges for which Sixth PRC Awards are applicable, Stages 1, 2, 3, 4and 5 correspond to scales as given with AGP of ₹ 6000, 7000, 8000, 9000 and 10000 respectively.

Table 8(B): Minimum Weightage Points (WP) norms of the APIs as provided in Table 7 to be applied for the Promotion of Library staff of Colleges and Weightages for Expert Assessment Under Career Advancement Scheme (CAS)

		College Librarian (Stage 1) College Librarian (senior scale) (Stage 2)	*College Librarian (senior scale) (Stage 2) to College Librarian (Selection Grade) (Stage 3)*	*College Librarian (selection Grade) (Stage 3 to Stage 4)*
1.	Procurement, organisation and delivery of knowledge and information thro' library services (category I)	75/Year	75/Year	75/year
2.	Extension and Profession related activities (Category II)	15/Year	15/Year	15/Year
3.	Minimum total average annual Score under Categories I and II*	100/Year	100/Year	100/Year
4.	Research and Academic Contribution (Category III) – Minimum Annual Score Required – to be assessed cumulatively	5/Year (40/assessment period)	10/Year (100/assessment period)	15/Year (90/assessment period)
	Expert Assessment System	*Screening Committee*	*Screening Committee*	*Selection Committee*
5.	Percentage of Distribution of Weightage Points in the Expert Assessment (Total weightage = 100. Minimum required 50)	No separate points. Screening committee to verify API scores	No separate points. Screening committee to verify API scores	30% - Library related research papers evaluation 50% - Assessment of domain knowledge on Library automation and Organizational skills 20% - Interview performance

Candidates may score 10 points from either Category I or Category II to achieve the minimum score required under Category I + II.

Note: For colleges for which Sixth PRC Awards are applicable, Stages 1, 2, 3 and 4 correspond to scales as provided with AGP of ₹ 6000, 7000, 8000 and 9000 respectively.

Table 8(C): Minimum APIS and other Norms for the Direct Recruitment of Librarian Positions in University Departments/Colleges

(To be considered along with other specified eligibility qualifications stipulated in this UGC regulation)

S. No. of Category	*Minimum Norm/Criteria*	*Assistant University Librarian/College Librarian (Stage 1)*	*Deputy Librarian in universities (Stage 4)*	*Librarian (university only) (Stage 5)*
I.	API score (Research and Academic Contribution – Category III)		Consolidated API score requirement of 300 points	Consolidated API score requirement of 400 points
II.	Selection Committee criteria/weightages (Total weightage = 100)	(a) Teaching/compute and communication skills by a Lecture demonstration (30%) (b) Record of Library management skills (20%) (c) Interview performance (50%)	(a) Library related Research/Theme papers (3 Nos) Evaluation: (50%) (b) Library automation skills and Organizational Plans (20%) (c) Interview performance (30%)	(a) Library Research papers (Five) evaluation (60%) (b) Organizational track record of innovation library service and vision plan (20%) (c) Interview performance (20%)

Note: For universities for which Sixth PRC Awards are applicable, Stages 1, 4, 5 and 5 correspond to scales as given and AGP of ₹ 6000, 7000, 8000, 9000, 10000 and 12000 respectively.

Table 9: Minimum Academic Performance and Service Requirements for Promotion of Librarian Cadres in Universities and Colleges

S. No.	*Promotion of Librarian Cadres through CAS*	*Service (as prescribed by the MHRD Notification) requirement*	*Minimum Academic Performance Requirements and Screening/Selection Criteria*
1.	Assistant University Librarian/College Librarian to Assistant Librarian (Senior Scale)/College Librarian (Senior Scale) (Stage 1 to Stage 2)	Assistant University Librarian/College Librarian (Stage 1) completed four years of service with Ph. D. or five years of service who are with M. Phil or six years of service who are without Ph. D./M.Phil.	1. Minimum API scores using PBAS scoring proforma developed by the university as per the norms provided in Table 8(A) for Librarian cadres in universities and Table 8(B) for college Librarian cadres. 2. One Orientation and one Refresher Course of 3/4 weeks duration 3. No separate interview points for the Screening cum Verification process of recommending promotion.

S. No.	*Promotion of Librarian Cadres through CAS*	*Service (as prescribed by the MHRD Notification) requirement*	*Minimum Academic Performance Requirements and Screening/Selection Criteria*
2.	Assistant university Librarian (Senior Scale)/college Librarian (senior scale) to Assistant university Librarian (Selection Grade)/ College Librarian/(selection grade) (Stage 2 to Stage 3)	Assistant university Librarian (Senior Scale)/college Librarian (senior scale) with completed service of five years in Stage 2	1. Minimum API scores using the PBAS scoring proforma developed by University as per the norms provided in Table 8(A) for Librarian Cadres in universities and Table 8(B) for college librarian cadres. 2. Additionally, two refresher courses, for a minimum period of 3 to 4 week duration to have been undergone during the assessment period. 3. No separate interview points for the Screening cum Verification process of recommending promotion.
3.	Deputy university Librarian/Assistant university Librarian (Selection Grade)/ College Librarian (Selection Grade) (Stage 3 to Stage 4)	Assistant university Librarian (Selection Grade)/College Librarian (Selection Grade) with three years of completed service in Stage 3.	1. Minimum API scores using the PBAS scoring proforma developed by university as per the norms provided in Table 8(A) for Librarian cadres in universities and in Table 8(B) for Librarian Cadres in Colleges. 2. Three publications over twelve years. In Colleges, an exemption of one publication will be given to M. Phil holders and two publications to Ph. D. Holders. 3. Additionally one course/training under the categories of Library automation/Analytical tool Development for academic documentation. 4. A selection committee process as stipulated in the Regulation and in Table 8(A) for university in Table 8(B) for librarian cadres in colleges.
4.	Librarian (university) (Stage 5) -	Deputy Librarian in university with three years of completed service in Stage 4.	1. Minimum API scores using the PBAS scoring proforma developed by the university as per the norms provided in Table 8(A) of for Librarian (university). Minimum API scores can also be considered over two assessment periods (Stages 3 and 4), if required. 2. A minimum of 5 publications over current and previous assessment periods. 3. Evidence of innovative library service and organization of published work 4. A selection committee process as stipulated in this regulation and in Table 8(A) for Librarian (university)

Note: The explanatory note provided for Tables 2(A) and (B) for CAS for teachers is also applicable for the librarian cadres as per the API score specified for this cadre.

Note: For universities for which Sixth PRC Awards are applicable, Stages 1, 2, 3, 4 and 5 correspond to scales as provided and AGP of ₹ 6000, 7000, 8000, 9000, 10000 and 12000 respectively.

ANNEXURE–C

In Indian Context: AICTE Norms for Infrastructure–2010

Norms for Land Requirement and Building Space for Technical Institution

4.1* LAND REQUIREMENTS FOR TECHNICAL INSTITUTIONS

	Land Area Requirement in Acres					
	Other than Rural Places (Competent Authority to certify that the place is not located in a rural area)			*Rural Places as Defined by Competent Authority*		
	UG Programs	*Diploma*	*Stand alone Post graduate Programs*	*UG Programs*	*Diploma*	*Stand alone Post Graduate Programs*
Engineering and Technology	2.50	1.50	2.5	10.0	5.00	10.0
Pharmacy	0.75	0.75	0.75	2.00	2.00	2.00
Architecture and Town Planning	1.00	1.00	1.00	2.50	2.50	2.50
Applied Arts and Crafts	0.75	0.75	0.75	2.00	2.00	2.00
HMCT	1.00	1.00	1.00	2.50	2.50	2.50
MCA	–	–	0.50	–	–	1.50
Management	–	–	0.50	–	–	1.00

4.1.1	a	Land area shall cover hostel facilities, if any
	b	Land shall be in one continuous piece.
	c	Considering hilly nature of land in North Eastern States, land may be made available in 3 pieces which are not away from each other by more than 1 Km

* AICTE's infrastructure details starts from 4.1 onward.

4.1.2	*Program*	*Number of students generally allowed per acre land available when FSI = 1*
a	Engineering and Technology	300
b	Pharmacy	250
c	Architecture and Town Planning	250
d	Applied Arts and Crafts	250
e	HMCT	300
f	MCA	300
g	Management	300

4.2 BUILT-UP AREA REQUIREMENTS

4.2	a	The Institution area is divided in, Instructional area (INA, carpet area in sq. m), Administrative area (ADA, carpet area in sq. m.), Amenities area (AMA, carpet area in sq. m).
	b	Circulation area (CIA) is equal to 0.25^x (INA+ADA+AMA).
	c	Total built up area in sq. m. is equal to (INA+ADA+AMA) + (CIA).

4.2.1 Instructional Area (Carpet Area) in sqm

Engineering/Technology (Degree Institute)

	Number of Divisions UG (Class of 60)	*Duration of course in Yrs*	*Class Rooms(C)*	*Tutorial Rooms(D) PG Class rooms (H)*	*Laboratory (including additional WS/Labs for category "X" courses)*	*Research Laboratory*	*Work Shop (for all courses)*	*Additional WS/Labs for Category "X" courses*	*Computer Centre*	*Drawing Hall*	*Library and Reading Room*	*Seminar Halls*
Carpet Area in sqm per room			66	33	66	66	200	200	150	132	400	132
Number of rooms required for new Institution	A	4	C=A	D=C/4	10	–	1	–	1	1	1	1
Total Number of rooms (UG)	A	4	C=Ax4	D=C/4	10/Course#	–	1	2/Course (Maximum 4)	1	1	1	1/Course
Total Number of rooms (PG)	F	2	–	H=Fx2	1/Specialisation	1/Specialisation						

1.	Category X of courses: Mechanical, Production, Civil, Electrical, Chemical, Textile, Marine, Aeronautical and allied courses of each.
2.	Classrooms, Tutorial rooms and Laboratories required for 2nd, 3rd and 4th year may be added progressively to achieve total number as stated.
3.	Additional Library (Reading room) area of 50 sq m/per 60 student (UG+PG) intake beyond 420.
4.	UG laboratories if shared for PG courses shall be upgraded to meet requirements of PG curriculum
5.	#Progressive requirement, 2nd year onwards shall be calculated as 3+3+2 labs/course
6.	#Additional 5 Labs/Course when number of divisions are more than 2/course
7.	Round off fraction in calculation to the next integer.

Engineering/Technology (Diploma and Post Diploma Institute)

	Number of Divisions (Class of 60)	*Duration of course in Yrs*	*Class Rooms(C)*	*Tutorial Rooms(D)*	*Laboratory (including additional WS/Labs for category "X" courses)*	*Work Shop (for all courses)*	*Additional WS/Labs for Category "X" courses*	*Computer Centre*	*Drawing Hall*	*Library and Reading Room*	*Seminar Halls*
Carpet Area in sqm per room			66	33	66	200	200	**100**	132	300	132
Number of rooms required for new Institution	A	Y	C=A	D=C/4	06	1	–	1	1	1	–
Total Number of rooms	A	Y	C=AxY	D=C/4	06/Course#	1	2/Course (Maximum 4)	1	1	1	1

1	Category X of courses: Mechanical, Production, Civil, Electrical, Chemical, Textile, Marine, Aeronautical and allied courses of each.
2	Classrooms, Tutorial rooms and Laboratories required for 2nd, 3rd and 4th year may be added progressively to achieve total number as stated.
3	Additional Library (Reading room) area of 50 sq m/per 60 student (UG+PG) intake beyond 420.
4	#Progressive requirement, 2nd year onwards shall be calculated as 2+2 labs/course
5	Round off fraction in calculation to the next integer.

Pharmacy (Degree Institute)

	Number of division UG (Class of 60) PG (Class of 18)	*Duration of course in yes*	*Class Rooms*	*Tutorial Rooms*	*Laboratory (includes Machine room & Instrumentation room)*	*Research Laboratory*	*Animal House*	*Computer Centre*	*Library and Reading Room*	*Seminar Hall*
Carpet Area in sqm per room			66	33	75	75	75	75	150	132
Number of Rooms required for new Institution	A	4	C=A	D=C/4	4	–	1	1	1	1
Total Number of rooms (UG)	A	4	C=Ax4	D=C/4	12	–	1	1	1	1
Total Number of rooms (PG)	F	2	–	H=F	1/Specialisation	1/Specialisation				

1.	Laboratories include Machine room & Instrumentation room
2.	Classrooms, Tutorial rooms and Laboratories required for 2nd, 3rd and 4th year may be added progressively (3+3+2) to achieve total number as stated.
3.	UG Laboratories if shared for PG courses shall be upgraded to meet requirements of PG curriculum.
4.	Round off fraction in calculation to the next integer

Pharmacy (Diploma/Post Diploma Institute)

	Divisions of 60)Number of (Class of 60)	*Duration of course in*	*Class Room*	*Tutorial Room*	*Laboratory (includes Machine room & Instrumentation room)*	*Animal House*	*Computer Centre*	*Library & Reading Room*	*Seminar Hall*
Carpet Area in sqm per room			66	33	75	75	75	150	132
Number of rooms required for new Institution	A	Y	C=A	D=C/4	4	1	1	1	–
Total Number of rooms	A	Y	C=AxY	D=C/4	9	1	1	1	1

1	Laboratories include Machine room and Instrumentation room
2.	Classrooms, Tutorial rooms and Laboratories required for 2nd and 3rd year may be added progressively (3+2) to achieve total number as stated.
3.	UG Laboratories if shared for PG courses shall be upgraded to meet requirements of PG curriculum.

Architecture and Town Planning (Degree Institute)

	Number of Divisions UG (Class of 60) PG (Class of 18)	*Duration of course in Yrs*	*Class Rooms(C)*	*Tutorial Rooms(D) PG Class rooms (H)*	*Laboratory including Computer Laboratory*	*Model making and Carpentry Workshop*	*Studio/Material Museum*	*Computer Centre*	*Library and Reading Room*	*Seminar Halls*
Carpet Area in sqm per room			66	33	66	200	132	75	150	132
Number of Rooms required for new Institution	A	5	C=A	D=A/4	1	1	1	1	1	–
Total Number of rooms UG)	A	5	C=Ax5	D=C/4	5	1	5	1	1	1
Total Number of rooms (PG)	F	2	–	H=Fx2	1/Specialisation					

1.	Classrooms, Tutorial rooms and Laboratories required for 2nd, 3rd, 4th and 5th year may be added progressively (1+1+1+1) to achieve total number as stated. UG laboratories if shared for PG courses shall be upgraded to meet requirements of PG curriculum.
2.	Round off fraction in calculation to the next integer

Architecture and Town Planning (Diploma/post Diploma Institute)

	Number of Divisions (Class of 60)	*Duration of course in Yrs*	*Class Rooms(C)*	*Tutorial Rooms(D) PG Class rooms (H)*	*Laboratory including Computer Laboratory*	*Model making and Carpentry Workshop*	*Studio/Material Museum*	*Computer Centre*	*Library and Reading Room*	*Seminar Halls*
Carpet Area in sqm per room			66	33	66	200	132	75	150	132
Number of Rooms required for new Institution	A	5	C=A	D=A/4	1	1	1	1	1	–
Total Number of rooms UG)	A	5	C=Ax5	D=C/4	5	1	5	1	1	1

1.	Classrooms, Tutorial rooms and Laboratories required for 2nd, 3rd, 4th and 5th year may be added progressively (1+1+1+1) to achieve total number as stated. UG laboratories if shared for PG courses shall be upgraded to meet requirements of PG curriculum.
2.	Round off fraction in calculation to the next integer

Architecture and Town Planning (Degree Institute)

	Number of Divisions0UG (Class of 60) PG (Class of 18)	*Duration of Course in Yrs*	*Class Rooms(C)*	*Tutorial Rooms(D) PG Class Rooms (H)*	*Laboratory Including C006Fmputer Laboratory*	*Model Making and Carpentry Workshop*	*Studio/Material Museum*	*Computer Centre*	*Library and Reading Room*	*Seminar Halls*
Carpet Area in sqm per room			66	33	66	200	132	75	150	132
Number of Rooms required for new Institution	A	5	C=A	D=A/4	1	1	1	1	1	–
Total Number of rooms UG)	A	5	C=Ax5	D=C/4	5	1	5	1	1	1
Total Number of rooms (PG)	F	2	–	H=Fx2	1/Specialisation					

1.	Classrooms, Tutorial rooms and Laboratories required for 2nd, 3rd, 4th and 5th year may be added progressively (1+1+1+1) to achieve total number as stated. UG laboratories if shared for PG courses shall be upgraded to meet requirements of PG curriculum.
2.	Round off fraction in calculation to the next integer

Applied Arts and Crafts (Diploma/Post Diploma Institute)

	Number of Divisions (Class of 60)	*Duration of Course in Yes*	*Class Rooms(C)*	*Tutorial Rooms(D)*	*Laboratory Including Photography and Computer Laboratory*	*Work shop*	*Studio/Display Room*	*Computer Centre*	*Library and Reading Room*	*Seminar Halls*
Carpet Area in sqm per room			66	33	66	200	132	75	150	132
Number of rooms required for new Institution	A	Y	C=A	D=A/4	1	1	1	1	1	–
Total Number of rooms	A	Y	C=AxY	D=C/4	3	1	1	1	1	1

1.	Classrooms, Tutorial rooms and Laboratories required for 2nd, 3rd, 4th and 5th year may be added progressively (1+1+1) to achieve total number as stated. UG laboratories if shared for PG courses shall be upgraded to meet requirement of PG curriculum courses shall be upgraded to meet requirements of PG curriculum.
2.	Round off fraction in calculation to the next integer.

Hotel Management and Catering Technology (Degree Institute)

	Number of Divisions UG (Class of 60) PG (Class of 18)	*Duration of course in Yrs*	*Class Rooms(C)*	*Tutorial Rooms(D) PG Class rooms (H)*	*Laboratory/Guest Room*	*Kitchen*	*Restaurant*	*Computer Centre*	*Library and Reading Room*	*Seminar Hall*
Carpet Area in sqm per room			66	33	66	132	66	75	150	132
Number of rooms required for new Institution		4	C=A	D=C/4	3	1	1	1	1	1
Total Number of rooms (UG)	A	4	C=Ax4	D=C/4	10	2	2	1	1	1
Total Number of rooms (PG)	F	G	–	H=FxG	1/Specialisation	1/Specialisation				

1.	Classrooms, Tutorial rooms and Laboratories required for 2nd, 3rd and 4th year may be added progressively (3+2+2) to achieve total number as stated. UG laboratories if shared for PG courses, shall be upgraded to meet requirements of PG curriculum
2.	Round off fraction in calculation to the next integer

Hotel Management and Catering Technology (Diploma/Post Diploma Institute)

	Number of Divisions UG (Class of 60) PG (Class of 18)	*Duration of course in Yrs*	*Class Rooms(C)*	*Tutorial Rooms(D)*	*Laboratory/Guest Room*	*Kitchen*	*Restaurant*	*Computer Centre*	*Library and Reading Room*	*Seminar Hall*
Carpet Area in sqm per room			66	33	66	132	66	75	150	132
Number of rooms required for new Institution	A	Y	C=A	D=C/4	3	1	1	1	1	–
Total Number of rooms	A	Y	C=AxY	D=C/4	6	1	1	1	1	1

1.	Classrooms, Tutorial rooms and Laboratories required for 2nd and 3rd year may be added progressively (3+3) to achieve total number as stated. UG laboratories if shared for PG courses, shall be upgraded to meet requirements of PG curriculum
2.	Round off fraction in calculation to the next integer

Management

	Number of Divisions UG (class of 60)	*Duration of course in Yrs*	*Class Rooms(C)*	*Tutorial Rooms (D)*	*Computer Centre*	*Library and Reading room*	*Seminar Halls (E)*
Carpet Area in sqm per room			66	33	150	100	132
Number of rooms required for new Institution	A	Y	C=A	D=C/4	1	1	1
Total Number of rooms	A	Y	C=AxY	D=C/4	1	1	E=C/4

1.	Classrooms, Tutorial rooms and Laboratories required for 2nd (and 3rd) year may be added progressively to achieve total number as stated
2.	Round off fraction in calculation to the next integer

MCA

	Number of Divisions UG Class s of 60)	*Duration of course in Yrs*	*Class Rooms(C)*	*Tutorial Rooms(D)*	*Computer Laboratories*	*Centre Computer*	*Library and Reading Room*	*Seminar Halls (E)*
Carpet Area in sqm per room			66	33	66	150	100	132
Number of rooms required for new Institution	A	3	C=A	D=C/4	2	1	1	1
Total Number of rooms	A	3	C=Ax3	D=C/4	4	1	1	E=C/4

1.	Classrooms, Tutorial rooms and Laboratories required for 2nd, 3rd year may be added progressively (1+1) to achieve total number as stated
2.	Round off fraction in calculation to the next integer

4.2.2 Administrative Area (Carpet Area) in sq m

	Principal/Director Office	*Board Room*	*Office all inclusive*	*Department Offices*	*Cabins for Head of Departments*	*Faculty Rooms*	*Central Stores*	*Maintenance*	*Security*	*Housekeeping*	*Pantry for staff*	*Examinations Control Office*	*Placement office*
Carpet Area in sqm per room	30	20	150*	20	10	5	30	10	10	10	10	30	30
Number of rooms required for New Technical Campus	1	1	1	–	–	First Year Student intake/15 One per	1	1	1	1	1	1	–
Total Number of rooms	1	1	1	1/Dept	1/Dept	teaching faculty (as per norms) in the Institution	1	1	1	1	1	1	1

1.	[$]Technical Campus having more than one Program
2.	* Technical Campus having one Program

Norms for Books, Journals, Library facilities, Computer, Software, Internet, Printers and Laboratory Equipments for Technical Institution

5.1 COMPUTERS, SOFTWARE, INTERNET AND PRINTERS

		Number of PCs to students ratio (Min 20 PCs)	*Legal System Software[@]*	*Legal Application Software**	*LAN and Internet*	*Main Server and Client*	*Internet Mbps/intake of 240 students with Bandwidth Contention of 1:1 (Min 1 Mbps)*	*Printers including Color Printer (% of total no of PC"s)*
Engineering/Technology	Dip	1:6	03	20	All	Desired	02	10%
	UG	1:4						

		Number of PCs to students ratio (Min 20 PCs)	Legal System Software[@]	Legal Application Software*	LAN and Internet	Main Server and Client	Internet Mbps/intake of 240 students with Bandwidth Contention of 1:1 (Min 1 Mbps)	Printers including Color Printer (% of total no of PC''s)
	PG	1:2						
Pharmacy	Dip	1:6	01	10	All	Desired	01	5%
	UG	1:6						
	PG	1:6						
Architecture and Town Planning	Dip	1:6	01	10	All	Desired	01	5%
	UG	1:5						
	PG	1:5						
Applied Arts and Crafts	Dip	1:5	01	10	All	Desired	01	5%
	UG	1:5						
	PG	1:5						
HMCT	Dip	1:6	01	10	All	Desired	01	5%
	UG	1:6						
Management	PG	1:2	01	10	All	Desired	02	10%
MCA	PG	1:2	03	20	All	Desired	02	10%

5.1	a	Utilization of Open Source Software may be encouraged
	b	Secured Wi Fi facility is highly recommended
	c	Purchase of most recent hardware is desired.
	d	Library, Administrative offices and Faculty members be provided with exclusive computing facilities along with LAN and Internet over and above the requirement meant for students
	e	[@]Adequate number of software licenses is required
	f	[#]Central Xeroxing facility for students is preferred

5.2 LABORATORY EQUIPMENTS AND EXPERIMENTS

5.2		a	The laboratories shall have equipments as appropriate for experiments as stated/suitable for the requirements of the affiliating University/Board's curriculum. It is desired that number of experiment set up be so arranged that maximum four students shall work on one set.

5.3 BOOKS, JOURNALS AND LIBRARY FACILITIES

Programme	*Total number of Divisions*	*Titles*	*Volumes*	*National Journals*	*International Journals*	*E Journals*	*Reading Room seating*	*Multimedia PCs for Digital Library\internet Surfing in reading room*
		Number					*% of total students*	*% of total students*
Engineering Technology(UG)	B	100	500xB			Required	15% (Max 150)	1% (Max 10)
		50 per course	250 per 6xB course – division	6xB	3xB			
Pharmacy(UG)	B	100	500xB	6xB	6xB			
		50	6xB 500xB	6xB				
Architecture and Town Planning (UG)	B	100	400xB	6xB	6xB			
		50	6xB 400xB	6xB				
Applied Arts and Crafts(UG)	B	100	500xB	6xB	3xB			
		50	6xB 500xB	6xB				
HMCT	B	100	500xB	6xB	3xB			
		50	6xB 500xB	6xB				
MBA/PGDM/ MCA (PG)	B	100	500xB	6xB	12xB		25% (Max 10)	
		50	12xB 500xB	6xB				
Engineering/Technology/ Architecture and Town Planning/Applied Arts and Crafts (PG)	B			6xB				
		50	200	6xB				
				6xB				
			5xB	6xB	5xB			
		As		6xB				
		Required		6xB				
				6xB				

Diploma in Engineering/Tech/Pharmacy/ Architecture and Town Planning Applied Arts and Crafts, HMCT	B	Half the number as required for UG course in the same programme	Half the number as required for UG course in the same programme	Half the number as required for UG course in the same programme		–	15% (Max 150)	1% (Max 10)

B = Number of divisions at 1st year (shift 1+2) + Number of 2nd year direct divisions (shift 1+2)

Book titles and volumes required at the time of starting new Institution.
Yearly increment.
Component for additional division/course.
Journals and Books shall also include subjects of Science and Humanities.
Digital Library facility with multimedia facility is essential.
Reprographic facility in the library is essential.
Document scanning facility in the library is essential.
Document printing facility in the library is essential.
Library books/non books classification as per standard classification methods is essential.
Availability of NPTEL facility at the library is essential.
Computerized indexing with bar coded/RF tagged book handling is desired.

Norms for Essential and Desired requirements for Technical Campus (Marked as essential need to be made available at the time of the Expert committee visit)

1.	*Language Laboratory* The Language Laboratory is used for language tutorials. These are attended by students who voluntarily opt for Remedial English classes. Lessons and exercises are recorded on a weekly basis so that the students are exposed to a variety of listening and speaking drills. This especially benefits students who are deficient in English and also aims at confidence-building for interviews and competitive examinations. The Language Laboratory sessions also include word games, quizzes, extemporary speaking, debates, skits etc. These sessions are complemented by online learning sessions which take place in the Multi-Purpose Computer Lab.	Essential
2.	Potable Water supply and outlets for drinking water at strategic locations	Essential
3.	Electric Supply	Essential
4.	Backup Electric Supply	As required

5.	Sewage Disposal	Essential
6.	Telephone and FAX	Essential
7.	First Aid facility	Essential
8.	Vehicle Parking	Essential
9.	Institution web site	Essential
10.	Barrier Free Built Environment for disabled and elderly persons including availability of specially designed toilets for ladies and gents separately. Refer guidelines and space standards for Barrier Free Built Environment for disabled and elderly persons by CPWD, Ministry of Urban Affairs and Employment, India.	Essential
11.	Safety provisions including fire and other calamities	Essential
12.	General Insurance provided for assets against fire, burglary and other calamities	Essential
13.	All weather approach road	Essential
14.	General Notice Board and Departmental Notice Boards	Essential
15.	Medical and Counseling Facilities	Essential
16.	Public announcement system at strategic locations for general announcements/paging and announcements in emergency.	Desired
17.	Enterprise Resource Planning (ERP) Software for Student-Institution-Parent interaction	Desired
18.	Transport	Desired
19.	Post, Banking Facility/ATM	Desired
20.	CCTV Security System	Desired
21.	LCD (or similar) projectors in classrooms	Desired
22.	Group Insurance to be provided for the employees	Desired
23.	Insurance for students	Desired
24.	Staff Quarters	Desired

Norms for Faculty requirements and Cadre Ratio for Technical campus

6.1 FACULTY REQUIREMENTS AND CADRE RATIO (DIPLOMA/POST DIPLOMA)

	Faculty: Student ratio	*Principal/ Director*	*Head of the Department*	*Lecturer*	*Total*
		A	*B*	*C*	*D*
Engineering/Tech/Pharmacy/Architecture and Town Planning Applied Arts and Crafts, HMCT	1:20	1	1per Department	S/20	A + B + C

6.1 S = Sum of number of students as per Approved Student Strength at all years

6.2 FACULTY REQUIREMENTS AND CADRE RATIO (UG)

	Faculty: Student ratio	*Principal/Director*	*Professor*	*Associate Professor*	*Assistant Professor*	*Total*
		A	*B*	*C*	*D*	*A+B+C+D*
Engineering/Technology	1:15	1	$\frac{S}{15\times R}-1$	$\frac{S}{15\times R}\times 2$	$\frac{S}{15\times R}\times 6$	$\frac{S}{15}$
Pharmacy	1:15	1	$\frac{S}{15\times R}-1$	$\frac{S}{15\times R}\times 2$	$\frac{S}{15\times R}\times 6$	$\frac{S}{15}$
Architecture and Town Planning	1:10	1	$\frac{S}{10\times R}-1$	$\frac{S}{10\times R}\times 2$	$\frac{S}{10\times R}\times 6$	$\frac{S}{10}$
Applied Arts and Crafts	1:10	1	$\frac{S}{10\times R}-1$	$\frac{S}{10\times R}\times 2$	$\frac{S}{10\times R}\times 6$	$\frac{S}{10}$
HMCT	1:15	1	$\frac{S}{15\times R}-1$	$\frac{S}{15\times R}\times 2$	$\frac{S}{15\times R}\times 6$	$\frac{S}{15}$

6.2 S = Sum of number of students as per Approved Student Strength at all years, R = (1+2+6).

6.3 FACULTY REQUIREMENT AND CADRE RATIO (PG)

	Faculty: Student ratio	*Principal/ Director*	*Professor*	*Associate Professor*	*Assistant Professor*	*Total*
		A	*B*	*C*	*D*	*A+B+C+D*
*Engineering/ Technology	1:12	–	$\frac{S}{12\times R}$	$\frac{S}{12\times R}$	$\frac{S}{12\times R}$	$\frac{S}{12}$
*Pharmacy	1:12	–	$\frac{S}{12\times R}$	$\frac{S}{12\times R}$	$\frac{S}{12\times R}$	$\frac{S}{12}$
*Architecture and Town Planning	1:10	–	$\frac{S}{10\times R}$	$\frac{S}{10\times R}$	$\frac{S}{10\times R}$	$\frac{S}{10}$
*Applied Arts and Crafts	1:10	–	$\frac{S}{10\times R}$	$\frac{S}{10\times R}$	$\frac{S}{10\times R}$	$\frac{S}{10}$
*HMCT	1:12	–	$\frac{S}{12\times R}$	$\frac{S}{12\times R}$	$\frac{S}{12\times R}$	$\frac{S}{12}$
#MBA/PGDM	1:15	1	$\frac{S}{15\times R}-1$	$\frac{S}{15\times R}-1$	$\frac{S}{15\times R}-6$	$\frac{S}{15}$
#MCA	1:15	1	$\frac{S}{15\times R}-1$	$\frac{S}{15\times R}-1$	$\frac{S}{15\times R}-6$	$\frac{S}{15}$

6.3 S = Sum of number of students as per Approved Student Strength at all years *R = (1+2), #R = (1+2+6).

ANNEXURE–D

Different Data Formats for University/College

FORM–1

LIST OF FACULTY

Department: Date:

S. No	Name	Date of Birth	Designation	Highest Qualification	Qualification Pursuing	Experience	Date of Joining the Institution	Date of Joining the Present Post	Scale and Total Emoluments Drawn	No. of Papers Published in Last 3 Years		Research Projects handled in last 3 years
										Journals Refereed	Conferences	

Faculty in-Charge *Head of the Department*

FORM–2

QUALIFICATION, EXPERIENCE, RATIO ANALYSIS AND RETENTION

Faculty: Student Ratio

Total Faculty Members -Full Time, Regular	*Sanctioned Students Strength–II, III and IV Years*	*Current Faculty: Student Ratio*

Qualification Profile

PhD Qualified	*PhD Pursing*	*ME/MTech/P.G Qualified*	*ME/MTech/P.G Pursing*	*BE/BTECH/U.G Qualified*	*Total*

Experience Profile

	Experience—Industry	*Experience—Academic*	*Cumulative*
Total			
Average			

Retention–1 Year

Total Faculty Members—Full Time, Regular	*Number of Faculty Members Joined in last One Year*	*1 Year Retention—Percentage*

Retention–3 Years

Total Faculty Members -Full Time, Regular	*Number of Faculty Members Joined in last Three Years*	*3 Years Retention—Percentage*

Faculty in-Charge *Head of the Department*

FORM–3

SUPPORT STAFF LIST

Department: Date:

Sl. No.	*Name*	*Date of Birth*	*Designation*	*Highest Qualification*	*Qualification Pursuing*	*Date of Joining the Institution*	*Date of Joining the Present Post*	*Total Emoluments Drawn*

Faculty in-Charge *Head of the Department*

FORM–4

FACULTY PROFILE

Photo

1. Name :
2. Date of Birth :
3. Highest Qualification :
4. Academic Performance (Descending Order)

S. No.	*Degree*	*University/ Institution*	*Year of Pass*	*% of Marks*	*Class*

5. Total Years of Experience

S. No.	*Period*		*Organization/ Institution*	*Position Held*
	From	*To*		

6. Date of joining in this Institution :
7. Status as on date of joining :
8. Salary as on date of joining :
9. Present Status :
10. Salary as on date :
11. Number of promotions since date of joining :

12. Achievements since date of joining:

S. No.	*Achievements*	*Year*	*Particulars*

13. Self-Appraisal

Major Strengths	*Major Weaknesses*
1. 2. 3.	1. 2. 3.

Signature

FORM–5

SUBJECT ALLOCATION AND RESPONSIBILITIES

Department: Semester:

Academic Year:

S. No.	*Name of the Faculty*	*Theory*			*Lab*			*Work Load/week*	*Other Responsibilities*	*Signature*
		Subject Title	*Branch*	*Semester*	*Subject Title*	*Branch*	*Semester*			

Faculty in-Charge *Head of the Department* *Principal*

FORM-6

FACULTY AND STAFF WORK LOAD

Department:

Semester:

Academic Year:

S. No.	*Faculty/ Staff Name*	*Theory 1*	*Theory 2*	*Theory 3*	*Lab 1*	*Lab 2*	*Lab 3*	*Work Load*				*Signature*
								Theory	*Lab*	*Project*	*Others*	

Faculty in-Charge

Head of the Department

FORM–7

FACULTY PERFORMANCE APPRAISAL

1. Name :
2. Designation :
3. Department :

Academic Works

4. Progress Report for the Semester:

   Academic Year:

	Subject 1	*Subject 2*	*Subject 3*
% of Syllabus Covered			
No. of Units Completed			
No. of Periods Conducted			
University Prescribed-Periods			
Percentage of Pass			
Percentage of Fail			

Personal Contribution

5 (a) Innovative methods (Class Room and Lab) :

(b) Extra Coaching Arranged :

6. Laboratory :

   No. of Session Conducted :

   No. of Experiments prescribed in the syllabus :

   No. of Experiments Completed :

7. List of Seminars/Workshops Attended During this Academic Year :
8. List of Papers/Articles Published/Presented during the Year :
9. List of Sponsorship/Consultancy/Project Work :
10. Any other Assignments (Non-Academic Works) pertaining to :

    (a) College

    (b) University

    (c) Any other Organization

11. (a) Appreciation/Awards/Recognition earned :

    (b) Disciplinary Actions faced :

12. Other activities Inside/Outside the campus towards development of self and students :

13. Any other Information :

14. Whether proficient with Rules, Regulations and Management system :

15. Leave Details

Period	*CL*	*Loss of Pay*	*Number of Lates*

Date: Signature of Faculty

(a) Remarks of the Head of the Department and Points Awarded

(Based on inter personal relationship with faculties and students, specific contribution to the department etc.)

Head of the Department

(b) Remarks of the Principal and Points Awarded

(Based on specific contribution to the institutional and departmental activities, on-time completion etc.)

Principal

Staff Appraisal—Points Earned

Students Feedback-20%	*University Results-50%*	*Self Appraisal 10%*	*HOD 10%*	*Principal 10%*	*Total*

Faculty Observation on Performance Appraisal

Faculty Member *Head* *Principal*

Support Staff Performance Appraisal

Department: Semester:

S. No.	*Name of the Support Staff*	*Lab/Work Entrusted*	*No. of Sessions Conducted*	*No. of Experiments Prescribed in the Syllabus*	*No. of Experiments Completed*

Any other Assignments	*Appreciation/ Awards/Recognition Earned*	*Disciplinary Action Faced*	*Other Activities Towards Development of Self and Students*	*Leave Details*		
				CL	*EL*	*LOP*

Faculty in-Charge *Head of the Department*

Incentives and Rewards

Department: Date:

Academic Year: Semester:

Faculties/Staff Incentives and Rewards

Sl. No.	*Subject*	*Class*	*Handled by*	*Pass Percentage*	*Cash Award*	*Remarks*
Yearly Expenditure for Academic Awards						

Faculties/Staff Incentives and Rewards—Others

S. No.	*Name of the Faculty Member*	*Details of Activities*	*Awards/Citations*

Faculty in-Charge *Head of the Department*

FORM–8

EXIT INTERVIEW

Department: Date:

Semester:

1. Name :
2. Designation :
3. Department :
4. Date of Joining :
5. Date of Leaving :
6. Reasons for leaving :
   (a)
   (b)
   (c)
7. Please mark your rating for the following

	Excellent	*Satisfactory*	*Average*
(a) Relation with higher authority			
(b) Relation with colleagues			
(c) Relation with students			
(d) Work load			
(e) Scope for personal growth			
(f) Work environment			
(g) Others if any			

Suggestions:

Signature

FORM–9

FACULTY DEVELOPMENT PROGRAMMES ATTENDED

Department: Date:

Academic Year:

S. No.	*Name of the Faculty*	*Dates*	*Name of the Programme*	*Host Institution*
1.				
2.				
3.				
4.				
5.				
6.				
7.				
8.				
9.				
10.				
11.				
12.				

Faculty in-Charge *Head of the Department*

FORM–10

FDP ATTENDED REPORT AND SEMINAR

Department: Date:

Faculty/Staff Name :

Title of Programme :

Institution/Organization :

Address :

Dates :

Report :

Signature

Internal Seminar Given on :

Participants :

Faculty in-Charge *Head of the Department*

Form–11

FDP ATTENDED-INTERNAL

Department: Date:

Title of Programme :

Resource Persons :

Institution/Organization :

Address :

Dates :

S. No.	*Name*	*Designation*	*Signature*

Faculty in-Charge *Head of the Department*

FORM–12

HIGHER EDUCATION—DEPUTATION

Department: Date:

Academic Year:

S. No.	*Name of the Faculty Member*	*Designation*	*Highest Qualification While Sponsoring*	*Sponsored for*	*Year of Sponsor*
1.					
2.					
3.					
4.					
5.					
6.					
7.					
8.					
9.					
10.					
11.					
12.					
13.					
14.					
15.					

Faculty in-Charge *Head of the Department*

FORM–13

QIP/INTERNSHIP/SABBATICAL LEAVE

Department: Date:

Academic Year:

S. No.	*Name of the Faculty Member*	*Designation*	*Highest Qualification While Sponsoring*	*Sponsored for*	*Year of Sponsor*
1.					
2.					
3.					
4.					
5.					
6.					
7.					
8.					
9.					
10.					
11.					
12.					
13.					
14.					
15.					

Faculty in-Charge *Head of the Department*

Form-14

FACULTY DEVELOPMENT—SUMMARY

Department: Date:

Faculty members deputed for specialized training/higher studies:

Schemes	*No. of Faculty Members Deputed During Last Three Years*		
	2011–2012	*2010–2011*	*2009–2010*
QIP/Study leave/Higher Education			
Seminars/Workshops/Conferences			
Summer schools/Winter schools			
Any others, please specify Refresher Courses/Short Term Training Programmes			

Faculty in-Charge *Head of the Department*

FORM-15

PUBLICATIONS—PAPERS, BOOKS

Department: Date:

Academic Year:

S. No.	*Name of Faculty Member*	*Paper/Book Title*	*Events/Journals/Publisher*
1.			
2.			
3.			
4.			
5.			
6.			
7.			
8.			
9.			
10.			
11.			
12.			
13.			
14.			
15.			

Faculty in-Charge *Head of the Department*

FORM–16

PROFESSIONAL SOCIETY MEMBERSHIPS

Department:

Academic Year:

Date:

S. No.	*Name of the Faculty Member*	*Designation*	*Professional Society*	*Membership No.*
1.				
2.				
3.				
4.				
5.				
6.				
7.				
8.				
9.				
10.				
11.				
12.				
13.				
14.				
15.				

Faculty in-Charge

Head of the Department

FORM-17

INVITED LECTURES BY FACULTY MEMBERS

Department:

Academic Year: Date:

S. No.	*Name of the Faculty Member*	*Date*	*Institution*	*Topic*

Faculty in-Charge *Head of the Department*

FORM–18

SUPPORT STAFF SKILLS UP-GRADATION

Department:

Academic Year: Date:

S. No	*Name of the Staff*	*Date*	*Details*

Faculty in-Charge *Head of the Department*

FORM–19

CONTINUING EDUCATION—ORGANIZED

Department: Date:

S. No.	*Title*	*Type*	*Duration*	*Sponsored by*
1.				
2.				
3.				

Faculty in-Charge *Head of the Department*

FORM–20

STUDENTS' LIST, ADDRESS

Department: Date:

Year of Admission:

S. No.	*Name of the Student*	*Roll No.*	*Reg. No.*	*Address*

Faculty in-Charge *Head of the Department*

FORM–21

STUDENTS' ADMISSION ANALYSIS

Department: Date:

Year of Admission:

(a) Admission Percentage

Sanctioned	*Admitted*	*Filled-Up %*	*Remarks*

(b) Students Rank

Admitted	*Best Rank*	*Last Rank*

(c) Boys and Girls

Admitted	*Boys*	*%*	*Girls*	*%*

(d) Hostellers and Dayscholars

Admitted	*Dayscholars*	*%*	*Hostellers*	*%*

(e) Urban and Rural

Admitted	*Urban*	*%*	*Rural*	*%*

Faculty Member in-Charge *Head of the Department*

FORM–22

STATISTICS ON SEATS FILLED-UP

Department: Date:

Year	*Sanctioned Strength*	*Admitted*	*% of Seats Filledup*

Faculty Member in-Charge *Head of the Department*

FORM–23

SEMESTERWISE, SUBJECTWISE RESULT ANALYSIS

Department: Date:

Semester:

Year/Semester	*Course*	*Name of Faculty*	*Number of Students*		*No. of Students Securing ≥ 60%*	*No. of Students Securing ≥ 75%*	*Pass%*	*Fail %*
			Appear	*Passed*				

Number of Subjects with ≥ 75%: pass Number of Subjects with ≤ 75% pass

Remedial Actions:

Faculty in-Charge *Head of the Department* *Principal*

FORM–24

ACADEMIC PERFORMANCE-CONSOLIDATED

Department: Date:

Academic Performance of Students Admitted in the Year

Year	*Semester*	*Subjects*	*Number of Subjects where results are*				*Toppers*
			100%	*90% and Above*	*75% and Above*	*Less than 75%*	
I	1st Year						
II	III						
	IV						
III	V						
	VI						
IV	VII						
	VIII						

Overall Pass Percentage (Current Batch) : ____________________

Overall Branch 1st Rank Holder : ____________________

Overall Branch 2nd Rank Holder : ____________________

Overall Branch 3rd Rank Holder : ____________________

University Ranks : ____________________

Faculty in-Charge *Head of the Department*

FORM-25

STATISTICS ON STUDENTS' DEGREE COMPLETION

Department: Date:

Batch	*Appeared*	*Passed*	*Pass %*	*Distinction*	*1st Class*	*2nd Class*

Batch	*1st Rank*	*2nd Rank*	*3rd Rank*	*University Ranks*

Faculty in-Charge *Head of the Department*

FORM–26

PERFORMANCE IN COMPETITIVE EXAMS

Department: Date:

Academic Year:

S. No.	*Name of the Student*	*Year*	*Exam*	*Rank/Mark*

Faculty in-Charge *Head of the Department*

FORM-27

STUDENTS HIGHER EDUCATION DETAILS

Department: Date:

Academic Year:

S. No.	*Name of the Student*	*Higher Study*	*Exam Attended*	*Institution/ University*	*India/ Abroad*

Faculty in-Charge *Head of the Department*

FORM–28

PLACEMENT REGISTRATION FORM

Department:

Affix the photograph

1. Roll No :
2. Reg. No :
3. Name (In Block Letters) :
4. Father Name :
5. Address for Communication (Permanent)
   Ph Mobile :
   E-mail :
6. Date of Birth and Age
7. Aggregate as on Date :
8. UG Academic Particulars

Semester	*Month/Year of Exam*	*No. of Subjects Passed*	*GPA*	*CGPA*	*Aggregate % (till that Exam)*
I					
II					
III					
IV					
V					
VI					
VII					
VIII					

9. Intermediate Particulars

Name of the Institution	*Place*	*Year of Pass*	*%*

10. SSC Particulars

Name of the School	*Place*	*Year of Pass*	*%*

11. Interesting Areas to work :
12. Computer Knowledge if any (for Non-CSE/IT) :
13. Academic achievements if any :
14. Co-Curricular Activities if any :
15. Hobbies :
16. References if any :

Declaration

I Mr/Ms ______________________________ hereby declare that

(1) The above given information is true to best of my knowledge and if any particulars are found false I am liable to be punished.

(2) I am solely interested to register my name with the T and P Cell and I abide to the rules and regulations of the cell which are in force from time to time and I undertake the responsibility to participate in all the PDP as well the other training activities being prepared by the cell with out fail and with at most interest.

(3) Recommendation of my candidature is at the discretion of the T and P Cell.

Place:

Date: Signature

FORM–29

ON/OFF CAMPUS PLACEMENT DETAILS

Department: Date:

Academic Year:

S. No.	*Name of the Student*	*Organisation*	*Designation*	*Salary*	*On/Off*

Students Passed	*Placement Eligible*	*Placed*	*% Placed*

Faculty in-Charge *Head of the Department*

FORM–30

SYLLABUS ANALYSIS

Department:

S. No.	*Year and Sem-ester*	*Course Title*	*Nature of Subject*	*Dept. Offering the Subject*	*Weekly Load (hours)*		
			Core (C)/Elective (E)		*L**	*T**	*P**
1.							
2.							
3.							
4.							
5.							
6.							
7.							
8.							
9.							
10.							
11.							
12.							
13.							
14.							
15.							
16.							
17.							
18.							
19.							

S. No.	*Year and Sem-ester*	*Course Title*	*Nature of Subject*	*Dept. Offering the Subject*	*Weekly Load (hours)*		
			Core (C)/Elective (E)		*L**	*T**	*P**
20.							
21.							
22.							
23.							
24.							
25.							
26.							
27.							
28.							
29.							
30.							

L-Lecture; T-Tutorial; P-Practical/Project

Number of Core Subjects :

Number of Practical :

Number of Elective Subjects :

Number of Inter Disciplinary Subjects :

Number of Science and Humanities Subjects :

Faculty in-Charge *Head of the Department*

FORM–31

DEPARTMENTAL ADVISORY COMMITTEE

Department: Date:

Nature of Meeting	*Departmental Advisory Committee*		
Venue		*Date*	*Time*
Members	*Name*	*Industry/Organization*	*Signature*
Members 1 2 3 4 5 6			
Circulated to:			

Agenda Points	*Details of Discussion + Action Points*	*Responsibility*	*Target date*
1			
2			
3			
4			
5			

Faculty in-Charge *Head of the Department* *Principal*

FORM-32

STUDENTS ADD-ON COURSE DETAILS

Department: Date:

Academic Year: Semester:

Period: From: To: Timing:

Title

S. No.	*Name*	*Signature*

Faculty in-Charge *Head of the Department*

FORM–33

RESOURCE PERSONS—EXTERNAL

Department: Date:

Semester:

S. No.	*Name, Designation Address, Phone Number*	*Topic*	*Date*	*Host Institution/Industry*

Faculty in-Charge *Head of the Department*

FORM–34

GUEST LECTURES/SEMINARS-INTIMATION

Department: Date:

Semester: Activity*:

Name of the speaker(s)	:
Designation	:
Institution/University/Organization	:
Title of the Seminar/Guest Lecture	:
Date and Time	:
Venue	:
Beneficiary	:

Activity*:

Adv. Topics/Subject/General/Placement/Higher Education/EDP/Ethics/Professional Society/Association

Faculty in-Charge *Head of the Department*

FORM–35

GUEST LECTURES—FEEDBACK

Department: Date:

Semester:

Name of the speaker(s)	:
Designation	:
Institution/University/Organization	:
Title of the Lecture	:
Date and Time	:
Venue	:
Beneficiary	:
Comments on Speaker(s)	:
Signature	:

Guest Address/Contact No.:

Names of Student who offered feedback (feedback enclosed)

1

2

3

4

5

Arranged by:

Date:

Faculty in-Charge *Head of the Department*

FORM-36

SEMESTER SUBJECTS LIST

Department of

Date:

Semester: Academic Year:

List of Subjects

S. No.	*Title of the Subject*	*Subject Code*	*Branch/Year*

Faculty in-Charge *Head of the Department*

FORM–37

Department of

SUBJECT/LAB OPTION FORM

Name of the Faculty :

Designation :

Academic Year :

Specialization :

Experience :

Sem :

S. No.	*Year*	*Interested Subjects*	*No of times handled*

Faculty in-Charge

Head of the Department

FOR OFFICE USE ONLY

Subject/Lab Allocated

S. No	*Class*	*Subject Allocated*	*Work Load*
1.			
2.			
3.			
4.			
5.			
6.			
7.			
8.			

Faculty in-Charge

Head of the Department

FORM-38

REQUISITION FOR INTER DEPARTMENTAL SUBJECTS

From: HOD, Dept. of *To:* HOD, Dept. of

Date:

The following subjects of our department are to be handled by your department, kindly allot the staff members for these subjects for ______________________ semester.

S. No.	*Subjects*
1.	
2.	
3.	
4.	

Faculty in-Charge *Head of the Department*

FORM-39

ALLOTMENT OF FACULTY MEMBERS FOR INTER DEPARTMENTAL SUBJECTS

From: HOD, Dept. of *To:* HOD, Dept. of

Date:

The following staff members are allotted to the subjects for ________ semester.

S. No.	*Subjects*	*Name of the Faculty Member*
1.		
2.		
3.		
4.		

Faculty Member in-Charge *Head of the Department*

FORM–40

CLASS TIME-TABLE

Department: Date:

Semester:

Day/ Hours	1 (9.00 am– 9.50 am)	2 (9.50 am– 10.40 am)	3 (10.40 am– 11.30 am)	4 (11.30 am– 12.20 pm)	5 (1.30 pm– 2.15 pm)	6 (2.15 pm– 3.00 pm)	7 (3.00 pm– 3.45 pm)	8 (3.45 pm– 4.30 am)
Mon								
Tue								
Wed								
Thurs								
Fri								

Subject Code	*Subject*	*Name of the Faculty Member*

Faculty in-Charge *Head of the Department*

FORM–41

MASTER TIME-TABLE

Department: Date:

Day	*Sem-*	*1 (9.00 am– 9.50 am)*	*2 (9.50 am– 10.40 am)*	*3 (10.40 am– 11.30 am)*	*4 (11.30 am– 12.20 pm)*	*5 (1.30 pm– 2.15 pm)*	*6 (2.15 pm– 3.00 pm)*	*7 (3.00 pm– 3.45 pm)*	*8 (3.45 pm– 4.30 am)*
Mon									
Tues									
Wed									
Thurs									
Fri									

Faculty in-Charge *Head of the Department*

FORM–42

INDIVIDUAL TIME-TABLE

Department: Date:

Name of the Faculty Member: Semester:

Day/ Hours	1 (9.00 am– 9.50 am)	2 (9.50 am– 10.40 am)	3 (10.40 am– 11.30 am)	4 (11.30 am– 12.20 pm)	5 (1.30 pm– 2.15 pm)	6 (2.15 pm– 3.00 pm)	7 (3.00 pm– 3.45 pm)	8 (3.45 pm– 4.30 am)
Mon								
Tue								
Wed								
Thurs								
Fri								

Faculty in-Charge *Head of the Department*

FORM–43

LAB TIME-TABLE

Department: Date:

Name of the Lab: Semester:

Day/ Hours	1 (9.00 am– 9.50 am)	2 (9.50 am– 10.40 am)	3 (10.40 am– 11.30 am)	4 (11.30 am– 12.20 pm)	5 (1.30 pm– 2.15 pm)	6 (2.15 pm– 3.00 pm)	7 (3.00 pm– 3.45 pm)	8 (3.45 pm– 4.30 am)
Mon								
Tue								
Wed								
Thurs								
Fri								

Faculty in-Charge *Head of the Department*

FORM-44

LESSON PLAN

Department of

Academic Year :

Semester :

Faculty Name :

Subject :

S. No. / *Unit/Topic No.*	*Sub Topic Names*	*No. of Classes Required*
I		
II		
III		
IV		
V		
Total No. of hours:		

Text/Reference Books

References

1

2

Faculty in-Charge *Head of the Department*

FORM–45

DELIVERY MONITORING

Department of:

Academic Year: Semester:

S. No.	*Subject Name*	*Faculty*	*Date*	*Preparedness*	*Doubts Clearing*	*Voice Audible*	*OHP/ LCD*

Faculty in Charge *Head of the Department* *Principal*

FORM–46

SYLLABUS COVERAGE—MONITORING

Department of:

Academic Year: Semester:

Date:

S. No.	*Subject Name*	*Faculty*	*No. of Classes Handled*	*% Syllabus Covered*	*Remarks*

Faculty in Charge *Head of the Department* *Principal*

FORM–47

STUDENTS' EXPERIMENTS COMPLETION

Semester: Period

Lab Name: Branch:

Year: Class:

S. No.	*Roll No.*	*Name of the Student*	*Experiments*														
			1	*2*	*3*	*4*	*5*	*6*	*7*	*8*	*9*	*10*	*11*	*12*	*13*	*14*	*15*
1.																	
2.																	
3.																	
4.																	
5.																	
6.																	
7.																	
8.																	
9.																	
10.																	
11.																	
12.																	
13.																	
14.																	
15.																	

Faculty Member in-Charge *Lab Faculty Member* *Head of the Department*

FORM-48

MAKEUP AND REMEDIAL CLASSES

Department of

Academic Year: Semester:

Makeup Classes Remedial Classes

Subject Name :

Faculty Name :

Reason :

Period: From: To Time: Total Duration:

Students Details

S. No.	*Reg. No.*	*Name of the Student*	*Signature*

Faculty *Faculty in-Charge* *Head of the Department*

FORM–49

SUBJECT FILES LIST

Department: Date:

Academic Year:

S. No.	*File Reference*	*Subject's Name*

Faculty in-Charge *Head of the Department*

FORM-50

LAB RESOURCES

Department: Date:

Departmental Laboratory Details

S. No	Name of the Lab	Available Floor Area (Sq. ft.)	Max. Batch Size	Weekly Hours Required as Per Curriculum	Number of Experiments		Recurring Expenditure (allotted per year)
					Prescribed	Conducted	
1.							
2.							
3.							
4.							
5.							

Faculty Member in-Charge *Head of the Department*

FORM–51

LAB EQUIPMENT LIST

Department: Date:

Academic Year:

Lab Name:

Major and Minor Equipments in the Laboratory:

Sl. No	*Equipment*		*Purchase*		*Installation Date*	*Present Condition*	
	Name	*Make and Qty*	*Date*	*Cost*		*Working*	*Non-Working*

Faculty in-Charge *Head of the Department*

FORM–52

LAB EXPERIMENTS LIST

Department: Date:

Class: Semester: I/II

Name of the Lab:

List of Experiments (As per syllabus)

S. No.	*Name of the Experiment*

Additional Experiments

S. No.	*Name of the Experiment*

Faculty in-Charge *Head of the Department*

Form–53

EQUIPMENTS HISTORY/MAINTENANCE

Department: Date:

Name of the Lab:

Equipment Name			
Asset Code			
Make			
Specification			
Installation Date			Value:
Guarantee/Warranty	From		To
Maintained by			

Calibration Done on

S. No.	*Date of Calibration/Master Reading*	*Remarks*

Maintenance History

Serviced on	*Nature of Complaint*	*Cost in Rs.*	*Serviced by*	*In-Charge*	*Remarks*

Faculty in-Charge *Head of the Department*

FORM-54

INFRASTRUCTURE, INSTRUCTIONAL AIDS

Department: Date:

S. No.	*Description*	*Quantity*
1.	No. of Class Rooms	
2.	No. of Laboratories	
3.	No. of OHP's	
4.	No. of LCD's	
5.	Built-up Area	
6.	Others	

Faculty in-Charge *Head of the Department*

FORM-55

COMPUTING, INTERNET AND SOFTWARE

Department: *Date:*

Computer Lab

S. No	*Equipment*		*Purchase*		*Installation Date*	*Present Condition*	
	Name	*Make*	*Date*	*Cost*		*Working*	*Non-Working*

Details of Internet:

List of Licensed Software

S. No.	*Software Details*	*Supplier*	*Users*	*Cost*

Faculty in-Charge *Head of the Department*

Form–56

BOOKS, JOURNALS, SELF LEARNING FACILITIES

Department: Date:

Central Library				
Books	*Journals*		*CDs, VCDs, Multimedia*	*Any other, please specify*
	National	*International*		

Departmental Library				
Books	*Journals*		*CDs, VCDs, Multimedia*	*Any other, please specify*
	National	*International*		

Self Learning Facilities

S. No.	*Details*

Faculty in-Charge *Head of the Department*

FORM–57

BOOKS EXCEPTION REPORT

Department: Date:

List of Prescribed Text/Reference Books Not Available in the Library:

S. No.	*Book Title*	*Author*	*Text/Reference*

Faculty in-Charge *Head of the Department*

FORM–58

MONTHLY ATTENDANCE

Department:

Semester:

S. No.	*Roll No.*	*Name*	*Subject*										*Percentage*
												Total	
		Total Classes Taken											
		Attended											

Counsellor *Faculty in-Charge* *Head of the Department*

FORM-59

DAILY WORK SHEET

Dept.:

Class: Date:

Hours	*Name of the Staff with Dept.*	*Subject Name with Code*	*Unit No.*	*Portion Covered*	*Staff Signature*	*Remarks*

FORM-60

STUDENT COUNSELLING RECORD

College Name

Address

College Logo

Counselling Record

Student's Name : ______________________________

Programme : ______________________________

Batch : ______________________________

Photo

Faculty Advisor: 1. ____________________ Period: ____________________

2. ____________________ ____________________

3. ____________________ ____________________

4. ____________________ ____________________

Mode of Joining: Regular/Lateral Entry

Admission Category: Govt. Quota/Management Quota

1. **Name** : ....
2. **Roll No.** :..
3. **University Reg. No.** : ....
4. **Course/Subject** : ....
5. **Date of Birth** : ....
6. **Blood Group** : ....
7. **Day Scholar/Hosteller** : ....
8. **Community** : ....
9. **College Bus/Private Bus/Vehicle** : ....
10. **Medium of Education (Last studied)** : ....
11. **Parent's Name** : ....
12. **Occupation** : ....
13. **Address for Communication** :

....

....

.... (P.O)

Pin Code ....

.... Taluk

.... District

Phone No. ....

Mobile ....

E-mail ID ....

14. Permanent Address

....

....

.... (P.O)

Pin Code ....

.... Taluk

.... District

Phone No. ....

Mobile ....

E-Mail ID..

15. Percentage of Marks:

10th: .... 12th: ....

Diploma: .... U.G.: ....

16. Cycle Test Marks & University Marks:

Semester I/II/III/IV/V/VI/VII/VIII

Sl. No	*Subject Code and Title*	*Cycle Test Marks*				*University Marks*			
		I	*II*	*RT*	*Model Exam*	*Max Marks*	*Marks Scored*	*Result*	*Month & Year of Pass*
Attendance %						Marks %			

Days of Leave:

No. of Days	*From*	*To*	*Reason*

Hosteller:

Outing Date	*Outing Time*

17. Industrial Visits

Year	*Name of the Company and Place*	*No. of Days*	*Area of Specialization*
I			
II			
III			
IV			
V			

18. In Plant Training

SEM	*Name of the Company And Place*	*No. of Days*	*SEM*	*Name of the Company and Place*	*No. of Days*
I			VI		
II			VII		
III			VIII		
IV			IX		
V			X		

19. Placement Training Programmes

Semester	*Programme Organised*	*Dates*	*Status (Attended/Not Attended)*

20. Placement Details

Sl. No.	*Name of the Company*	*Semester*	*Status (Selected/Not Selected)*

21. Extra Curricular Activities

Semester	*Name of the Activity*	*Nature of Participation/Awards*

22. Co-Curricular Activities

Semester	*Name of the Activity*	*Nature of Participation/Awards*

23. Projects

Semester	*Project Type (Mini/Major/Sponsored)*	*Title of the Project*	*Name of the Company/Organization*	*Financial Assistance*	*Project Guide*

24. Parents' Meeting

SEM	*Date of Meeting*	*Status (Attended/Not Attended)*	*SEM*	*Date of Meeting*	*Status (Attended/Not Attended)*
I			VI		
II			VII		
III			VIII		
IV					
V					

25. Regular Counselling

Sl. No.	*Date*	*Nature of Counselling*	*Signature of the Staff*	*Signature of the Student*

26. Other Counselling Details

Date	*Nature of Problem*	*Intimation to Parents (Y/N)*	*Type of Action*	*Undertaking*	*Signature of the Parent*	*Signature of the Student*

27. Hobbies and Special Talents

(a) ....

(b) ....

(c) ....

28. General Comments

Initials of Faculty Advisor with Date										
Initials of Director/HOD with Date										
Initials of Faculty Advisor with Date										

Form-61

PROGRESS REPORT—MONTHLY

Department: Date:

Semester:

Dear Parent/Guardian,

Name of the Student:

Branch: Roll No:

Your Son's/Daughter's attendance up to ______________ is as follows. Advise him/her to attend all the classes so that he/she can maintain more than 90% attendance. Please note that he/she will not be allowed to write university exams, unless he/she maintains a minimum of 75% attendance.

No. of Classes Handled:

No. of Classes Attended:

% of Attendance:

Class Test No: **Marks:**

S. No.	*Test dates*	*Subject*	*Marks (Maximum 20)*	*Attendance Period*			*Remarks*
				No. of Classes Handled	*No of Classes Attended*	*Percentage of Attendance*	
1.							
2.							
3.							
4.							
5.							
6.							
7.							
8.							
9.							
10.							

Your Son's/Daughter's performance is ______________

You are requested to meet the HOD at the earliest.

You are requested to advise your ward to study well and improve performance in the subsequent tests.

Counselor in-Charge *Head of the Department*

FORM–62

CUMULATIVE ATTENDANCE-SUBJECTWISE

Department: Date:

Name of the Subject: Semester:

Subject Handled by:

S. No.	*Roll No.*	*Name*	*Up to the Month of*					*May*	*Total*	*%*
			Dec.	*Jan.*	*Feb.*	*Mar.*	*Apr.*			
	Total Classes Taken									
						Attended				
1.										
2.										
3.										
4.										
5.										
6.										
7.										
8.										
9.										
10.										
11.										
12.										
13.										
14.										
15.										
16.										
17.										
18.										
19.										
20.										
21.										
22.										
23.										
24.										
25.										
26.										
27.										
28.										
29.										
30.										

Faculty in-Charge *Head of the Department*

FORM–63

DISCIPLINARY ACTIONS ON STUDENTS

Date:

Originator	*Head, Disciplinary Committee*
Circulated to	1.
	2.
	3.
	4.
	5.

Sub:

Ref.:

Signature

FORM–64

TEST SCHEDULES

Semester: Date:

Monthly Tests

	Test1/Quiz1	*Test2/Quiz2*	*Test3/Quiz3*	*Test4/Quiz4*	*Test5/Quiz5*
From					
To					
Timing					
Syllabus					

Model Exams

Date	*Subject*	*Timing*

Lab Model Exams

Date	*Subject*	*Timing*

Faculty in-Charge *Head of the Department*

FORM-65

TEST MARKS ANALYSIS

Department: Date:

Test: Semester:

Year/Semester	*Course*	*Name of Faculty*	*Number of Students*		*No. of Students Securing ≥ 60%*	*No. of Students Securing ≥ 75%*	*Pass%*	*Fail %*
			Appear	*Passed*				

Remedial Actions:

Faculty in-Charge *Head of the Department*

FORM–66

SUBJECT WISE MARKS-INTERNAL

Department: Date:

Subject: Semester:

S. No.	*Roll No.*	*Name*	*T1*	*T2*	*T3*	*Assig*	*Att*	*Total*
				← 10 →		5	5	

Faculty in-Charge *Head of the Department*

FORM-67

LAB WISE MARKS-INTERNAL

Department: Date:

Semester:

Name of the Lab

S. No.	*Roll No*	*Name of the Student*	*Model Test (5 M)*	*Viva (5 M)*	*Evaluation of Practical (5 M)*	*Record And Neatness (5 M)*	*Attend Ance (5 M)*	*Total (25 M)*

Faculty in-Charge *Head of the Department*

FORM–68

STUDENTS MINI PROJECTS

Department: Date:

Semester: Batch No:

S. No.	*Roll No.*	*Student Name*	*Project Title*	*Internal Guide*

Signature of Project Co-Ordinator *Head of the Department*

FORM–69

PROJECT GUIDE ALLOTMENT

Department: Date:

Semester:

Batch No.	*Student Name*	*Project Title*	*Internal Guide*

Project Co-Ordinator *Head of the Department*

FORM–70

PROJECT REVIEW

Department:

Semester: Review Date:

Batch No.	*Students Name*	*Project Title*	*Internal Guide*	*Date*	*Grade*

Faculty in-Charge *Head of the Department*

Form–71

PROJECT INTERNAL ASSESSMENT

Department: Date:

Semester:

Batch No.	*Roll No.*	*Students Name*	*Project Title*	*Internal Guide*	*Marks*			*Total (50)*	*Grade*
					R1	*R2*	*R3*		

Project Co-Ordinator *Head of the Department*

FORM–72

STUDENT FEEDBACK ON-FACULTIES

Name (Optional): Branch:

Semester:

I–VIII → Subject's Code

Choose → 5-Excellent; 4-V.Good; 3-Good; 2-Fair; 1-Poor

S. No.	*Description*	*I*	*II*	*III*	*IV*	*V*	*VI*	*VII*	*VIII*
1.	Teacher comes to Class on time								
2.	Teaching is well planned								
3.	Teacher makes objectives clear								
4.	Subject matter organized in logical sequence								
5.	Teacher comes well prepared in the subject								
6.	Teacher speaks clearly and audibly								
7.	Teacher writes and draws legibly								
8.	Teacher explains with examples clearly								
9.	Teaching pace is good; Not very fast								
10.	Teacher offers assistance and counseling								
11.	Teacher asks relevant questions for interaction								
12.	Teacher encourages raising doubts								
13.	Teacher ensures learning of subject								
14.	Teacher encourages originality and creativity								
15.	Teacher is courteous and impartial								
16.	Teacher is regular and maintains discipline								
17.	Teacher covers the syllabus at appropriate pace								
18.	Teacher holds quizzes, seminars regularly								
19.	Teacher's correction of scripts fair and impartial								
20.	Teacher promptly values and returns papers								

Date:

Faculty in-Charge *Head of the Department*

FORM–73

FEEDBACK ANALYSIS AND ACTIONS

Department Date:

Academic Year: Semester:

S. No.	*Faculty Name*	*Subject*	*Percentile*	*Remarks*

Remedial Action Suggested:

Faculty in-Charge *Head of the Department* *Principal*

FORM–74

STUDENTS FEEDBACK ON LABS

Department: Date:

Semester:

Academic Year:

Title of Lab			
What was your batch Size?			
Are you satisfied with your batch Size?	Yes/No	Yes/No	Yes/No
Are the experiments of the Lab Classes conducted as per schedule provided?	Yes/No	Yes/No	Yes/No
Are the Equipments provided sufficient?	Yes/No	Yes/No	Yes/No
Are the Equipments provided in working condition?	Yes/No	Yes/No	Yes/No
Are the Lab Consumables provided of Good Quality?	Yes/No	Yes/No	Yes/No
How many experiments were conducted as per University Norms?			
How many experiments were conducted over and Above the University Syllabus?			
The Lab Manual Provided was complete in covering the Syllabus and informative?	Yes/No	Yes/No	Yes/No
Whether the lab assistant/technician are assisting you	Yes/No	Yes/No	Yes/No
Whether the lab in-charges (Faculties) are helpful in the Lab	Yes/No	Yes/No	Yes/No

Your Suggestion for improvements:

Signature of Student

Name of the Student

Form–75

LABS FEEDBACK ANALYSIS AND ACTIONS

Department: Date:

Academic Year: Semester:

S. No.	*Lab Name*	*Lab in-Charge and Lab Assistant*	*Remarks*

Remedial Action Suggested:

Faculty in-Charge *Head of the Department* *Principal*

FORM–76

FEEDBACK FROM FACULTY MEMBERS AND STAFF

Department: Date:

Academic Year: Semester:

(a) Name :

(b) Number of Years in the College :

(c) Please provide your comments on the following:

1. Management Attitude	: ☐ Excellent	☐ Good	☐ Average	☐ Fair
2. Attitude of the Administration	: ☐ Excellent	☐ Good	☐ Average	☐ Fair
3. Motivational Incentives	: ☐ Excellent	☐ Good	☐ Average	☐ Fair
4. Salary and other emoluments	: ☐ Excellent	☐ Good	☐ Average	☐ Fair
5. Service Conditions	: ☐ Excellent	☐ Good	☐ Average	☐ Fair
6. Opportunities for Professional Growth	: ☐ Excellent	☐ Good	☐ Average	☐ Fair
7. Opportunities for Personal Growth	: ☐ Excellent	☐ Good	☐ Average	☐ Fair
8. Infrastructure Facilities	: ☐ Excellent	☐ Good	☐ Average	☐ Fair
9. Library Facilities	: ☐ Excellent	☐ Good	☐ Average	☐ Fair
10. Computing and Internet Facilities	: ☐ Excellent	☐ Good	☐ Average	☐ Fair
11. Opportunities for R&D	: ☐ Excellent	☐ Good	☐ Average	☐ Fair
12. Sports, Extra Curricular Facilities	: ☐ Excellent	☐ Good	☐ Average	☐ Fair
13. Mess/Canteen Facilities	: ☐ Excellent	☐ Good	☐ Average	☐ Fair
14. Transport Facilities	: ☐ Excellent	☐ Good	☐ Average	☐ Fair
15. Overall rating of the College	: ☐ Excellent	☐ Good	☐ Average	☐ Fair

(d) Your Positive/Negative Comments:

(e) Your suggestions for the Improvement of the Institution/Department:

Date:

Signature

FORM-77

FEEDBACK FROM PARENTS

(a) Name of the Parent :

(b) Present Address :

Phone Number :

E-mail :

(c) Name of the Student :

(d) Branch and Year :

(e) Please provide your comments on the following:

1.	College Infrastructure	: ☐ Excellent	☐ Good	☐ Average	☐ Fair
2.	Teaching imparted to your ward	: ☐ Excellent	☐ Good	☐ Average	☐ Fair
3.	Department Resources	: ☐ Excellent	☐ Good	☐ Average	☐ Fair
4.	Faculties helpfulness	: ☐ Excellent	☐ Good	☐ Average	☐ Fair
5.	Library Facilities	: ☐ Excellent	☐ Good	☐ Average	☐ Fair
6.	Computing and Internet Facilities	: ☐ Excellent	☐ Good	☐ Average	☐ Fair
7.	Sports, Extra Curricular Facilities	: ☐ Excellent	☐ Good	☐ Average	☐ Fair
8.	Personality/Communications Skills Development Facilities	: ☐ Excellent	☐ Good	☐ Average	☐ Fair
9.	Placement Opportunities	: ☐ Excellent	☐ Good	☐ Average	☐ Fair
10.	Transport Facilities	: ☐ Excellent	☐ Good	☐ Average	☐ Fair
11.	Mess/Canteen Facilities	: ☐ Excellent	☐ Good	☐ Average	☐ Fair
12.	Feedback on ward's Progress	: ☐ Excellent	☐ Good	☐ Average	☐ Fair
13.	Discipline standards in the College	: ☐ Excellent	☐ Good	☐ Average	☐ Fair
14.	Overall rating of the College	: ☐ Excellent	☐ Good	☐ Average	☐ Fair

(e) Your comments/remarks/additional points:

(f) Your suggestions for the Improvement of the Institution/Department:

Date:

Signature

FORM-78

FEEDBACK FROM ALUMNI

(a) Name :

(b) Year of Graduation :

(c) Branch :

(d) Present Address :

E-mail :

(e) Present Occupation :

(Please send appointment letter copy to the HOD at the earliest)

(f) Whether undergone higher education: Yes/No

(If Yes, please send Admission details at the earliest)

(g) Please provide your comments on the following:

1. College Infrastructure	: ☐ Excellent	☐ Good	☐ Average	☐ Fair
2. Effectiveness of Teaching Processes	: ☐ Excellent	☐ Good	☐ Average	☐ Fair
3. Department Resources	: ☐ Excellent	☐ Good	☐ Average	☐ Fair
4. Faculties helpfulness	: ☐ Excellent	☐ Good	☐ Average	☐ Fair
5. Library Facilities	: ☐ Excellent	☐ Good	☐ Average	☐ Fair
6. Computing and Internet Facilities	: ☐ Excellent	☐ Good	☐ Average	☐ Fair
7. Sports, Extra Curricular Facilities	: ☐ Excellent	☐ Good	☐ Average	☐ Fair
8. Personality/Communications Skills Development Facilities	: ☐ Excellent	☐ Good	☐ Average	☐ Fair
9. Placement Cell	: ☐ Excellent	☐ Good	☐ Average	☐ Fair
10. Overall rating of the College	: ☐ Excellent	☐ Good	☐ Average	☐ Fair

(h) Your Positive/Negative Comments:

(i) Your suggestions for the Improvement of the Institution:

Date:

Signature

FORM–79

FEEDBACK FROM EMPLOYER

(a) Name of the Organization :

(b) Name of the Officer and Designation :

(c) Name of the Employee :

(d) Please provide your comments on the following:

1. Performance of the staff : ☐ Excellent ☐ Good ☐ Average ☐ Fair
2. Technical Skills : ☐ Excellent ☐ Good ☐ Average ☐ Fair
3. Attitude : ☐ Excellent ☐ Good ☐ Average ☐ Fair
4. Interpersonal Skills : ☐ Excellent ☐ Good ☐ Average ☐ Fair
5. Passion for Growth : ☐ Excellent ☐ Good ☐ Average ☐ Fair

(e) Would you like to consider our students for future employment: Yes/No.

(f) What are your advices for further improvements on our candidates?

Date:

Signature

Seal:

FORM-80

FEEDBACK-HOSTELLERS

Name (Optional): Branch:

Semester: Room:

(a) Please provide your comments on the following :

1. Hostel Infrastructure Comments	: ☐ Excellent	☐ Good	☐ Average	☐ Fair
2. Facilities in the Room Comments	: ☐ Excellent	☐ Good	☐ Average	☐ Fair
3. Mess Facilities Comments	: ☐ Excellent	☐ Good	☐ Average	☐ Fair
4. Food Quality Comments	: ☐ Excellent	☐ Good	☐ Average	☐ Fair
5. Medical Facilities Comments	: ☐ Excellent	☐ Good	☐ Average	☐ Fair
6. Computing and Internet Facilities Comments	: ☐ Excellent	☐ Good	☐ Average	☐ Fair
7. Sports, Extra Curricular Facilities Comments	: ☐ Excellent	☐ Good	☐ Average	☐ Fair
8. Library Access and Facilities Comments	: ☐ Excellent	☐ Good	☐ Average	☐ Fair
9. Study Hours Comments	: ☐ Excellent	☐ Good	☐ Average	☐ Fair
10. Overall rating of the Hostel Comments	: ☐ Excellent	☐ Good	☐ Average	☐ Fair

(b) Your suggestions for the Improvement of the Hostel:

Date:

Signature

Form–81

FEEDBACK ANALYSIS AND ACTION

Department: Date:

Academic Year: Semester:

Feedback Form

☐ Faculty ☐ Parents ☐ Alumni ☐ Employer ☐ Hostellers

Consolidated Feedback Points

Remedial Action Suggested:

Faculty in-Charge *Head of the Department* *Principal*

FORM–82

EXTRA/CO-CURRICULAR ACTIVITIES

Department: ____________________ Date: __________

Academic Year: ____________________

S. No.	*Date of Event*	*Event Description*	*Event Venue*	*Event Level (Unit/State/ National)*	*Type of Event (Indi/Team)*	*Student Details*		*Awards*	*Remarks*
						Student Name	*Year- I/II/III/IV*		

Faculty in-Charge *Head of the Department*

FORM–83

PERSONALITY DEVELOPMENT PROGRAMS

Department: Academic Year:

Personality Development Programs-External

S. No.	*Resource Person*	*Name of the Topic*	*Dates*	*No. of Hours*	*Beneficiary*	*Number of Students*	*Amount Spent*

Personality Development Programs-Internal

S. No.	*Resource Person*	*Name of the Topic*	*Number of Days*	*Number of Hours*	*Beneficiary*	*Number of Students*

Faculty in-Charge *Head of the Department*

FORM-84

ENTREPRENEURSHIP/ETHICS PROGRAMS

Department: Academic Year:

Entrepreneurship Programs

S. No.	*Resource Person*	*Name of the Topic*	*Dates*	*No. of Hours*	*Beneficiary*	*Number of Students*	*Amount Spent*

Ethics Programs

S. No.	*Resource Person*	*Name of the Topic*	*Dates*	*No of Hours*	*Beneficiary*	*Number of Students*	*Amount Spent*

Faculty in-Charge *Head of the Department*

FORM-85

PROFESSIONAL SOCIETY MEMBERSHIP-STUDENTS

Department: Date:

Professional Society:

S. No.	*Name of the Student*	*Year*	*Reg. No.*	*Membership Number*	*Period*

Faculty in-Charge *Head of the Department*

FORM–86

ALUMNI MEETS

Department:

Alumni Meet: Held At: Date:

S. No.	*Name of the Alumni*	*Year*	*Reg. No.*	*Membership Number*	*Feedback (Yes/No)*

Faculty in-Charge *Head of the Department*

FORM-87

STUDENT-INCENTIVES AND REWARDS

Department: Date:

Semester:

Students Incentives and Rewards-Academic

Sl. No.	*Name*	*Year*	*Details*	*Marks*	*Award*	*Remarks*
Expenditure for Academic Awards						

Students Incentives and Rewards-Others

Sl. No.	*Name*	*Year*	*Details*	*Award*	*Remarks*

Students Publications and Awards

Faculty in-Charge *Head of the Department*

FORM-88

STUDENT'S RESEARCH ACTIVITY

Department: Date:

Academic Year:

S. No.	*Name of the Student and Class*	*Title of the Work*	*Period*	*Funding*
1.				
2.				
3.				
4.				
5.				

Faculty in-Charge *Head of the Department*

FORM-89

RESEARCH ACTIVITY–IN HOUSE

Department: Date:

Academic Year:

S. No.	*Name of the Faculty*	*Title of the Work*	*Period*	*Funds Availed*
1.				
2.				
3.				
4.				
5.				

Faculty in-Charge *Head of the Department*

FORM–90

RESEARCH ACTIVITY–EXTERNAL

Department: Date:

Academic Year:

S. No.	*Name of the Faculty*	*Title of the Work and Sponsoring Organization*	*Period*	*Funds Availed*
1.				
2.				
3.				
4.				
5.				

Faculty in-Charge *Head of the Department*

FORM–91

RESEARCH PUBLICATION, PATENTS

Department: Date:

Academic Year:

Research Publication

S. No.	*Name of the Faculty*	*Title of the Publication*	*Journal*
1.			
2.			
3.			
4.			
5.			

Patents

S. No.	*Name of the Faculty*	*Patent Title*	*Status*
1.			
2.			
3.			
4.			
5.			

Faculty I Member N-Charge *Head of the Department*

FORM-92

INDUSTRY–INSTITUTION INTERACTION, MOU

Department: Date:

Academic Year:

Resource persons from Industries invited for lectures and seminars:

Year (Y)	*Names of Resource Person*	*Background Industry/ Academic/R&D*	*Topics Covered*

Memorandum of Undertaking with Industry/Research Bodies:

1.
2.
3.
4.

Faculty in-Charge *Head of the Department*

Form–93

STUDENTS' INPLANT TRAINING

Department: Date:

Academic Year:

Sl. No.	*Name of the Student*	*Year*	*Industry*	*Period*	*Report Yes/No*

Faculty in-Charge *Head of the Department*

FORM–94

STUDENTS' INDUSTRIAL VISIT AND FEEDBACK

Department:

Semester: Date:

Name and address of industry visited:

Date:

Time Duration:

Beneficiary Dept:

Semester:

Total No. of Students:

Industrial visit organized by:

Name of the in charge and other Faculty who accompanied the students:

Contact Person at Industry:

Visit related to the subject:

During visit the students were taken to following Departments in the Industry

Feedback obtained from the following students (to be enclosed as annexure)

Signature of Industrial Visit in-Charge: *Head of the Department*

FORM–95

CONSULTANCY/TESTING ACTIVITY–STAFF

Department: Date:

Academic Year:

Consultancy:

Testing Activity:

Faculty in-Charge *Head of the Department*

FORM–96

MINUTES OF CLASS COMMITTEE MEETING

Department: Date:

Semester

Nature of Meeting	*Class Committee Meeting*	
Venue	*Date*	*Time*
Present 1 2 3 4 5 6		
Absent 1 2 3 4		
Circulated to:		

Points Discussed	*Actions to be Initiated*	*Responsibility*	*Target Date*
1.			
2.			
3.			

Faculty in-Charge *Class Teacher* *Head of the Department*

FORM–97

MINUTES OF DEPARTMENT REVIEW MEETING

Department: Date:

Semester:

Nature of Meeting	*Department Review Meeting*							
Venue					*Date*		*Time*	
Present								
1								
2								
3								
4								
5								
6								
7								
8								
9								
10								
11								
12								
13								
14								
15								
16								
Absent								
1								
2								
3								
Circulated to:								

Points Discussed	*Actions to be Initiated*	*Responsibility*	*Target Date*

Faculty in-Charge *Head of the Department*

FORM-98

MINUTES OF MANAGEMENT REVIEW MEETING

Department: Date:

Semester:

Nature of Meeting	*Management Review Meeting*	
Venue	*Date*	*Time*
Present 1 2 3 4 5 6		
Absent 1 2 3 4		
Circulated to:		

Points Discussed	*Actions to be Initiated*	*Responsibility*	*Target Date*
1.			
2.			
3.			

Faculty in-Charge *Principal*

FORM–99

DEPARTMENT BUDGET PROPOSAL

YYYY/DDD/MP/B&U/PRO

Department: Date:

Academic Year:

Department Budget-Proposal

S. No	*Budget Heads*	*Budget Amt*	*Total*
1.	Laboratory/Department Development ❑ Major Equipment ❑ Minor Equipment ❑ Furniture ❑ Maintenance/Calibration/Lab Consumable ❑ Teaching Aids		
2.	Faculty/Staff Development ❑ Seminars/Workshops/Conferences ❑ Summer/Winter Schools ❑ Organizing Faculty Developmental Programs ❑ Professional Society Membership ❑ Incentives and Rewards		
3.	Research—Inhouse ❑ In house Research Activities ❑ Research Publication		
4.	Faculty/Staff Operational Expenses ❑ Salary of Teaching Staff ❑ Salary of Non-Teaching Staff ❑ Other Benefits		
5.	Students Development ❑ Paper Presentation/Quiz Etc ❑ Organizing Inter Dept. Events ❑ Organizing Inter Institute Events ❑ Professional Society Memberships ❑ Organizing Personality Developmental. Programs ❑ Organizing Programs on Ethics and Entrepreneurship. ❑ Organizing Alumni Events ❑ Students' Incentives and Rewards		

Faculty in-Charge *Head of the Department*

FORM-100

DEPARTMENT BUDGET SANCTION

Department: Date:

Academic Year:

Department Budgets-Sanction

S. No.	*Budget Heads*	*Budget Sanctioned*	*Total*
1.	Laboratory/Department Development ❑ Major Equipment ❑ Minor Equipment ❑ Furniture ❑ Maintenance/Calibration/Lab Consumable ❑ Teaching Aids		
2.	Faculty/Staff Development ❑ Seminars/Workshops/Conferences ❑ Summer/Winter Schools ❑ Organizing Faculty Developmental Programs ❑ Professional Society Membership ❑ Incentives and Rewards		
3.	Research—Inhouse ❑ In house Research Activities ❑ Research Publication		
4.	Faculty/Staff Operational Expenses ❑ Salary of Teaching Staff ❑ Salary of Non-Teaching Staff ❑ Other Benefits		
5.	Students Development ❑ Paper Presentation/Quiz Etc ❑ Organizing Inter Dept. Events ❑ Organizing Inter Institute Events ❑ Professional Society Memberships ❑ Organizing Personality Developmental Programs ❑ Organizing Programs on Ethics and Entrepreneurship. ❑ Organizing Alumni Events ❑ Students' Incentives and Rewards		

Head of the Department *Principal*

FORM–101

DEPARTMENT BUDGET UTILIZATION

Department:

Date:

Academic Year:

Department Budgets-Utilization

S. No	*Budget Heads*	*Budget Sanctioned*	*Budget Utilized*	*Funds Available*
1	Laboratory/Department Development ❑ Major Equipment ❑ Minor Equipment ❑ Furniture ❑ Maintenance/Calibration/Lab Consumable ❑ Teaching Aids			
2	Faculty/Staff Development ❑ Seminars/Workshops/Conferences ❑ Summer/Winter Schools ❑ Organizing Faculty Development. Programs ❑ Professional Society Membership ❑ Incentives and Rewards			
3	Research—Inhouse ❑ In house Research Activities ❑ Research Publication			
4	Faculty/Staff Operational Expenses ❑ Salary of Teaching Staff ❑ Salary of Non-Teaching Staff ❑ Other Benefits			
5	Students Development ❑ Paper Presentation/Quiz Etc ❑ Organizing Inter Dept. Events ❑ Organizing Inter Institutional. Events ❑ Professional Society Memberships ❑ Organizing Personality Developmental Programs ❑ Organizing Programs on Ethics and Entrepreneurship ❑ Organizing Alumni Events ❑ Students' Incentives and Rewards			

Faculty in-Charge

Head of the Department

FORM-102

STUDENT LIST—TRANSPORT

Department:

Academic Year: Semester:

S. No.	*Student Name*	*Roll Number*	*Year*	*Route And Stage*

Faculty in-Charge *Head of the Department*

FORM–103

STUDENT LIST—HOSTEL

Department:

Academic Year: Semester:

S. No.	*Student Name*	*Roll Number*	*Year*	*Hostel, Room Number*

Faculty in-Charge *Head of the Department*

FORM-104

BUS STATUS REPORT

Year:

S. No.	*Vehicle Number*	*Owner*	*Insurance by*	*Permit Due Date*	*Fitness Certificate*	*Insurance Due Date*	*Tax Due Date*	*Pollution Due Date*	*Driver Name*	*Driving License*

Transport in-Charge

References

1. Aronowitz, Stanley (2000). *The Knowledge Factory: Dismantling the Corporate University and Creating True Higher Learning*. Boston: Beacon Press. ISBN 978-0-8070-3122-3.
2. Barrow, Clyde W. (1990). *Universities and the Capitalist State: Corporate Liberalism and the Reconstruction of American Higher Education, 1894–1928*. Madison, Wis: University of Wisconsin Press. ISBN 978-0-299-12400-7.
3. Diamond, Sigmund (1992). *Compromised Campus: The Collaboration of Universities with the Intelligence Community, 1945–1955*. New York, NY: Oxford Univ. Press. ISBN 978-0-19-505382-1.
4. Pedersen, Olaf (1997). *The First Universities: Studium Generale and the Origins of University Education in Europe*. Cambridge: Cambridge Univ. Press. ISBN 978-0-521-59431–8.
5. Ridder-Symoens, Hilde de, ed. (1992). *A History of the University in Europe*. Volume 1: Universities in the Middle Ages. Ruegg, Walter (general ed.). Cambridge: Cambridge University Press. ISBN 0-521-36105-2.
6. Ridder-Symoens, Hilde de, ed. (1996). *A History of the University in Europe*. Volume 2: Universities in Early Modern Europe (1500–1800). Rüegg, Walter (general ed.). Cambridge: Cambridge University Press. ISBN 0-521-36106-0.
7. Ruegg, Walter, ed. (2004). *A History of the University in Europe*. Volume 3: Universities in the Nineteenth and Early Twentieth Centuries (1800–1945). Cambridge: Cambridge University Press. ISBN 0-521-36107-9.
8. http://en.wikipedia.org/wiki/University.
9. *Google eBook of "Encyclopædia Britannica"*. Books.google.com. 2006-09-22. Retrieved 2010-05-28.
10. Lewis, Charlton T. and Short, Charles (1966) [1879], *A Latin Dictionary*, Oxford: Clarendon Press
11. Marcia L. Colish, *Medieval Foundations of the Western Intellectual Tradition, 400–1400,* (New Haven: Yale Univ. Pr., 1997), p. 267.
12. Rüegg, W. (2003). Mythologies and Historiogaphy of the Beginnings, pp. 4–34 in H. De Ridder-Symoens, editor, A History of the University in Europe; Vol. 1, Cambridge University Press.
13. Watson, P. (2005). Ideas. London: Weidenfeld and Nicolson, p. 373.
14. Riche, Pierre (1978). "Education and Culture in the Barbarian West: From the Sixth through the Eighth Century", Columbia: University of South Carolina Press, ISBN 0-87249-376-8, pp. 126–7, 282–98.
15. Johnson, P. (2000). The Renaissance: A short history. Modern Library Chronicles (Modern Library ed.). New York: Modern Library, p. 9.

16. "The Origin of Universities". www.utexas.edu. Retrieved 2010-05-28.
17. University of Coimbra founded in Lisbon and was based there in 1290–1308, 1338–54 and 1377–1537.Medieval Universities And the Origin of the College.
18. Makdisi, G. (1981). Rise of Colleges: Institutions of Learning in Islam and the West. Edinburgh: Edinburgh University Press.
19. Daun, H. and Arjmand, R. (2005). Islamic Education, pp. 377–388 in J. Zajda, editor, International Handbook of Globalisation, Education and Policy Research. Netherlands: Springer.
20. Huff, T. (2003). The Rise of Early Modern Science. Cambridge University Press, p. 122.
21. Kerr, C. (2001). The Uses of the University. P Harvard University Press, p. 16 and 145.
22. Ruegg, W. (2003). Mythologies and Historiogaphy of the Beginnings, pp. 4–34 in H. De Ridder-Symoens, editor, A History of the University in Europe; Vol 1, Cambridge University Press, p. 12.
23. Grendler, P.F. (2004). "The Universities of the Renaissance and Reformation". Renaissance Quarterly, 57, pp. 2.
24. Rubenstein, R.E. (2003). Aristotle's Children: How Christians, Muslims and Jews rediscovered ancient wisdom and illuminated the dark ages (1st ed.). Orlando, Fla: Harcourt, pp. 16–17.
25. Dales, R.C. (1990). Medieval discussions of the eternity of the world (Vol. 18). Brill Archive, p. 144.
26. Grendler, P.F. (2004). "The Universities of the Renaissance and Reformation". Renaissance Quarterly, 57, pp. 2–8.
27. Scott, J.C. (2006). The Mission of the University: Medieval to Postmodern transformations. Journal of Higher Education, 77(1), p. 6.
28. Arnold H. Green. "The History of Libraries in the Arab World: A Diffusionist Model". *Libraries and the Cultural Record* 23(4): 459.
29. Hossein Nasr. *Traditional Islam in the Modern World.* Taylor and Francis, p. 125.
30. Daniel, Norman (1984). "Review of "The Rise of Colleges. Institutions of Learning in Islam and the West by George Makdisi"". *Journal of the American Oriental Society* 104 (3): 586–8. JSTOR 601679.
31. George Makdisi, "Madrasa and University in the Middle Ages", *Studia Islamica*, No. 32 (1970), pp. 255–264.
32. Toby Huff, *Rise of Early Modern Science: Islam, China and the West,* 2nd ed., Cambridge 2003, ISBN 0-521-52994-8, p. 133–139, 149–159, 179–189.
33. William J. Courtenay, de: Jurgen Miethke, David B. Priest. *Universities and schooling in medieval society.* Brill. pp. 95–99.
34. Ruegg, Walter, "Foreword. The University as a European Institution", *A History of the University in Europe. Vol. 1: Universities in the Middle Ages,* Cambridge University Press, 1992, ISBN 0-521-36105-2, pp. XIX–XX.
35. Nuria Sanz, Sjur Bergan, *The Heritage of European Universities,* Vol. 548. Council of Europe, p. 121.
36. Nuria Sanz, Sjur Bergan. *The Heritage of European Universities,* Vol. 548. Council of Europe, p. 28.

37. Makdisi, George (April–June 1989). "Scholasticism and Humanism in Classical Islam and the Christian West". *Journal of the American Oriental Society* (Journal of the American Oriental Society, Vol. 109, No. 2) 109 (2): 175–182 [175–77]. doi:10.2307/604423. JSTOR 604423.
38. Goddard, Hugh (2000). *A History of Christian-Muslim Relations.* Edinburgh University Press. p. 99. ISBN 0-7486-1009-X.
39. Daniel, Norman (1984). "Review of "The Rise of Colleges. Institutions of Learning in Islam and the West by George Makdisi"". *Journal of the American Oriental Society* 104 (3): 586–8.JSTOR 601679.
40. Grendler, P.F. (2004). The Universities of the Renaissance and Reformation. Renaissance Quarterly, 57, pp. 1–3.
41. Frijhoff, W. (1996). Patterns. In H.D. Ridder-Symoens (Ed.), Universities in early modern Europe, 1500–1800, A history of the University in Europe. Cambridge, Cambridge University Press, p. 75.
42. Frijhoff, W. (1996). Patterns. In H.D. Ridder-Symoens (Ed.), Universities in early modern Europe, 1500–1800, A history of the University. Cambridge, Cambridge University Press, p. 47.
43. Grendler, P.F. (2004). The Universities of the Renaissance and Reformation. Renaissance Quarterly, 57, p. 23.
44. Scott, J.C. (2006). The mission of the University: Medieval to Postmodern transformations. Journal of Higher Education, 77(1), pp. 10–13.
45. Frijhoff, W. (1996). Patterns. In H.D. Ridder-Symoens (Ed.), Universities in early modern Europe, 1500–1800, A history of the university in Europe. Cambridge, Cambridge University Press, p. 65.
46. Ruegg, W. (1992). Epilogue: the rise of humanism. In H. D. Ridder-Symoens (Ed.), Universities in the Middle Ages, A history of the university in Europe. Cambridge, Cambridge University Press.
47. Grendler, P.F. (2002). The Universities of the Italian renaissance. Baltimore: Johns Hopkins University Press, p. 223.
48. Grendler, P.F. (2002). The Universities of the Italian renaissance. Baltimore: Johns Hopkins University Press, p. 197.
49. Ruegg, W. (1996). Themes. In H.D. Ridder-Symoens (Ed.), Universities in Early Modern Europe, 1500–1800, A history of the University in Europe. Cambridge, Cambridge University Press, pp. 33–39.
50. Grendler, P.F. (2004). The Universities of the Renaissance and Reformation. Renaissance Quarterly, 57, pp. 12–13.
51. Bylebyl, J.J. (2009). Disputation and description in the renaissance pulse controversy. In A. Wear, R.K. French and I. M. Lonie (Eds.), The medical renaissance of the sixteenth century (1st ed., pp. 223–245). Cambridge University Press.
52. FUssel, S. (2005). Gutenberg and the Impact of Printing (English ed.). Aldershot, Hampshire: Ashgate Pub., p. 145.
53. Westfall, R.S. (1977). The Construction of Modern Science: mechanisms and Mechanics, Cambridge, Cambridge University Press, p. 105.

54. Ornstein, M. (1928). The Role of Scientific Societies in the Seventeenth Century. Chicago, IL: University of Chicago Press.
55. Gascoigne, J. (1990). A Reappraisal of the role of the Universities, The Scientific Revolution. In D.C. Lindberg and R.S. Westman (Eds.), Reappraisals of the Scientific Revolution, pp. 208–209.
56. Gascoigne, J. (1990). A Reappraisal of the Role of the Universities, The Scientific Revolution. In D.C. Lindberg and R. S. Westman (Eds.), Reappraisals of the Scientific Revolution, pp. 210–229.
57. Gascoigne, J. (1990). A Reappraisal of the role of the Universities, The Scientific Revolution. In D.C. Lindberg and R.S. Westman (Eds.), Reappraisals of the Scientific Revolution, pp. 245–248.
58. Feingold, M. (1991). Tradition vs novelty: universities and scientific societies in the early modern period. In P. Barker and R. Ariew (Eds.), Revolution and continuity: essays in the history and philosophy of early modern science, Studies in philosophy and the history of philosophy. Washington, D.C: Catholic University of America Press, pp. 53–54.
59. Feingold, M. (1991). Tradition vs novelty: universities and scientific societies in the early modern period. In P. Barker and R. Ariew (Eds.), Revolution and continuity: essays in the history and philosophy of early modern science, Studies in philosophy and the history of philosophy. Washington, D.C: Catholic University of America Press, pp. 46–50.
60. Baldwin, M. (1995). The Snakestone Experiments: an Early Modern Medical Debate, ISIS, 86(3), 394–418.
61. "Oxford Dictionary of National Biography". Oxforddnb.com. Retrieved 2010-05-28.
62. Anderson, Robert (March 2010). "The 'Idea of a University' today", *History and Policy*. United Kingdom: History and Policy. Retrieved 9 December 2010.
63. "Basic Classification Technical Details". Carnegie Foundation for the Advancement of Teaching. Retrieved 2007-03-20.
64. "Massachusetts Board of Education: Degree-Granting Regulations for Independent Institutions of Higher Education" . Retrieved 2010-05-28.
65. Peter Drucker. "'Deemed' Status Distributed Freely During Arjun Singh's Tenure - LearnHub News". Learnhub.com. Retrieved 2010-07-29.
66. "Grading Student Loans". Federal Reserve Bank of New York. Retrieved 6 December 2012.
67. "First Class In The University: Is It Hard? - Education". Nairaland. Retrieved 2012-08-14.
68. "THE QS World University Rankings". Top Universities. Retrieved 14 August 2012.
69. "Private Universities - University Grants Commission". 30 June 2011. Retrieved 30 June 2011.
70. Bhagwant University AUHS web site.
71. O.P. Jindal University web site.
72. Amity University web site.
73. Education in Lebanon, CSRD report, Lebanese American University, 2004
74. Diane Stone, "Market Principles, Philanthropic Ideals and Public Service Values: The Public Policy Program at the Central European University", *PS: Political Science and Politics*, July 2007: 545–551.

75. "Meer dan tachtig jaar; IVA Driebergen". Iva-driebergen. Retrieved 14 August 2012.
76. "Private university - eNotes.com Reference". Enotes. Retrieved 14 August 2012.
77. "List of universities in Turkey - Wikipedia, the free encyclopedia". En.wikipedia.org. Retrieved 2012-12-09.
78. "The University Debate: What the Ivy League can teach Britain". The Independent. 16 February 2011. Retrieved 3 March 2011.
79. *OxCHEPS Occasional Paper No. 39.* Oxford Centre for Higher Education Policy Studies. Retrieved 20 March 2011.
80. Paton, Graeme (5 January 2012). "Taxpayer Funding of Universities 'to drop to 100 year low'". *The Telegraph*. Retrieved 6 January 2012.
81. "Higher Education". Privy Council Office. Retrieved 6 December 2007.
82. Luzer, Daniel (13 April 2012). "Can We Make College Cheaper?". *Washington Monthly*. Retrieved 17 April 2012.
83. Gladwell, Malcolm. (2005) "Getting In: the social logic of Ivy League admissions." The New Yorker, 10 October 2005 [2].
84. "Princeton University Financial Aid without Loans". Princeton.edu. Retrieved 2012-12-09.
85. Burrows, Toby (1993). *Serials Management in Australia and New Zealand.* Binghamton, NY: Haworth Press. p. 19.ISBN 1-56024-453-4.
86. Princeton Review (2004). *Guide to Studying Abroad.* New York, NY: The Princeton Review. p. 105. ISBN 978-0-375-76371-7.
87. "Private Universities". Ministry of Higher Education. Retrieved 14 August 2012.
88. http://en.wikipedia.org/wiki/Vocational_university.
89. en.wikipedia.org/wiki/Private_university.
90. "University Grants Commission Act, 1956"Union Human Resource Development Ministry. Retrieved 3 September 2011.
91. "Professional Councils-Inside H E - University Grants Commission", *ugc.ac.in.* Retrieved 18 December 2011.
92. http://www.innovationinbusiness.research.hu.nl/Onderzoek.aspx
93. Renaud-Coulon, Annick (2008). *Corporate Universities, A Lever of Corporate Responsibility.* GlobalCCU Publisher. ISBN 978-2-9531667-0-5.
94. Paton, Rob; Geoff Peters, John Storey and Scott Aszza (2005). *Handbook of Corporate University Development: Managing Strategic Learning Initiatives in Public and Private Domains.* Gower Publishing Ltd., ISBN 978-0-566-08583-3.
95. Allen, Mark (2002). *The Corporate University Handbook.* AMACOM Div American Mgmt Assn. pp. 9. ISBN 978-0-8144-0711-0.
96. Hearn, Denise R. (2002-05-10). "Education in the Workplace: An Examination of Corporate University Models". Retrieved 2009-01-27.
97. Meister, Jeanne C. (1998). *Corporate Universities: Lessons in Building a World-class Work Force.* McGraw-Hill. ISBN 978-0-7863-0787-6.
98. Tanner, Lisa (2003-07-25). "Corporate University Approach Taking Hold". Dallas Business Journal. Retrieved 2009-01-27.

99. Preston, Rob (May 16, 2011). "Down To Business: Higher Education is Ripe for Technology Disruption". *InformationWeek* (UMB): 60. Retrieved 2011-05-31.
100. Wolfe, C. and Wolfe, C.R. (2001). Learning and teaching on the World Wide Web. San Diego, Calif.; London: Academic.
101. Delanty, G. (2001). Challenging Knowledge, Open University Press, London.
102. King, R. (2004). The University in the Global Age, Palgrave Macmillan, London.
103. Tavangarian, D., Leypold, M., Nolting, K. and Roser, M. (2004). Is E-learning the Solution for Individual Learning? Journal of e-learning, 2004.
104. "Technology Impact on Learning". Retrieved 26 December 2012.
105. Nagy, A. (2005). The Impact of E-Learning, in: Bruck, P.A.; Buchholz, A.; Karssen, Z.; Zerfass, A. (Eds). E-Content: Technologies and Perspectives for the European Market. Berlin: Springer-Verlag, pp. 79–96.
106. Allen, I.E. and Seaman, J. (2008). Staying the Course: Online Education in the United States, 2008 Needham MA: Sloan Consortium.
107. Allen, I.E. and Seaman, J. (2003). Sizing the Opportunity: The Quality and Extent of Online Education in the United States, 2002 and 2003 Wellesley, MA: The Sloan Consortium.
108. Ambient Insight Research (2009). US Self-paced e-Learning Market Monroe WA: Ambient Insight Research.
109. Hebert, D.G. (2007). "Five Challenges and Solutions in Online Music Teacher Education". *Research and Issues in Music Education* 5 (1).
110. "The Rise of Cyber-Schools". The New Atlantis. Retrieved 2012-10-24.
111. "Research Center: Charter Schools". Edweek.org. Retrieved 2012-10-24.
112. Hiltz, S. (1990). 'Evaluating the Virtual Classroom', in Harasim, L. (ed.) Online Education: Perspectives on a New Environment New York: Praeger, pp. 133–169.
113. Mason. R. and Kaye, A. (1989). Mindweave: Communication, Computers and Distance Education Oxford, UK: Pergamon Press.
114. Bates, A. (2005). Technology, e-Learning and Distance Education London: Routledge.
115. Johnson, Henry M. Dialogue and the construction of knowledge in e-learning: Exploring students' perceptions of their learning while using Blackboard's asynchronous discussion board. European Journal of Open, Distance and E-Learning 05.01.2007 (2007), ISSN 10275–207.
116. Harasim, L., Hiltz, S., Teles, L. and Turoff, M. (1995) Learning Networks: A Field Guide to Teaching and Learning Online Cambridge, MA: MIT Press.
117. Pumilia-Gnarini, Paolo (2012). *Didactic Strategies and Technologies for Education: Incorporating Advancements.*
118. Curriculum and Pedagogy in Technology Assisted Learning.
119. Redecker, Christine (2009). "Review of Learning 2.0 Practices: Study on the Impact of Web 2.0 Innovations on Education and Training in Europe". *JRC Scientific and technical report* (EUR 23664 EN – 2009).
120. Seely Brown, John; Adler, Richard P. (2008). "Minds on Fire:Open Education, the Long Tail and Learning 2.0". *Educause review* (January/February 2008): 16–32.

121. Manprit Kaur (2011). "Using Online Forums in Language Learning and Education". StudentPulse.com. Retrieved 2012-08-22.
122. Crane, Beverley E., "Using Web 2.0 Tools in the k-12 Classroom" Neal-Shuman Publishers Inc., 2009, p. 3.
123. Bates, A., Poole, G. Effective Teaching with Technology in Higher Education San Francisco: Jossey-Bass, John Wiley, 2003.
124. Whyte, Cassandra Bolyard (1989). Student Affairs—The Future, Journal of College Student Development, 30, 86–89.
125. Sendall, P.; Ceccucci, W. and Peslak, A. (December 2008). "Web 2.0 Matters: An Analysis of Implementing Web 2.0 in the Classroom". *Information Systems Education Journal* 6 (64). Retrieved 04/12/12.
126. Whyte, Cassandra B. and Lauridsen, Kurt (editor) (1980). An Integrated Learning Assistance Center. New Directions Sourcebook, Jossey-Bass, Inc.
127. Diecker, Lisa; Lane, Allsopp, O'Brien, Butler, Kyger, Fenty (May 2009). "Evaluating Video Models of Evidence-Based Instructional Practices to Enhance Teacher Learning". *Teacher Education and Special Education* 32 (2): 180–196. Retrieved 9/17/2011.
128. E-moderating: The Key to Teaching and Learning Online – Gilly Salmon, Kogan Page, 2000,ISBN 0-7494-4085-6.
129. Bloom, B.S. and Krathwohl, D.R. (1956). Taxonomy of Educational Objectives: Handbook 1.
130. Baath, J.A. (1982). "Distance Students' Learning – Empirical Findings and Theoretical Deliberations".
131. Areskog, N.-H. (1995). The Tutorial Process – the Roles of Student Teacher and Tutor in a Long Term Perspective.
132. Black, J. and McClintock, R. (1995). "An Interpretation Construction Approach to Constructivist Design."
133. Smith, B., Reed, P. and Jones, C. (2008) 'Mode Neutral' pedagogy. European Journal of Open, Distance and E-learning."
134. J. Scott Armstrong (2012). "Natural Learning in Higher Education". *Encyclopedia of the Sciences of Learning.*
135. http://en.wikipedia.org/wiki/List_of_academic_ranks.
136. http://en.wikipedia.org/wiki/Academic_ranks_(United_States).
137. Ruegg, Walter (1992). *A History of the University in Europe. Vol. 1: Universities in the Middle Ages.* Cambridge University Press. pp. XIX–XX. ISBN 0-521-36105-2.
138. Verger, J. (1999). "Doctor, doctoratus". *Lexikon des Mittelalters.* 3. Stuttgart: J.B. Metzler.
139. TimesUnion.com: "Women surpassing men by degrees." Hope Yen. April 27, 2011.
140. Bologna Secretariat, Brussels (2010). "Welcome to the website of the European Higher Education Area: The official Bologna Process website 2007–2010". Benelux Bologna Secretariat. Archived from the original on 19 June 2010. Retrieved 2010-06-21.
141. Wadsack, Ingrid; Kasparovsky, Heinz (2004). *Higher Education in Austria* (2nd ed.). Vienna: Austrian Federal Ministry of Education, Science and Culture. ISBN 3-85456-453-8.

142. A diploma supplement by University of West Bohemia, see section 8 - Information of National Higher Educational System.

143. Association of American Universities Data Exchange. Glossary of Terms for Graduate Education. Accessed May 26, 2008; National Science Foundation (2006).

144. "Time to Degree of U.S. Research Doctorate Recipients," *InfoBrief, Science Resource Statistics* NSF 06–312, 2006, p. 7. (Under "Data notes" mentions that the J.D. is a professional doctorate); San Diego County Bar Association (1969).

145. *Ethics Opinion 1969–5*. Accessed May 26, 2008. (Under "other references" discusses differences between academic and professional doctorate and statement that the J.D. is a professional doctorate); University of Utah (2006).

146. University of Utah – The Graduate School – Graduate Handbook. Accessed May 28, 2008 (the J.D. degree is listed under doctorate degrees); German Federal Ministry of Education.

147. *U.S. Higher Education/Evaluation of the Almanac Chronicle of Higher Education*. Accessed May 26, 2008. (report by the German Federal Ministry of Education analysing the Chronicle ocff Higher Education from the U.S. and stating that the J.D. is a professional doctorate);

148. Encyclopædia Britannica. (2002).*Encyclopædia Britannica*, 3:962:1a.

149. Massachusetts Institute of Technology (MIT), www.mit.edu.

150. University of Cambridge, www.cam.ac.uk.

151. Harvard University, www.harvard.edu.

152. Stanford University, www.stanford.edu.

153. UCL (University College London), www.ucl.ac.uk.

154. University of Oxford, www.ox.ac.uk.

155. Imperial College London, www.imperial.ac.uk.

156. Yale University, www.yale.edu.

157. University of Chicago, www.uchicago.edu.

158. Princeton University, www.princeton.edu.

159. California Institute of Technology (Caltech), www.caltech.edu.

160. www.iitm.ac.in.

161. www.iisc.ernet.in.

162. www.annauniv.edu.

163. www.unom.ac.in.

164. Internationalization of Higher Education Practices and Priorities: 2003 Survey Report, Jane KNIGHT, International Association of Universities (IAU).

165. Top 100 Bio-Medicine Universities, Harvard shows it has winning in the genes', The Times Higher, March 2005.

166. 'World University Ranking', Times Higher Education Supplement - www.thes.co.uk

167. 'The Top American Research Universities', An Annual Report from The Lombardi Program on Measuring University, Performance. Gainesville, Florida: The Center, University of Florida. http://thecenter.ufl.edu.

168. Academic Ranking of World Universities', Institute of Higher Education, Shanghai, Jiao Tong University, http://ed.sjtu.edu.cn/ranking.htm

169. 'The 2006 Sunday Times league table of UK universities'.
170. 'The Top American ResearchUniversities',2006 Annual Report, The Center for Measuring University Performance at Arizona State University, John V. Lombardi, Elizabeth D. Capaldi, Craig W. Abbey.
171. www.IHEP.org.
172. www.cepes.ro/hed/meetings/berlin06.
173. http://www.topuniversities.com.
174. http://www.qaa.ac.uk/academicinfrastructure/default.asp.
175. Educational Interest and Intellectual Commitment, Darshana P. Sharma, Anmol Publications PVT. LTD., 2004, ISBN 8126119535, 9788126119530.
176. Webometrics Ranking of World Universities - www.webometrics.info.
177. World Education News and Reviews (WENR) http://www.wes.org/ewenr/06aug/practical.htm
178. 2007 Web Popularity Rankings http://www.4icu.org.
179. CHE-Excellence Ranking. Europe-wide ranking. http://www.excellenceranking.eu.
180. Asia's Best Universities (Asiaweek) discontinued 2000. www.asiaweek.com/asiaweek/features/universities2000/schools/multi.overall.html.
181. The International Standing of Australian Universities - www.melbourneinstitute.com/publications/reports/aus_uni.
182. Good University Guide (Hobsons) - www.thegoodguides.com.au/misc/university_ratings.
183. Canada's Best Schools (Maclean's) - www.macleans.ca/universities.
184. Chinese University Rankings - http://rank2006.netbig.com.
185. FOCUS Uni-Ranking 2007 http://www.focus.de/wissen/campus/hochschulen.
186. DFG Forder-Rankings 2006 www.dfg.de/en/ranking.
187. Humboldt-Ranking 2006 http://www.humboldt-stiftung.net/de/aktuelles/presse/doc/2006ranking72.pdf.
188. Education18 - www.education18.com.
189. National Assessement and Accreditation Council (NAAC) - www.naacindia.org.
190. India Today College Rankings - www.india-today.com/itoday/20000619/cover2.html .
191. JAM College Rankings - www.jammag.com/campus/rankings/jam%20rankings.htm
192. Japan University Accreditation Association (JUAA) - www.juaa.or.jp.
193. World Education News and Reviews (WES) Japan http://www.wes.org/ewenr/PF/06aug/pfjapan.htm#media.
194. The Good University Guide (The Times, London) - www.timesonline.co.uk/section/716,00.html.
195. Guardian University Guide - http://education.guardian.co.uk/universityguide2006.
196. Financial Times - Global MBA rankings 2007 http://rankings.ft.com/global-mbarankings
197. Financial Times - EMBA rankings 2007 http://rankings.ft.com/emba-rankings.
198. HEFCE Report: Counting what is measured or measuring what counts? League tablesand their impact on higher education institutions in England - www.hefce.ac.uk/pubs/hefce/2008/08_14.

199. America's Best Colleges (US News and World Report) - www.usnews.com/usnews/edu/college/rankings/rankindex_brief.php.
200. Council for Higher Education Accreditation (CHEA) - www.cheaorg.
201. The Princeton Review - 2008 Best 366 Colleges Rankings. http://www.princetonreview.com/college/research/rankings/rankings.asp.
202. Carnegie Foundation for the Advancement of Teaching http://www.carnegiefoundation.org/classifications.
203. http://gse.buffalo.edu/org/inthigheredfinance/files/Publications/foundation_papers/%282009%29_Financing_Higher_Education.pdf.
204. Helena Agnes S. Valderrama, "Estimates of Direct Cost of Undergraduate Instruction at the University of the Philippines", Philippine Management Review, 2005, Vol. 12, pp. 105–119.
205. http://www.ugc.ac.in.
206. www.aicte-india.org.